Rousseau and Romanticism

Rousseau and Romanticism

BY IRVING BABBITT

Foreword by Harry Levin

University of Texas Press, Austin & London

International Standard Book Number 0-292-77012-x

Library of Congress Catalog Card Number 76-57080

Printed in the United States of America

L'imagination dispose de tout. PASCAL

Le bon sens est le maître de la vie humaine. BOSSUET

L'homme est un être immense, en quelque sorte, qui peut exister partiellement, mais dont l'existence est d'autant plus délicieuse qu'elle est plus entière et plus pleine. JOUBERT

CONTENTS

FOREWORD

Survival for two generations can be a good test of a book's value, and it is now almost sixty years since this book originally appeared. Much has been written about romanticism during that interval; and many of those more recent writers, in taking their own positions, have felt the need to account for Babbitt's, *pro* or *contra*. Often the attitude of the earlier generation—like his, like that of his best-known former disciple, T. S. Eliot—has been classicistic and antiromantic. If the current generation has witnessed some revival of romantic sympathies, this implies that we still feel the impact of the movement and confirms the relevance of Babbitt's critique. Novelists or dramatists like Beckett, even more than those whom Babbitt criticized in a formulation he borrowed from Paul Bourget, "roll in abysses of despair and ennui." Poets like Robert Lowell do rather more than their predecessors of 1830 did to fulfill the conception, cited by Babbitt from Goethe, of "hospital poetry." Thus, the many citations and pointed allusions with which Babbitt's arguments are always richly studded can be amplified and updated by cross-reference to matters that concern us at the moment—visualized, as everything was for him, in the light of traditional verities.

One of his contemporaries with whom he engaged in controversy, A. O. Lovejoy, argued that the term *romanticism*, since it covered a multitude of ideas, should be used in the plural. René Wellek subsequently responded, and returned to the semantic ground from which Babbitt started, by affirming the historical unity of that complex sequence of manifestations which has dominated Western culture since the time of Rousseau. Rousseau was not its propagator so much as its prototype; as such he is less the subject of the book than, so to speak, a set of illustrations. Yet it remains an extraordinary fact that this sentimental novelist, this narcissistic autobiographer, should have been so great an influence in shaping the modern consciousness of ethics, politics, and education. He is necessarily "the most important single figure," though Babbitt's cast of characters includes significant roles for Byron, Wordsworth, Chateaubriand, and Schiller, on the one hand, and for Plato, Aristotle, Horace, and Dr. Johnson, on the other. Among the many additional witnesses, we are struck by frequent quotations from Confucius and other wise men of the East. Babbitt was something of a pioneer in looking toward that horizon. It will be observed that the writers he discusses are called upon to illuminate his themes, rather than to be illuminated by literary criticism.

That he was not deeply involved in aesthetic appreciation has given rise to some misunderstanding. He himself warns his readers that they should seek elsewhere for "rounded estimates," and he personally took greater pleasure in reading certain romantics than his immediate purposes allowed him to convey. Gathering his testimony from literature, it was his main concern to anatomize a pervasive state of mind. He was frankly a moralist as well as an anatomist, and he offered a prescription along with his diagnosis. It was the very broadest of recommendations: nothing less than humanism itself, a credo easy to accept but difficult to practice in the face of increasing pressures—biological and technological—to neutralize the hard-won distinctions between civilization and nature, human beings and things. In drawing and maintaining that line, religion had been an enabling force, though Babbitt never professed a specific religious commitment. Science, though he respected it as a major form of intellectual inquiry, posed the hazard of confounding men with animals.

And, writing through the period of the First World War, he was painfully conscious of "living in a world that has gone wrong on first principles." He could scarcely have been less so, had he lived through later decades, which have further sharpened the nature of his challenge.

Somewhat paradoxically but consistently, Babbitt thought of himself as a positivist because he strongly believed in those principles, those affirmative values grounded on centuries of human experience, which the classics had summed up and handed down. Seeing them so widely and swiftly repudiated in favor of facile instinct, self-indulgent materialism, and disheveled permissiveness, he could not but speak out in terms of critical negation. Melville had complained many years before that America was pervaded by "*yes*-gentry" and had praised the independent Hawthorne for saying "*No!* in thunder." Babbitt too must be reckoned among the courageous band of dissenting voices that has sustained the dialectical energies of American thought. Bergson, whom he viewed as the characteristic twentieth-century philosopher, had based his ethic on a "vital urge" (*élan vital*), a naturalistic source of motivation for man and beast alike. Babbitt sought to differentiate by stressing man's *frein vital*—a reversal of Bergson which he roughly translated with an apt phrase from Emerson, "inner check," pointing back toward the New England conscience for better or worse. We should notice what Babbitt's critics sometimes neglected: that the change of adjectives shifted his emphasis to *self*-control. He was never comfortable with efforts to ally his views with the authoritarian ideologies of the political right.

Irving Babbitt (1865–1933) did not come by stable background or direct inheritance to the traditionalism he was to expound. Though of Yankee stock, he was born in the Middle West to a dispersing family, so that he had to rely upon himself and set his own sights from adolescence. Nearly all of his career as student and teacher would be associated with the nation's oldest university. Harvard, under President Eliot, had been modernizing—or, as Babbitt felt, diluting—its curriculum. The part he played on the faculty, as a kind of Socratic gadfly, appreciably delayed his advancement to professorial tenure. Yet his courses in French literature, which he regarded as the strategic link between modernity and the Greco-Roman heritage, and especially in the new field of comparative literature, which he did so much to develop, were increasingly large and influential. Much of his notable teaching has been distilled into the eight volumes he left us. Three are lively collections of essays and lectures, one is a lucid translation of a Buddhist text. *Democracy and Leadership* is his profession of political faith, *The New Laokoön* his treatise on latter-day aesthetics, *The Masters of Modern French Criticism* his most purely literary achievement. All are well worth reading and re-reading, but *Rousseau and Romanticism* forms the best introduction and comprises the most central statement.

Harry Levin
Irving Babbitt Professor
of Comparative Literature,
Harvard University

Rousseau & Romanticism

INTRODUCTION

Many readers will no doubt be tempted to exclaim on seeing my title: "Rousseau and no end!" The outpour of books on Rousseau had indeed in the period immediately preceding the war become somewhat portentous.[1] This preoccupation with Rousseau is after all easy to explain. It is his somewhat formidable privilege to represent more fully than any other one person a great international movement. To attack Rousseau or to defend him is most often only a way of attacking or defending this movement.

It is from this point of view at all events that the present work is conceived. I have not undertaken a systematic study of Rousseau's life and doctrines. The appearance of his name in my title is justified, if at all, simply because he comes at a fairly early stage in the international movement the rise and growth of which I am tracing, and has on the whole supplied me with the most significant illustrations of it. I have already put forth certain views regarding this movement in three previous volumes.[2] Though each one of these volumes attempts to do justice to a particular topic, it is at the same time intended to be a link in a continuous argument. I hope that I may be allowed to speak here with some frankness of the main trend of this argument both on its negative and on its positive, or constructive, side.

Perhaps the best key to both sides of my argument is found in the lines of Emerson I have taken as epigraph for "Literature and the American College":

> *There are two laws discrete*
> *Not reconciled, —*
> *Law for man, and law for thing;*
> *The last builds town and fleet,*
> *But it runs wild,*
> *And doth the man unking.*

On its negative side my argument is directed against this undue emphasis on the "law for thing," against the attempt to erect on naturalistic foundations a complete philosophy of life. I define two main forms of naturalism—on the one hand, utilitarian and scientific and, on the other, emotional naturalism. The type of romanticism I am studying is inseparably bound up with emotional naturalism.

This type of romanticism encouraged by the naturalistic movement is only one of three main types I distinguish, and I am dealing for the most part with only one aspect of it. But even when thus circumscribed the subject can scarcely be said to lack importance; for if I am right in my conviction as to the unsoundness of a Rousseauistic philosophy of life, it follows that the total tendency of the Occident at present is away from rather than towards civilization.

On the positive side, my argument aims to reassert the "law for man," and its special discipline against the various forms of naturalistic excess. At the very mention of the word discipline I shall be set down in certain quarters as reactionary. But does it necessarily follow from a plea for the human law that one is a reactionary or in general a traditionalist? An American writer of distinction was once heard to remark that he saw in the world to-day but two classes of persons,—the mossbacks and the mountebanks, and that for his part he preferred to be a mossback. One should think twice before thus consenting to seem a mere relic of the past. The ineffable smartness of our young radicals is due to the conviction that, whatever else they may be, they are the very pink of modernity. Before sharing their conviction it might be well to do a little preliminary defining of such terms as modern and the modern spirit. It may then turn out that the true difficulty with our young radicals is not that they are too modern but that they are not modern enough. For, though the word modern is often and no doubt inevitably used to describe the more recent or the most recent thing, this is not its sole use. It is not in this sense alone that the word is used by writers like Goethe and Sainte-Beuve and Renan and Arnold. What all these writers mean by the modern spirit is the positive and critical spirit, the spirit that refuses to take things on authority. This is what Renan means, for example, when he calls Petrarch the "founder of the modern spirit in literature," or Arnold when he explains why the Greeks of the great period seem more modern to us than the men of the Middle Ages.[3]

Now what I have myself tried to do is to be thoroughly modern in this sense. I hold that one should not only welcome the efforts of the man of science at his best to put the natural law on a positive and critical basis, but that one should strive to emulate him in one's dealings with the human law; and so become a complete positivist. My main objection to the movement I am studying is that it has failed to produce complete positivists. Instead of facing honestly the emergency created by its break with the past the leaders of this movement have inclined to deny the duality of human nature, and then sought to dissimulate this mutilation of man under a mass of intellectual and emotional sophistry. The proper procedure in refuting these incomplete positivists is not to appeal to some dogma or outer authority but rather to turn against them their own principles. Thus Diderot, a notable example of the incomplete positivist and a chief source of naturalistic tendency, says that "everything is experimental in man." Now the word experimental has somewhat narrowed in meaning since the time of Diderot. If one takes the saying to mean that everything in man is a matter of experience one should accept it unreservedly and then plant oneself firmly on the facts of experience that Diderot and other incomplete positivists have refused to recognize.

The man who plants himself, not on outer authority but on experience, is an individualist. To be modern in the sense I have defined is not only to be positive and critical, but also—and this from the time of Petrarch—to be individualistic. The establishment of a sound type of individualism is indeed the specifically modern problem. It is right here that the failure of the incomplete positivist, the man who is positive only according to the natural law, is most conspicuous. What prevails in the region of the natural law is endless change and relativity; therefore the naturalistic positivist attacks all the traditional creeds and dogmas for the very reason that they aspire to fixity. Now all the ethical values of civilization have been associated with these fixed beliefs; and so it has come to pass that with their undermining by naturalism the ethical values themselves are in danger of being swept away in the everlasting flux. Because the individual who views life positively must give up unvarying creeds and dogmas "anterior, exterior, and superior" to himself, it has been assumed that he must also give up standards. For standards imply an element of oneness somewhere, with reference to which it is possible to measure the mere manifoldness and change. The naturalistic individualist, however, refuses to recognize any such element of oneness. His own private and personal self is to be the measure of all things and this measure itself, he adds, is constantly changing. But to stop at this stage is to be satisfied with the most dangerous of half-truths. Thus Bergson's assertion that "life is a perpetual gushing forth of novelties" is in itself only a dangerous half-truth of this kind. The constant element in life is, no less than the element of novelty and change, a matter of observation and experience. As the French have it, the more life changes the more it is the same thing.

If, then, one is to be a sound individualist, an individualist with human standards—and in an age like this that has cut loose from its traditional moorings, the very survival of civilization would seem to hinge on its power to produce such a type of individualist—one must grapple with what Plato terms the problem of the One and the Many. My own solution of this problem, it may be well to point out, is not purely Platonic. Because one can perceive immediately an element of unity in things, it does

not follow that one is justified in establishing a world of essences
or entities or "ideas" above the flux. To do this is to fall away
from a positive and critical into a more or less speculative attitude; it is to risk setting up a metaphysic of the One. Those who
put exclusive emphasis on the element of change in things are
in no less obvious danger of falling away from the positive and
critical attitude into a metaphysic of the Many.[4] This, for example, is the error one finds in the contemporary thinkers who
seem to have the cry, thinkers like James and Bergson and
Dewey and Croce. They are very far from satisfying the requirements of a complete positivism; they are seeking rather to build
up their own intoxication with the element of change into a
complete view of life, and so are turning their backs on one
whole side of experience in a way that often reminds one of the
ancient Greek sophists. The history of philosophy since the
Greeks is to a great extent the history of the clashes of the metaphysicians of the One and the metaphysicians of the Many. In
the eyes of the complete positivist this history therefore reduces
itself largely to a monstrous logomachy.

Life does not give here an element of oneness and there an
element of change. It gives a *oneness that is always changing.*
The oneness and the change are inseparable. Now if what is
stable and permanent is felt as real, the side of life that is always
slipping over into something else or vanishing away entirely is,
as every student of psychology knows, associated rather with the
feeling of illusion. If a man attends solely to this side of life he
will finally come, like Leconte de Lisle, to look upon it as a
"torrent of mobile chimeras," as an "endless whirl of vain appearances." To admit that the oneness of life and the change
are inseparable is therefore to admit that such reality as man
can know positively is inextricably mixed up with illusion.
Moreover man does not observe the oneness that is always
changing from the outside; he is a part of the process, he is
himself a oneness that is always changing. Though imperceptible at any particular moment, the continuous change that is
going on leads to differences—those, let us say, between a
human individual at the age of six weeks and the same individual at the age of seventy—which are sufficiently striking:
and finally this human oneness that is always changing seems

to vanish away entirely. From all this it follows that an enormous element of illusion—and this is a truth the East has always accepted more readily than the West—enters into the idea of personality itself. If the critical spirit is once allowed to have its way, it will not rest content until it has dissolved life into a mist of illusion. Perhaps the most positive and critical account of man in modern literature is that of Shakespeare:

> *We are such stuff*
> *As dreams are made on, and our little life*
> *Is rounded with a sleep.*

But, though strictly considered, life is but a web of illusion and a dream within a dream, it is a dream that needs to be managed with the utmost discretion, if it is not to turn into a nightmare. In other words, however much life may mock the metaphysician, the problem of conduct remains. There is always the unity at the heart of the change; it is possible, however, to get at this real and abiding element and so at the standards with reference to which the dream of life may be rightly managed only through a veil of illusion. The problem of the One and the Many, the ultimate problem of thought, can therefore be solved only by a right use of illusion. In close relation to illusion and the questions that arise in connection with it is all that we have come to sum up in the word imagination. The use of this word, at least in anything like its present extension, is, one should note, comparatively recent. Whole nations and periods of the past can scarcely be said to have had any word corresponding to imagination in this extended sense. Yet the thinkers of the past have treated, at times profoundly, under the head of fiction or illusion the questions that we should treat under the head of imagination.[5] In the "Masters of Modern French Criticism" I was above all preoccupied with the problem of the One and the Many and the failure of the nineteenth century to deal with it adequately. My effort in this present work is to show that this failure can be retrieved only by a deeper insight into the imagination and its all-important rôle in both literature and life. Man is cut off from immediate contact with anything abiding and therefore worthy to be called real and condemned to live in an element of fiction or illusion, but he may, I have tried to show, lay hold with the aid of the imagination on the element of oneness that is inextricably blended with the manifoldness and change and to just that extent may build up a sound model for imitation. One tends to be an individualist with true standards, to put the matter somewhat differently, only in so far as one understands the relation between appearance and reality—what the philosophers call the epistemological problem. This problem, though it cannot be solved abstractly and metaphysically, can be solved practically and in terms of actual conduct. Inasmuch as modern philosophy has failed to work out any such solution, it is hard to avoid the conclusion that modern philosophy is bankrupt, not merely from Kant, but from Descartes.

The supreme maxim of the ethical positivist is: By their fruits shall ye know them. If I object to a romantic philosophy it is because I do not like its fruits. I infer from its fruits that this philosophy has made a wrong use of illusion. "All those who took the romantic promises at their face value," says Bourget, "rolled in abysses of despair and ennui." [6] If any one still holds, as many of the older romanticists held, that it is a distinguished thing to roll in abysses of despair and ennui, he should read me no further. He will have no sympathy with my point of view. If any one, on the other hand, accepts my criterion but denies that Rousseauistic living has such fruits, it has been my aim so to accumulate evidence that he will be confronted with the task of refuting not a set of theories but a body of facts. My whole method, let me repeat, is experimental, or it might be less ambiguous to say if the word were a fortunate one, experiential. The illustrations I have given of any particular aspect of the movement are usually only a small fraction of those I have collected—themselves no doubt only a fraction of the illustrations that might be collected from printed sources. M. Maigron's investigation[7] into the fruits of romantic living suggests the large additions that might be made to these printed sources from manuscript material.

My method indeed is open in one respect to grave misunderstanding. From the fact that I am constantly citing passages from this or that author and condemning the tendency for which these passages stand, the reader will perhaps be led to in-

fer a total condemnation of the authors so quoted. But the in-
ference may be very incorrect. I am not trying to give rounded
estimates of individuals—delightful and legitimate as that type
of criticism is—but to trace main currents as a part of my
search for a set of principles to oppose to naturalism. I call attention for example to the Rousseauistic and primitivistic elements in Wordsworth but do not assert that this is the whole
truth about Wordsworth. One's views as to the philosophical
value of Rousseauism must, however, weigh heavily in a total
judgment of Wordsworth. Criticism is such a difficult art because one must not only have principles but must apply them
flexibly and intuitively. No one would accuse criticism at present of lacking flexibility. It has grown so flexible in fact as to
become invertebrate. One of my reasons for practicing the present type of criticism is the conviction that because of a lack of
principles the type of criticism that aims at rounded estimates
of individuals is rapidly ceasing to have any meaning.

I should add that if I had attempted rounded estimates, they
would often have been more favorable than might be gathered
from my comments here and elsewhere on the romantic leaders. One is justified in leaning towards severity in the laying
down of principles, but should nearly always incline to indulgence in the application of them. In a sense one may say with
Goethe that the excellencies are of the individual, the defects of
the age. It is especially needful to recall distinctions of this kind
in the case of Rousseau himself and my treatment of him.
M. Lanson has dwelt on the strange duality of Rousseau's nature. "The writer," he says, "is a poor dreamy creature who approaches action only with alarm and with every manner of pre-
caution, and who understands the applications of his boldest
doctrines in a way to reassure conservatives and satisfy oppor-
tunists. But the work for its part detaches itself from the
author, lives its independent life, and, heavily charged with revolutionary explosives which neutralize the moderate and concil-
iatory elements Rousseau has put into it for his own satisfaction, it exasperates and inspires revolt and fires enthusiasms and
irritates hatreds; it is the mother of violence, the source of all
that is uncompromising, it launches the simple souls who give
themselves up to its strange virtue upon the desperate quest of

the absolute, an absolute to be realized now by anarchy and now by social despotism." 8 I am inclined to discover in the Rousseau who, according to M. Lanson, is merely timorous, a great deal of shrewdness and at times something even better than shrewdness. The question is not perhaps very important, for M. Lanson is surely right in affirming that the Rousseau who has moved the world—and that for reasons I shall try to make plain—is Rousseau the extremist and foe of compromise; and so it is to this Rousseau that as a student of main tendencies I devote almost exclusive attention. I am not, however, seeking to make a scapegoat even of the radical and revolutionary Rousseau. One of my chief objections, indeed, to Rousseauism, as will appear in the following pages, is that it encourages the making of scapegoats.

If I am opposed to Rousseauism because of its fruits in experience, I try to put what I have to offer as a substitute on the same positive basis. Now experience is of many degrees: first of all one's purely personal experience, and infinitesimal fragment; and then the experience of one's immediate circle, of one's time and country, of the near past and so on in widening circles. The past which as dogma the ethical positivist rejects, as experience he not only admits but welcomes. He can no more dispense with it indeed than the naturalistic positivist can dispense with his laboratory. He insists moreover on including the remoter past in his survey. Perhaps the most pernicious of all the conceits fostered by the type of progress we owe to science is the conceit that we have outgrown this older experience. One should endeavor, as Goethe says, to oppose to the aberrations of the hour the masses of universal history. There are special reasons just now why this background to which one appeals should not be merely Occidental. An increasing material contact between the Occident and the Far East is certain. We should be enlightened by this time as to the perils of material contact between men and bodies of men who have no deeper understanding. Quite apart from this consideration the experience of the Far East completes and confirms in a most interesting way that of the Occident. We can scarcely afford to neglect it if we hope to work out a truly ecumenical wisdom to oppose to the sinister one-sidedness of our current naturalism. Now the ethical experience of the Far East may be summed up for practical purposes in the teachings and influence of two men, Confucius and Buddha.[9] To know the Buddhistic and Confucian teachings in their true spirit is to know what is best and most representative in the ethical experience of about half the human race for over seventy generations.

A study of Buddha and Confucius suggests, as does a study of the great teachers of the Occident, that under its bewildering surface variety human experience falls after all into a few main categories. I myself am fond of distinguishing three levels on which a man may experience life—the naturalistic, the humanistic, and the religious. Tested by its fruits Buddhism at its best confirms Christianity. Submitted to the same test Confucianism falls in with the teaching of Aristotle and in general with that of all those who from the Greeks down have proclaimed decorum and the law of measure. This is so obviously true that Confucius has been called the Aristotle of the East. Not only has the Far East had in Buddhism a great religious movement and in Confucianism a great humanistic movement, it has also had in early Taoism[10] a movement that in its attempts to work out naturalistic equivalents of humanistic or religious insight offers almost startling analogies to the movement I am here studying.

Thus both East and West have not only had great religious and humanistic disciplines which when tested by their fruits confirm one another, bearing witness to the element of oneness, the constant element in human experience, but these disciplines have at times been conceived in a very positive spirit. Confucius indeed, though a moral realist, can scarcely be called a positivist; he aimed rather to attach men to the past by links of steel. He reminds us in this as in some other ways of the last of the great Tories in the Occident, Dr. Johnson. Buddha on the other hand was an individualist. He wished men to rest their belief neither on his authority[11] nor on that of tradition.[12] No one has ever made a more serious effort to put religion on a positive and critical basis. It is only proper that I acknowledge my indebtedness to the great Hindu positivist: my treatment of the problem of the One and the Many, for example, is nearer to Buddha than to Plato. Yet even if the general thesis be granted that it is desirable to put the "law for man" on a positive and critical basis, the question remains whether the more crying need just now is for positive and critical humanism or for positive and critical religion. I have discussed this delicate and difficult question more fully in my last chapter, but may give at least one reason here for inclining to the humanistic solution. I have been struck in my study of the past by the endless self-deception to which man is subject when he tries to pass too abruptly from the naturalistic to the religious level. The world, it is hard to avoid concluding, would have been a better place if more persons had made sure they were human before setting out to be superhuman; and this consideration would seem to apply with special force to a generation like the present that is wallowing in the trough of naturalism. After all to be a good humanist is merely to be moderate and sensible and decent. It is much easier for a man to deceive himself and others regarding his supernatural lights than it is regarding the degree to which he is moderate and sensible and decent.

The past is not without examples of a positive and critical humanism. I have already mentioned Aristotle. If by his emphasis on the mediatory virtues he reminds one of Confucius, by his positive method and intensely analytical temper he reminds one rather of Buddha. When Aristotle rises to the religious level and discourses on the "life of vision" he is very Buddhistic. When Buddha for his part turns from the religious life to the duties of the layman he is purely Aristotelian. Aristotle also deals positively with the natural law. He is indeed a complete positivist, and not, like the man of the nineteenth century, positive according to the natural law alone. The Aristotle that should specially concern us, however, is the positive and critical humanist—the Aristotle, let us say, of the "Ethics" and "Politics" and "Poetics." Just as I have called the point of view of the scientific and utilitarian naturalist Baconian,[13] and that of the emotional naturalist Rousseauistic, so I would term the point of view that I am myself seeking to develop Aristotelian. Aristotle has laid down once for all the principle that should guide the ethical positivist. "Truth," he says, "in matters of moral action is judged from facts and from actual life. . . . So what we should do is to examine the preceding statements [of

Solon and other wise men] by referring them to facts and to actual life, and when they harmonize with facts we may accept them, when they are at variance with them conceive of them as mere theories." [14]

It is in this sense alone that I aspire to be called an Aristotelian; for one risks certain misunderstandings in using the name of Aristotle.[15] The authority of this great positivist has been invoked innumerable times throughout the ages as a substitute for direct observation. Aristotle was not only the prop and mainstay of dogma for centuries during the Middle Ages, but dogmatic Aristotelianism survived to no small extent, especially in literature, throughout the neo-classical period. It was no doubt natural enough that the champions of the modern spirit should have rejected Aristotle along with the traditional order of which he had been made a support. Yet if they had been more modern they might have seen in him rather a chief precursor. They might have learned from him how to have standards and at the same time not be immured in dogma. As it is, those who call themselves modern have come to adopt a purely exploratory attitude towards life. "On desperate seas long wont to roam," they have lost more and more the sense of what is normal and central in human experience. But to get away from what is normal and central is to get away from wisdom. My whole argument on the negative side, if I may venture on a final summing up, is that the naturalistic movement in the midst of which we are still living had from the start this taint of eccentricity. I have tried to show in detail the nature of the aberration. As for the results, they are being written large in disastrous events. On its constructive side, my argument, if it makes any appeal at all, will be to those for whom the symbols through which the past has received its wisdom have become incredible, and who, seeing at the same time that the break with the past that took place in the eighteenth century was on unsound lines, hold that the remedy for the partial positivism that is the source of this unsoundness, is a more complete positivism. Nothing is more perilous than to be only half critical. This is to risk being the wrong type of individualist—the individualist who has repudiated outer control without achieving inner control. "People mean nowadays by a philosopher," says Rivarol, "not the man who learns the great art of mastering his passions or adding to his insight, but the man who has cast off prejudices without acquiring virtues." That view of philosophy has not ceased to be popular. The whole modern experiment is threatened with breakdown simply because it has not been sufficiently modern. One should therefore not rest content until one has, with the aid of the secular experience of both the East and the West, worked out a point of view so modern that, compared with it, that of our smart young radicals will seem antediluvian.

CHAPTER ONE

THE TERMS CLASSIC AND ROMANTIC

The words classic and romantic, we are often told, cannot be defined at all, and even if they could be defined, some would add, we should not be much profited. But this inability or unwillingness to define may itself turn out to be only one aspect of a movement that from Rousseau to Bergson has sought to discredit the analytical intellect—what Wordsworth calls "the false secondary power by which we multiply distinctions." However, those who are with Socrates rather than with Rousseau or Wordsworth in this matter, will insist on the importance of definition, especially in a chaotic era like the present; for nothing is more characteristic of such an era than its irresponsible use of general terms. Now to measure up to the Socratic standard, a definition must not be abstract and metaphysical, but experimental; it must not, that is, reflect our opinion of what a word should mean, but what it actually has meant. Mathematicians may be free at times to frame their own definitions, but in the case of words like classic and romantic, that have been used innumerable times, and used not in one but in many countries, such a method is inadmissible. One must keep one's eye on actual usage. One should indeed allow for a certain amount of freakishness in this usage. Beaumarchais, for example, makes classic synonymous with barbaric.[1] One may disregard an oc-

casional aberration of this kind, but if one can find only confusion and inconsistency in all the main uses of words like
classic and romantic, the only procedure for those who speak
or write in order to be understood is to banish the words from
their vocabulary.

Now to define in a Socratic way two things are necessary:
one must learn to see a common element in things that are apparently different and also to discriminate between things that
are apparently similar. A Newton, to take the familiar instance
of the former process, saw a common element in the fall of an
apple and the motion of a planet; and one may perhaps without
being a literary Newton discover a common element in all the
main uses of the word romantic as well as in all the main uses
of the word classic; though some of the things to which the
word romantic in particular has been applied seem, it must be
admitted, at least as far apart as the fall of an apple and the
motion of a planet. The first step is to perceive the something
that connects two or more of these things apparently so diverse,
and then it may be found necessary to refer this unifying trait
itself back to something still more general, and so on until we
arrive, not indeed at anything absolute—the absolute will always elude us—but at what Goethe calls the original or underlying phenomenon (*Urphänomen*). A fruitful source of false
definition is to take as primary in a more or less closely allied
group of facts what is actually secondary—for example, to fix
upon the return to the Middle Ages as the central fact in romanticism, whereas this return is only symptomatic; it is very
far from being the original phenomenon. Confused and incomplete definitions of romanticism have indeed just that origin—they seek to put at the centre something that though
romantic is not central but peripheral, and so the whole subject is thrown out of perspective.

My plan then is to determine to the best of my ability, in
connection with a brief historical survey, the common element
in the various uses of the words classic and romantic; and then,
having thus disposed of the similarities, to turn to the second
part of the art of defining and deal, also historically, with the
differences. For my subject is not romanticism in general, but
only a particular type of romanticism, and this type of romanti-

cism needs to be seen as a recoil, not from classicism in general, but from a particular type of classicism.

I

The word romantic when traced historically is found to go back to the old French *roman* of which still older forms are *romans* and *romant*. These and similar formations derive ultimately from the mediæval Latin adverb *romanice*. *Roman* and like words meant originally the various vernaculars derived from Latin, just as the French still speak of these vernaculars as *les langues romanes;* and then the word *roman* came to be applied to tales written in the various vernaculars, especially in old French. Now with what features of these tales were people most struck? The reply to this question is found in a passage of a fifteenth-century Latin manuscript:[2] "From the reading of certain romantics, that is, books of poetry composed in French on military deeds which are for the most part fictitious." [3] Here the term romantic is applied to books that we should still call romantic and for the very same reason, namely, because of the predominance in these books of the element of fiction over reality.

In general a thing is romantic when, as Aristotle would say, it is wonderful rather than probable; in other words, when it violates the normal sequence of cause and effect in favor of adventure. Here is the fundamental contrast between the words classic and romantic which meets us at the outset and in some form or other persists in all the uses of the word down to the present day. A thing is romantic when it is strange, unexpected, intense, superlative, extreme, unique,[4] etc. A thing is classical, on the other hand, when it is not unique, but representative of a class. In this sense medical men may speak correctly of a classic case of typhoid fever, or a classic case of hysteria. One is even justified in speaking of a classic example of romanticism. By an easy extension of meaning a thing is classical when it belongs to a high class or to the best class.

The type of romanticism referred to in the fifteenth-century manuscript was, it will be observed, the spontaneous product of the popular imagination of the Middle Ages. We may go further and say that the uncultivated human imagination in all times and places is romantic in the same way. It hungers for the thrilling and the marvelous and is, in short, incurably melodramatic. All students of the past know how, when the popular imagination is left free to work on actual historical characters and events, it quickly introduces into these characters and events the themes of universal folk-lore and makes a ruthless sacrifice of reality to the love of melodramatic surprise. For example, the original nucleus of historical fact has almost disappeared in the lurid melodramatic tale "Les quatre fils Aymon," which has continued, as presented in the "Bibliothèque Bleue," to appeal to the French peasant down to our own times. Those who look with alarm on recent attacks upon romanticism should therefore be comforted. All children, nearly all women and the vast majority of men always have been, are and probably always will be romantic. This is true even of a classical period like the second half of the seventeenth century in France. Boileau is supposed to have killed the vogue of the interminable romances of the early seventeenth century which themselves continue the spirit of the mediæval romances. But recent investigations have shown that the vogue of these romances continued until well on into the eighteenth century. They influenced the imagination of Rousseau, the great modern romancer.

But to return to the history of the word romantic. The first printed examples of the word in any modern tongue are, it would seem, to be found in English. The Oxford Dictionary cites the following from F. Greville's "Life of Sidney" (written before 1628, published in 1652): "Doe not his Arcadian romantics live after him?"—meaning apparently ideas or features suggestive of romance. Of extreme interest is the use of the word in Evelyn's "Diary" (3 August, 1654): "Were Sir Guy's grot improved as it might be, it were capable of being made a most romantic and pleasant place." The word is not only used in a favorable sense, but it is applied to nature; and it is this use of the word in connection with outer nature that French and German literatures are going to derive later from England. Among the early English uses of the word romantic may be noted: "There happened this extraordinary case—one of the most romantique that ever I heard in my life and could not have believed," [5] etc. "Most other authors that I ever read either have wild romantic tales wherein they strain Love and Honor to that ridiculous height that it becomes burlesque," [6] etc. The word becomes fairly common by the year 1700 and thousands of examples could be collected from English writers in the eighteenth century. Here are two early eighteenth-century instances:

"The gentleman I am married to made love to me in rapture but it was the rapture of a Christian and a man of Honor, not a romantic hero or a whining coxcomb." [7]

> *Whether the charmer sinner it or saint it*
> *If folly grow romantick I must paint it.*[8]

The early French and German uses of the word romantic seem to derive from England. One important point is to be noted as to France. Before using the word *romantique* the French used the word *romanesque* in the sense of wild, unusual, adventurous—especially in matters of sentiment—and they have continued to employ *romanesque* alongside *romantique,* which is now practically used only of the romantic school. A great deal of confusion is thus avoided into which we fall in English from having only the one word romantic, which must do duty for both *romantique* and *romanesque.* An example of *romantique* is found in French as early as 1675;[9] but the word owed its vogue practically to the anglomania that set in about the middle of the eighteenth century. The first very influential French example of the word is appropriately found in Rousseau in the Fifth Promenade (1777): "The shores of the Lake of Bienne are more wild and romantic than those of the Lake of Geneva." The word *romantique* was fashionable in France especially as applied to scenery from about the year 1785, but without any thought as yet of applying it to a literary school.

In Germany the word *romantisch* as an equivalent of the French *romanesque* and modern German *romanhaft* appears at the end of the seventeenth century and plainly as a borrowing from the French. Heidigger, a Swiss, used it several times in his "Mythoscopia romantica," [10] an attack on romances and the wild and vain imaginings they engender. According to Heidigger the only resource against romanticism in this sense is religion. In Germany as in France the association of romantic with natural scenery comes from England, especially from the imitations and translations of Thomson's "Seasons."

In the second half of the eighteenth century the increasingly favorable use of words like Gothic and enthusiastic as well as the emergence of words like sentimental and picturesque are among the symptoms of a new movement, and the fortunes of the word romantic were more or less bound up with this movement. Still, apart from its application to natural scenery, the word is as yet far from having acquired a favorable connotation if we are to believe an essay by John Foster on the "Application of the Epithet Romantic" (1805). Foster's point of view is not unlike that of Heidigger. Romantic, he says, had come to be used as a term of vague abuse, whereas it can be used rightly only of the ascendency of imagination over judgment, and is therefore synonymous with such words as wild, visionary, extravagant. "A man possessing so strong a judgment and so subordinate a fancy as Dean Swift would hardly have been made romantic . . . if he had studied all the books in Don Quixote's library." It is not, Foster admits, a sign of high endowment for a youth to be too coldly judicial, too deaf to the blandishments of imaginative illusion. Yet in general a man should strive to bring his imagination under the control of sound reason. But how is it possible thus to prevail against the deceits of fancy? Right knowing, he asserts very un-Socratically, is not enough to ensure right doing. At this point Foster changes from the tone of a literary essay to that of a sermon, and, maintaining a thesis somewhat similar to that of Pascal in the seventeenth century and Heidigger in the eighteenth, he concludes that a man's imagination will run away with his judgment or reason unless he have the aid of divine grace.

II

When Foster wrote his essay there was no question as yet in England of a romantic school. Before considering how the word came to be applied to a particular movement we need first to bring out more fully certain broad conflicts of tendency during the seventeenth and eighteenth centuries, conflicts that are not sufficiently revealed by the occasional uses during this period of the word romantic. In the contrast Foster established between judgment and imagination he is merely following a long series of neo-classical critics and this contrast not only seemed to him and these critics, but still seems to many, the essential contrast between classicism and romanticism. We shall be helped in understanding how judgment (or reason) and imagination came thus to be sharply contrasted if we consider briefly the changes in the meaning of the word wit during the neo-classical period, and also if we recollect that the contrast between judgment and imagination is closely related to the contrast the French are so fond of establishing between the general sense (*le sens commun*) and the private sense or the sense of the individual (*le sens propre*).

In the sixteenth century prime emphasis was put not upon common sense, but upon wit or conceit or ingenuity (in the sense of quickness of imagination). The typical Elizabethan strove to excel less by judgment than by invention, by "high-flying liberty of conceit"; like Falstaff he would have a brain "apprehensive, quick, forgetive, full of nimble, fiery, and delectable shapes." Wit at this time, it should be remembered, was synonymous not only with imagination but with intellect (in opposition to will). The result of the worship of wit in this twofold sense was a sort of intellectual romanticism. Though its origins are no doubt mediæval, it differs from the ordinary romanticism of the Middle Ages to which I have already referred in being thus concerned with thought rather than with action. Towards the end of the Renaissance and in the early seventeenth century especially, people were ready to pursue the strange and surprising thought even at the risk of getting too far away from the workings of the normal mind. Hence the "points" and "conceits" that spread, as Lowell put it, like a "cutaneous eruption" over the face of Europe; hence the Gongorists and Cultists, the Marinists and Euphuists, the *précieux* and the "metaphysical" poets. And then came the inevitable swing away from all this fantasticality towards common sense. A demand arose for something that was less rare and "precious" and more representative.

This struggle between the general sense and the sense of the individual stands out with special clearness in France. A model was gradually worked out by aid of the classics, especially the Latin classics, as to what man should be. Those who were in the main movement of the time elaborated a great convention, that is they *came together* about certain things. They condemned in the name of their convention those who were too indulgent of their private sense, in other words, too eccentric in their imaginings. A Théophile, for example, fell into disesteem for refusing to restrain his imagination, for asserting the type of "spontaneity" that would have won him favor in any romantic period.[11]

The swing away from intellectual romanticism can also be traced in the changes that took place in the meaning of the word wit in both France and England. One of the main tasks of the French critics of the seventeenth century and of English critics, largely under the lead of the French, was to distinguish between true and false wit. The work that would have been complimented a little earlier as "witty" and "conceited" is now censured as fantastic and far-fetched, as lacking in judicial control over the imagination, and therefore in general appeal. The movement away from the sense of the individual towards common sense goes on steadily from the time of Malherbe to that of Boileau. Balzac attacks Ronsard for his individualistic excess, especially for his audacity in inventing words without reference to usage. Balzac himself is attacked by Boileau for his affectation, for his straining to say things differently from other people. In so far his wit was not true but false. La Bruyère, in substantial accord with Boileau, defines false wit as wit which is lacking in good sense and judgment and "in which the imagination has too large a share."[12]

What the metaphysical poets in England understood by wit, according to Dr. Johnson, was the pursuit of their thoughts to their last ramifications, and in this pursuit of the singular and the novel they lost the "grandeur of generality." This imaginative quest of rarity led to the same recoil as in France, to a demand for common sense and judgment. The opposite extreme from the metaphysical excess is reached when the element of invention is eliminated entirely from wit and it is reduced, as it is by Pope, to rendering happily the general sense—

What oft was thought but ne'er so well expressed.

Dr. Johnson says that the decisive change in the meaning of the word wit took place about the time of Cowley. Important evidences of this change and also of the new tendency to depreciate the imagination is also found in certain passages of Hobbes. Hobbes identifies the imagination with the memory of outer images and so looks on it as "decaying sense." [13] "They who observe similitudes," he remarks elsewhere, making a distinction that was to be developed by Locke and accepted by Addison, "in case they be such as are but rarely observed by others are said to have a good wit; by which, in this occasion, is meant a good fancy" (wit has here the older meaning). "But they who distinguish and observe differences," he continues, "are said to have a good judgment. Fancy without the help of judgment is not worthy of commendation, whereas judgment is commended for itself without the help of fancy. Indeed without steadiness and direction to some end, a great fancy is one kind of madness." "Judgment without fancy," he concludes, "is wit" (this anticipates the extreme neo-classical use of the word wit), "but fancy without judgment, not."

Dryden betrays the influence of Hobbes when he says of the period of incubation of his "Rival Ladies": "Fancy was yet in its first work, moving the sleeping images of things towards the light, there to be distinguished and either chosen or rejected by judgment." Fancy or imagination (the words were still synonymous), as conceived by the English neo-classicists, often shows a strange vivacity for a faculty that is after all only "decaying sense." "Fancy without judgment," says Dryden, "is a hot-mouthed jade without a curb." "Fancy," writes Rymer in a similar vein, "leaps and frisks, and away she's gone; whilst reason rattles the chain and follows after." The following lines of Mulgrave are typical of the neo-classical notion of the relation between fancy and judgment:

As all is dullness when the Fancy's bad,
So without Judgment, Fancy is but mad.

Reason is that substantial, useful part
Which gains the Head, while t' other wins the Heart.[14]

The opposition established by the neo-classicist in passages of
this kind is too mechanical. Fancy and judgment do not seem
to coöperate but to war with one another. In case of doubt the
neo-classicist is always ready to sacrifice fancy to the "substantial, useful part," and so he seems too negative and cool and
prosaic in his reason, and this is because his reason is so largely
a protest against a previous romantic excess. What had been
considered genius in the time of the "metaphysicals" had too
often turned out to be only oddity. With this warning before
them men kept their eyes fixed very closely on the model of
normal human nature that had been set up, and imitated it very
literally and timorously. A man was haunted by the fear that
he might be "monstrous," and so, as Rymer put it, "satisfy nobody's maggot but his own." Correctness thus became a sort
of tyranny. We suffer to the present day from this neo-classical
failure to work out a sound conception of the imagination in
its relation to good sense. Because the neo-classicist held the
imagination lightly as compared with good sense the romantic
rebels were led to hold good sense lightly as compared with imagination. The romantic view in short is too much the neo-
classical view turned upside down; and, as Sainte-Beuve says,
nothing resembles a hollow so much as a swelling.

III

Because the classicism against which romanticism rebelled
was inadequate it does not follow that every type of classicism
suffers from a similar inadequacy. The great movement away
from imaginative unrestraint towards regularity and good
sense took place in the main under French auspices. In general
the French have been the chief exponents of the classic spirit
in modern times. They themselves feel this so strongly that a
certain group in France has of late years inclined to use inter-
changeably the words classicist and nationalist. But this is a
grave confusion, for if the classic spirit is anything at all it is
in its essence not local and national, but universal and human.
To be sure, any particular manifestation of classicism will of
necessity contain elements that are less universal, elements that

reflect merely a certain person or persons, or a certain age and country. This is a truth that we scarcely need to have preached to us; for with the growth of the historical method we have come to fix our attention almost exclusively on these local and relative elements. The complete critic will accept the historical method but be on his guard against its excess. He will see an element in man that is set above the local and the relative; he will learn to detect this abiding element through all the flux of circumstance; in Platonic language, he will perceive the One in the Many.

Formerly, it must be admitted, critics were not historical enough. They took to be of the essence of classicism what was merely its local coloring, especially the coloring it received from the French of the seventeenth century. If we wish to distinguish between essence and accident in the classic spirit we must get behind the French of the seventeenth century, behind the Italians of the sixteenth century who laid the foundations of neo-classical theory, behind the Romans who were the immediate models of most neo-classicists, to the source of classicism in Greece. Even in Greece the classic spirit is very much implicated in the local and the relative, yet in the life of no other people perhaps does what is universal in man shine forth more clearly from what is only local and relative. We still need, therefore, to return to Greece, not merely for the best practice, but for the best theory of classicism; for this is still found in spite of all its obscurities and incompleteness in the Poetics of Aristotle. If we have recourse to this treatise, however, it must be on condition that we do not, like the critics of the Renaissance, deal with it in an abstract and dogmatic way (the form of the treatise it must be confessed gave them no slight encouragement), but in a spirit akin to Aristotle's own as revealed in the total body of his writings—a spirit that is at its best positive and experimental.

Aristotle not only deals positively and experimentally with the natural order and with man so far as he is a part of this order, but he deals in a similar fashion with a side of man that the modern positivist often overlooks. Like all the great Greeks Aristotle recognizes that man is the creature of two laws: he has an ordinary or natural self of impulse and desire and a human self that is known practically as a power of control over impulse and desire. If man is to become human he must not let impulse and desire run wild, but must oppose to everything excessive in his ordinary self, whether in thought or deed or emotion, the law of measure. This insistence on restraint and proportion is rightly taken to be of the essence not merely of the Greek spirit but of the classical spirit in general. The norm or standard that is to set bounds to the ordinary self is got at by different types of classicists in different ways and described variously: for example, as the human law, or the better self, or reason (a word to be discussed more fully later), or nature. Thus when Boileau says, "Let nature be your only study," he does not mean outer nature, nor again the nature of this or that individual, but representative human nature. Having decided what is normal either for man or some particular class of men the classicist takes this normal "nature" for his model and proceeds to imitate it. Whatever accords with the model he has thus set up he pronounces natural or probable, whatever on the other hand departs too far from what he conceives to be the normal type or the normal sequence of cause and effect he holds to be "improbable" and unnatural or even, if it attains an extreme of abnormality, "monstrous." Whatever in conduct or character is duly restrained and proportionate with reference to the model is said to observe decorum. Probability and decorum are identical in some of their aspects and closely related in all.[15] To recapitulate, a general nature, a core of normal experience, is affirmed by all classicists. From this central affirmation derives the doctrine of imitation, and from imitation in turn the doctrines of probability and decorum.

But though all classicists are alike in insisting on nature, imitation, probability and decorum, they differ widely, as I have already intimated, in what they understand by these terms. Let us consider first what Aristotle and the Greeks understand by them. The first point to observe is that according to Aristotle one is to get his general nature not on authority or second hand, but is to disengage it directly for himself from the jumble of particulars that he has before his eyes. He is not, says Aristotle, to imitate things as they are, but as they ought to be. Thus conceived imitation is a creative act. Through all the welter of the actual one penetrates to the real and so succeeds without ceasing to be individual in suggesting the universal. Poetry that is imitative in this sense is, according to Aristotle, more "serious" and "philosophical" than history. History deals merely with what has happened, whereas poetry deals with what may happen according to probability or necessity. Poetry, that is, does not portray life literally but extricates the deeper or ideal truth from the flux of circumstance. One may add with Sydney that if poetry is thus superior to history in being more serious and philosophical it resembles history and is superior to philosophy in being concrete.

The One that the great poet or artist perceives in the Many and that gives to his work its high seriousness is not a fixed absolute. In general the model that the highly serious man (ὁ σπουδαῖος) imitates and that keeps his ordinary self within the bounds of decorum is not to be taken as anything finite, as anything that can be formulated once for all. This point is important for on it hinges every right distinction not merely between the classic and the romantic, but between the classic and the pseudoclassic. Romanticism has claimed for itself a monopoly of imagination and infinitude, but on closer examination, as I hope to show later, this claim, at least so far as genuine classicism is concerned, will be found to be quite unjustified. For the present it is enough to say that true classicism does not rest on the observance of rules or the imitation of models but on an immediate insight into the universal. Aristotle is especially admirable in the account he gives of this insight and of the way it may manifest itself in art and literature. One may be rightly imitative, he says, and so have access to a superior truth and give others access to it only by being a master of illusion. Though the great poet "breathes immortal air," though he sees behind the shows of sense a world of more abiding relationships, he can convey his vision not directly but only imaginatively. Aristotle, one should observe, does not establish any hard and fast opposition between judgment and imagination, an opposition that pervades not only the neo-classical movement but also the romantic revolt from it. He simply affirms a supersensuous order which one can perceive only with the help of fiction. The best art, says Goethe in the true spirit of Aristotle, gives us the "illusion of a higher reality." This has the advantage of being experimental. It is merely a statement of what one feels in the presence of a great painting, let us say, or in reading a great poem.

IV

After this attempt to define briefly with the help of the Greeks the classical spirit in its essence we should be prepared to understand more clearly the way in which this spirit was modified in neo-classical times, especially in France. The first thing that strikes one about the classicism of this period is that it does not rest on immediate perception like that of the Greeks but on outer authority. The merely dogmatic and traditional classicist gave a somewhat un-Greek meaning to the doctrines of nature and imitation. Why imitate nature directly, said Scaliger, when we have in Virgil a second nature? Imitation thus came to mean the imitation of certain outer models and the following of rules based on these models. Now it is well that one who aims at excellence in any field should begin by a thorough assimilation of the achievements of his great predecessors in this field. Unfortunately the neo-classical theorist tended to impose a multitude of precepts that were based on what was external rather than on what was vital in the practice of his models. In so far the lesson of form that the great ancients can always teach any one who approaches them in the right spirit degenerated into formalism. This formalistic turn given to the doctrine of imitation was felt from the outset to be a menace to originality; to be incompatible, and everything hinges at last on this point, with the spontaneity of the imagination. There was an important reaction headed by men like Boileau, within the neo-classical movement itself, against the oppression of the intuitive side of human nature by mere dogma and authority, above all against the notion that "regularity" is in itself any guarantee of literary excellence. A school of rules was succeeded by a school of taste. Yet even to the end the neo-classicist was too prone to reject as unnatural or even monstrous everything that did not fit into one of the traditional pigeon-holes. One must grant, indeed, that much noble work was achieved under the neo-classical dispensation, work that shows a genuine insight into the universal, but it is none the less evident that the view of the imagination held during this period has a formalistic taint.

This taint in neo-classicism is due not merely to its dogmatic and mechanical way of dealing with the doctrine of imitation but also to the fact that it had to reconcile classical with Christian dogma; and the two antiquities, classical and Christian, if interpreted vitally and in the spirit, were in many respects divergent and in some respects contradictory. The general outcome of the attempts at reconciliation made by the literary casuists of Italy and France was that Christianity should have a monopoly of truth and classicism a monopoly of fiction. For the true classicist, it will be remembered, the two things are inseparable—he gets at his truth through a veil of fiction. Many of the neo-classicists came to conceive of art as many romanticists were to conceive of it later as a sort of irresponsible game or play, but they were, it must be confessed, very inferior to the romanticists in the spontaneity of their fiction. They went for this fiction as for everything else to the models, and this meant in practice that they employed the pagan myths, not as imaginative symbols of a higher reality—it is still possible to employ them in that way—but merely in Boileau's phrase as "traditional ornaments" (*ornements reçus*). The neo-classicist to be sure might so employ his "fiction" as to inculcate a moral; in that case he is only too likely to give us instead of the living symbol, dead allegory; instead of high seriousness, its caricature, didacticism. The traditional stock of fiction became at last so intolerably trite as to be rejected even by some of the late neo-classicists. "The rejection and contempt of fiction," said Dr. Johnson (who indulged in it himself on occasion) "is rational and manly." But to reject fiction in the larger sense is to miss the true driving power in human nature—the imagination. Before concluding, however, that Dr. Johnson had no notion of the rôle of the imagination one should read his attack on the theory of the three unities[16] which was later to be turned to account by the romanticists.

Now the three unities may be defended on an entirely legitimate ground—on the ground namely that they make for concentration, a prime virtue in the drama; but the grounds on which they were actually imposed on the drama, especially in connection with the Quarrel of the Cid, illustrate the corruption of another main classical doctrine, that of probability or verisimilitude. In his dealings with probability as in his dealings with imitation, the neo-classical formalist did not allow sufficiently for the element of illusion. What he required from the drama in the name of probability was not the "illusion of a higher reality," but strict logic or even literal deception. He was not capable of a poetic faith, not willing to suspend his disbelief on passing from the world of ordinary fact to the world of artistic creation. Goethe was thinking especially of the neo-classical French when he said: "As for the French, they will always be arrested by their reason. They do not recognize that the imagination has its own laws which are and always must be problematic for the reason."

It was also largely under French influence that the doctrine of decorum, which touches probability at many points, was turned aside from its true meaning. Decorum is in a way the peculiar doctrine of the classicist, is in Milton's phrase "the grand masterpiece to observe." The doctrines of the universal and the imitation of the universal go deeper indeed than decorum, so much deeper that they are shared by classicism with religion. The man who aspires to live religiously must no less than the humanist look to some model set above his ordinary self and imitate it. But though the classicist at his best meditates, he does not, like the seeker after religious perfection, see in meditation an end in itself but rather a support for the mediatory virtues, the virtues of the man who would live to the best advantage in this world rather than renounce it; and these virtues may be said to be summed up in decorum. For the best type of Greek humanist, a Sophocles let us say, decorum was a vital and immediate thing. But there enters into decorum even from the time of the Alexandrian Greeks, and still more into French neo-classical decorum, a marked element of artificiality. The all-roundness and fine symmetry, the poise and dignity that come from working within the bounds of the human law, were taken to be the privilege not of man in general but of a special social class. Take for instance verbal decorum: the French neo-classicists assumed that if the speech of poetry is to be noble and highly serious it must coincide with the speech of the aristocracy. As Nisard puts it, they confused nobility of language with the language of the nobility. Decorum was thus more or less merged with etiquette, so that the standards of the stage and of literature in general came to coincide, as Rousseau complains, with those of the drawing-room. More than anything else this narrowing of decorum marks the decline from the classic to the pseudo-classic, from form to formalism.

While condemning pseudo-decorum one should remember that even a Greek would have seen something paradoxical in a poem like Goethe's "Hermann und Dorothea" and its attempt to invest with epic grandeur the affairs of villagers and peasants. After all, dignity and elevation and especially the opportunity for important action, which is the point on which the classicist puts prime emphasis, are normally though not invariably associated with a high rather than with a mean social estate. In general one should insist that the decorum worked out under French auspices was far from being merely artificial. The French gentleman (*honnête homme*) of the seventeenth century often showed a moderation and freedom from over-emphasis, an exquisite tact and urbanity that did not fall too far short of his immediate model, Horace, and related him to the all-round man of the Greeks (καλὸς κάγαθός). To be sure an ascetic Christian like Pascal sees in decorum a disguise of one's ordinary self rather than a real curb upon it, and feels that the gap is not sufficiently wide between even the best type of the man of the world and the mere worldling. One needs, however, to be very austere to disdain the art of living that has been fostered by decorum from the Greeks down. Something of this art of living survives even in a Chesterfield, who falls far short of the best type of French gentleman and reminds one very remotely indeed of a Pericles. Chesterfield's half-jesting definition of decorum as the art of combining the useful appearances of virtue with the solid satisfactions of vice points the way to its ultimate corruption. Talleyrand, who marks perhaps this last stage, was defined by Napoleon as "a silk stocking filled with mud." In some of its late exemplars decorum

had actually become, as Rousseau complains, the "mask of hy
pocrisy" and the "varnish of vice."

One should not however, like Rousseau and the romanticists,
judge of decorum by what it degenerated into. Every doctrine
of genuine worth is disciplinary and men in the mass do not
desire discipline. "Most men," says Aristotle, "would rather
live in a disorderly than in a sober manner." But most men do
not admit any such preference—that would be crude and in-
artistic. They incline rather to substitute for the reality of discipline some art of going through the motions. Every great
doctrine is thus in constant peril of passing over into some hollow semblance or even, it may be, into some mere caricature
of itself. When one wishes therefore to determine the nature of
decorum one should think of a Milton, let us say, and not of a
Talleyrand or even of a Chesterfield.

Milton imitated the models, like any other neo-classicist, but
his imitation was not, in Joubert's phrase, that of one book
by another book, but of one soul by another soul. His decorum
is therefore imaginative; and it is the privilege of the imagination to give the sense of spaciousness and infinitude. On the
other hand, the unimaginative way in which many of the
neo-classicists held their main tenets—nature, imitation, probability, decorum—narrowed unduly the scope of the human
spirit and appeared to close the gates of the future. "Art
and diligence have now done their best," says Dr. Johnson
of the versification of Pope, "and what shall be added will be
the effort of tedious toil and needless curiosity." Nothing is
more perilous than thus to seem to confine man in some pin-
fold; there is something in him that refuses to acquiesce in any
position as final; he is in Nietzsche's phrase the being who
must always surpass himself. The attempt to oppose external
and mechanical barriers to the freedom of the spirit will create
in the long run an atmosphere of stuffiness and smugness, and
nothing is more intolerable than smugness. Men were guillo-
tined in the French Revolution, as Bagehot suggests, simply
because either they or their ancestors had been smug. Inert acceptance of tradition and routine will be met sooner or later by
the cry of Faust: *Hinaus ins Freie!*

Before considering the value of the method chosen by Rousseau and the romanticists for breaking up the "tiresome old heavens" and escaping from smugness and stuffiness, one should note that the lack of originality and genius which they lamented in the eighteenth century—especially in that part of it known as the Enlightenment—was not due entirely to pseudo-classic formalism. At least two other main currents entered into the Enlightenment: first the empirical and utilitarian current that goes back to Francis Bacon, and some would say to Roger Bacon; and secondly the rationalistic current that goes back to Descartes. English empiricism gained international vogue in the philosophy of Locke, and Locke denies any super-sensuous element in human nature to which one may have access with the aid of the imagination or in any other way. Locke's method of precise naturalistic observation is in itself legitimate; for man is plainly subject to the natural law. What is not truly empirical is to bring the whole of human nature under this law. One can do this only by piecing out precise observation and experiment with dogmatic rationalism. One side of Locke may therefore be properly associated with the father of modern rationalists, Descartes. The attempt of the rationalist to lock up life in some set of formulæ produces in the imaginative man a feeling of oppression. He gasps for light and air. The very tracing of cause and effect and in general the use of the analytical faculties—and this is to fly to the opposite extreme—came to be condemned by the romanticists as inimical to the imagination. Not only do they make endless attacks on Locke, but at times they assail even Newton for having mechanized life, though Newton's comparison of himself to a child picking up pebbles on the seashore would seem to show that he had experienced "the feeling infinite."

The elaboration of science into a closed system with the aid of logic and pure mathematics is as a matter of fact to be associated with Descartes rather than with Newton. Neither Newton nor Descartes, one scarcely needs add, wished to subject man entirely to the natural law and the nexus of physical causes; they were not in short determinists. Yet the superficial rationalism of the Enlightenment was in the main of Cartesian origin. This Cartesian influence ramifies in so many directions and is related at so many points to the literary movement, and there has been so much confusion about this relationship, that we need to pause here to make a few distinctions.

Perhaps what most strikes one in the philosophy of Descartes is its faith in logic and abstract reasoning and the closely allied processes of mathematical demonstration. Anything that is not susceptible of clear proof in this logical and almost mathematical sense is to be rejected. Now this Cartesian notion of clearness is fatal to a true classicism. The higher reality, the true classicist maintains, cannot be thus demonstrated; it can only be grasped, and then never completely, through a veil of imaginative illusion. Boileau is reported to have said that Descartes had cut the throat of poetry; and this charge is justified in so far as the Cartesian requires from poetry a merely logical clearness. This conception of clearness was also a menace to the classicism of the seventeenth century which rested in the final analysis not on logic but on tradition. This appeared very clearly in the early phases of the quarrel between ancients and moderns when literary Cartesians like Perrault and Fontenelle attacked classical dogma in the name of reason. In fact one may ask if any doctrine has ever appeared so fatal to every form of tradition—not merely literary but also religious and political—as Cartesianism. The rationalist of the eighteenth century was for dismissing as "prejudice" everything that could not give a clear account of itself in the Cartesian sense. This riot of abstract reasoning (*la raison raisonnante*) that prepared the way for the Revolution has been identified by Taine and others with the classic spirit. A more vicious confusion has seldom gained currency in criticism. It is true that the French have mixed a great deal of logic with their conception of the classic spirit, but that is because they have mixed a great deal of logic with everything. I have already mentioned their tendency to substitute a logical for an imaginative verisimilitude; and strenuously logical classicists may be found in France from Chapelain to Brunetière. Yet the distinction that should keep us from confusing mere logic with the classic spirit was made by a Frenchman who was himself violently logical and also a great geometrician—Pascal. One should keep distinct, says Pascal, the *esprit de géométrie* and the *esprit de finesse*. The *esprit de finesse* is not, like the *esprit de géométrie*, abstract, but very concrete.[17] So far as a man possesses the *esprit de finesse* he is enabled to judge correctly of the ordinary facts of life and of the relationships between man and man. But these judgments rest upon such a multitude of delicate perceptions that he is frequently unable to account for them logically. It is to intuitive good sense and not to the *esprit de géométrie* that the gentleman (*honnête homme*) of the neo-classical period owed his fine tact. Pascal himself finally took a stand against reason as understood both by the Cartesian and by the man of the world. Unaided reason he held is unable to prevail against the deceits of the imagination; it needs the support of intuition—an intuition that he identifies with grace, thus making it inseparable from the most austere form of Christianity. The "heart," he says, and this is the name he gives to intuition, "has reasons of which the reason knows nothing." A Plato or an Aristotle would not have understood this divorce between reason and intuition.[18]

Pascal seems to get his insight only by flouting ordinary good sense. He identifies this insight with a type of theological dogma of which good sense was determined to be rid; and so it tended to get rid of the insight along with the dogma. Classical dogma also seemed at times to be in opposition to the intuitive good sense of the man of the world. The man of the world therefore often inclined to assail both the classical and the Christian tradition in the name of good sense, just as the Cartesian inclined to assail these traditions in the name of abstract reason. Perhaps the best exponent of anti-traditional good sense in the seventeenth century was Molière. He vindicated nature, and by nature he still meant in the main normal human nature, from arbitrary constraints of every kind whether imposed by an ascetic Christianity or by a narrow and pedantic classicism. Unfortunately Molière is too much on the side of the opposition. He does not seem to put his good sense into the service of some positive insight of his own. Good sense may be of many degrees according to the order of facts of which it has a correct perception. The order of facts in human nature that Molière's good sense perceived is not the highest and so this good sense appears at times too ready to justify the bourgeois against the man who has less timid and conventional views. So at least Rousseau thought when he made his famous attack on Molière.[19] Rousseau assailed Molière in the name of instinct as Pascal would have assailed him in the name of insight, and fought sense with sensibility. The hostility of Rousseau to Molière, according to M. Faguet, is that of a romantic Bohemian to a philistine of genius.[20] One hesitates to call Molière a philistine, but one may at least grant M. Faguet that Molière's good sense is not always sufficiently inspired.

I have been trying to build up a background that will make clear why the reason of the eighteenth century (whether we understand by reason logic or good sense) had come to be superficial and therefore oppressive to the imagination. It is only with reference to this "reason" that one can understand the romantic revolt. But neo-classical reason itself can be understood only with reference to its background—as a recoil namely from a previous romantic excess. This excess was manifested not only in the intellectual romanticism of which I have already spoken, but in the cult of the romantic deed that had flourished in the Middle Ages. This cult and the literature that reflected it continued to appeal, even to the cultivated, well on into the neo-classical period. It was therefore felt necessary to frame a definition of reason that should be a rebuke to the extravagance and improbability of the mediæval romances. When men became conscious in the eighteenth century of the neo-classical meagerness on the imaginative side they began to look back with a certain envy to the free efflorescence of fiction in the Middle Ages. They began to ask themselves with Hurd whether the reason and correctness they had won were worth the sacrifice of a "world of fine fabling." [21] We must not, however, like Heine and many others, look on the romantic movement as merely a return to the Middle Ages. We have seen that the men of the Middle Ages themselves understood by romance not simply their own kind of speech and writing in contrast with what was written in Latin, but a kind of writing in which the pursuit of strangeness and adventure predominated. This pursuit of strangeness and adventure will be found to predominate in all types of romanticism. The type of romanticism, however, which came in towards the end of the eighteenth century did not, even when professedly mediæval, simply revert to the older types. It was primarily not a romanticism of thought or of action, the types we have encountered thus far, but a romanticism of feeling. The beginnings of this emotional romanticism antedate considerably the application of the word romantic to a particular literary school. Before considering how the word came to be thus applied we shall need to take a glance at eighteenth-century sentimentalism, especially at the plea for genius and originality that, from about the middle of the century on, were opposed to the tameness and servile imitation of the neo-classicists.

CHAPTER TWO

ROMANTIC GENIUS

Romanticism, it has been remarked, is all that is not Voltaire. The clash between Rousseau and Voltaire is indeed not merely the clash between two men, it is the clash between two incompatible views of life. Voltaire is the end of the old world, as Goethe has put it, Rousseau the beginning of the new.

One is not to suppose, however, that Voltaire was a consistent champion of the past. He is indeed with all his superficial clearness one of the most incoherent of writers. At the same time that he defended classical tradition he attacked Christian tradition, spreading abroad a spirit of mockery and irreverence that tended to make every traditional belief impossible. The "reason" to which he appeals has all the shallowness that I have noticed in the "reason" of the eighteenth century. Though he does not fall into the Cartesian excess of abstract reasoning, and though the good sense that he most often understands by reason is admirably shrewd within certain bounds, he nevertheless falls very far short of the standards of a true classicism. He delights in the philosophy of Locke and has little sense for Greek philosophy or for the higher aspects of Greek literature. He is quite lacking in the quality of imagination that is needful if one is to communicate with what is above the ordinary rational level. So far from being capable of high seriousness, he is scarcely capable of ordinary seriousness. And so the nobility, elegance, imitation, and decorum that he is constantly preaching have about them a taint of formalism. Perhaps this taint appears most conspicuously in his conception of decorum. A man may be willing to impose restrictions on his ordinary self —and every type of decorum is restrictive—if he is asked to do so for some adequate end. The end of the decorum that an Aristotle, for example, would impose is that one may become more human and therefore, as he endeavors to show in a highly positive fashion, happier. The only art and literature that will please a man who has thus become human through the observance of true decorum is an art and literature that are themselves human and decorous. Voltaire for his part wishes to subject art and literature to an elaborate set of restrictions in the name of decorum, but these restrictions are not joined to any adequate end. The only reward he holds out to those who observe all these restrictions is "the merit of difficulty overcome." At bottom, like so many of the Jesuits from whom he received his education, he looks upon art as a game—a very ingenious and complicated game. The French muse he compares to a person executing a difficult clog dance on a tight rope, and he argues from this comparison, not that the French muse should assume a less constrained posture, but that she should on the contrary be exemplary to the nations. No wonder the romanticists and even Dr. Johnson demurred at Voltaire's condemnation of Shakespeare in the name of this type of decorum.

Voltaire is therefore, in spite of all his dazzling gifts, one of the most compromising advocates of classicism. Pope also had eminent merits, but from the truly classical point of view he is about as inadequate as Voltaire; and this is important to remember because English romanticism tends to be all that is not Pope. The English romanticists revolted especially from the poetic diction of which Pope was one of the chief sources, and poetic diction, with its failure to distinguish between nobility of language and the language of the nobility, is only an aspect of artificial decorum. However, the revolt from poetic diction and decorum in general is not the central aspect of the great movement that resulted in the eclipse of the wit and man of the world and in the emergence of the original genius. What the genius wanted was spontaneity, and spontaneity, as he understood it, involves a denial, not merely of decorum, but of something that, as I have said, goes deeper than decorum—namely the doctrine of imitation. According to Voltaire genius is only judicious imitation. According to Rousseau the prime mark of genius is refusal to imitate. The movement away from imitation, however, had already got well started before it thus came to a picturesque head in the clash between Rousseau and Voltaire, and if we wish to understand this movement we need to t ke a glance at its beginnings—especially in England.

There are reasons why this supposed opposition between imitation and genius should have been felt in England more keenly than elsewhere. The doctrine of imitation in its neo-classical form did not get established there until about the time of Dryden. In the meanwhile England had had a great creative literature in which the freedom and spontaneity of the imagination had not been cramped by a too strict imitation of models. Dryden himself, though he was doing more than any one else to promote the new correctness that was coming in from France, felt that this correctness was no equivalent for the Elizabethan inspiration. The structure that he and his contemporaries were erecting might be more regular, but lacked the boldness and originality of that reared by the "giant race before the flood":

> *Our age was cultivated thus at length;*
> *But what we gained in skill we lost in strength.*
> *Our builders were with want of genius cursed;*
> *The second temple was not like the first.*[1]

This contrast between the imitator and the inspired original was developed by Addison in a paper ("Spectator," 160) that was destined to be used against the very school to which he himself belonged. For Addison was in his general outlook a somewhat tame Augustan. Nevertheless he exalts the "natural geniuses" who have something "nobly wild and extravagant" in them above the geniuses who have been "refined by conversation, reflection and the reading of the most polite authors"; who have "formed themselves by rules and submitted the greatness of their natural talents to the corrections and restraints of art." "The great danger in these latter kind of geniuses, is lest they cramp their own abilities too much by imitation, and form themselves altogether upon models, without giving full play to their own natural parts. An imitation of the best authors is not to compare with a good original; and I believe we may observe that very few writers make an extraordinary figure in the world, who have not something in their way of thinking or expressing themselves that is peculiar to them, and entirely their own."

Another main influence that was making against the doctrine of imitation was also largely of English origin. This was the idea of progress through scientific observation and experiment. As a result of this type of positivism, discovery was being added to discovery. Science was kindling man's imagination and opening up before him what he really craves, the vista of an endless advance. Why should not literature likewise do something new and original instead of sticking forever in the same rut of imitation? In its Greek form the doctrine of imitation was, as I have tried to show, not only flexible and progressive, but in its own way, positive and experimental. But in modern times the two main forms of imitation, the classical and the Christian, have worked within the limits imposed by tradition and traditional models. The imitation of models, the Christian imitation of Christ, let us say, or the classical imitation of Horace, may indeed be a very vital thing, the imitation of one soul by another soul; but when carried out in this vital way, the two main forms of imitation tend to clash, and the compromise between them, as I have already said, resulted in a good deal of formalism. By its positive and critical method science was undermining every traditional belief. Both the Christian and the classical formalists would have been the first to deny that the truths of imitation for which they stood could be divorced from tradition and likewise put on a positive and critical basis. The fact is indubitable in any case that the discrediting of tradition has resulted in a progressive lapse from the religious and the humanistic to the naturalistic level. An equally indubitable fact is that scientific or rationalistic naturalism tended from the early eighteenth century to produce emotional naturalism, and that both forms of naturalism were hostile to the doctrine of imitation.

The trend away from the doctrine of imitation towards emotional naturalism finds revolutionary expression in the literary field in such a work as Young's "Conjectures on Original Composition" (1759). Addison had asserted, as we have seen, the superiority of what is original in a man, of what comes to him spontaneously, over what he acquires by conscious effort and culture. Young, a personal friend of Addison's, develops this contrast between the "natural" and the "artificial" to its extreme consequences. "Modern writers," he says, "have a choice to make. . . . They may soar in the regions of liberty, or move in the soft fetters of easy imitation." "An original may be said to be of a vegetable nature; it rises spontaneously from the vital root of genius; it grows, it is not made; imitations are often a sort of manufacture, wrought up by those mechanics, art and labor, out of preëxistent materials not their own." "We may as well grow good by another's virtue, or fat by another's food, as famous by another's thought." One evidence that we are still living in the movement of which Young is one of the initiators is that his treatise will not only seem to most of us a very spirited piece of writing—that it certainly is—but doctrinally sound. And yet it is only one of those documents very frequent in literary history which lack intrinsic soundness, but which can be explained if not justified as a recoil from an opposite extreme. The unsoundness of Young's work comes out clearly if one compares it with the treatise on the "Sublime" attributed to Longinus which is not a mere protest against a previous excess, but a permanently acceptable treatment of the same problem of genius and inspiration. Longinus exalts genius, but is at the same time regardful of culture and tradition, and even emphasizes the relation between inspiration and the imitation of models. Young insinuates, on the contrary, that one is aided in becoming a genius by being brainless and ignorant. "Some are pupils of nature only, nor go further to school." "Many a genius probably there has been which could neither write nor read." It follows almost inevitably from these premises that genius flourishes most in the primitive ages of society before originality has been crushed beneath the super-

incumbent weight of culture and critics have begun their pernicious activities. Young did not take this step himself, but it
was promptly taken by others on the publication of the Ossianic poems (1762). Ossian is at once added to the list of
great originals already enumerated by Addison—Homer,
Pindar, the patriarchs of the Old Testament and Shakespeare
(whom Young like the later romanticists opposes to Pope).
"Poetry," says Diderot, summing up a whole movement, "calls
for something enormous, barbaric and savage."

This exaltation of the virtues of the primitive ages is simply
the projection into a mythical past of a need that the man of
the eighteenth century feels in the present—the need to let
himself go. This is what he understands by his "return to
nature." A whole revolution is implied in this reinterpretation
of the word nature. To follow nature in the classical sense is to
imitate what is normal and representative in man and so to
become decorous. To be natural in the new sense one must
begin by getting rid of imitation and decorum. Moreover, for
the classicist, nature and reason are synonymous. The primitivist, on the other hand, means by nature the spontaneous play
of impulse and temperament, and inasmuch as this liberty is
hindered rather than helped by reason, he inclines to look on
reason, not as the equivalent but as the opposite of nature.

If one is to understand this development, one should note
carefully how certain uses of the word reason, not merely by
the neo-classicists but by the anti-traditionalists, especially in
religion, tended to produce this denial of reason. It is a curious
fact that some of those who were attacking the Christian religion in the name of reason, were themselves aware that mere
reason, whether one understood by the word abstract reasoning
or uninspired good sense, does not satisfy, that in the long run
man is driven either to ⌐ise higher or to sink lower than reason. St. Evremond, for example, prays nature to deliver man
from the doubtful middle state in which she has placed him—
either to "lift him up to angelic radiance," or else to "sink him
to the instinct of simple animals." [2] Since the ascending path,
the path that led to angelic radiance, seemed to involve the acceptance of a mass of obsolete dogma, man gradually inclined
to sink below the rational level and to seek to recover the

"instinct of simple animals." Another and still more fundamental fact that some of the rationalists perceived and that
militated against their own position, is that the dominant element in man is not reason, but imagination, or if one prefers,
the element of illusion. "Illusion," said Voltaire himself, "is
the queen of the human heart." The great achievement of
tradition at its best was to be at once a limit and a support to
both reason and imagination and so to unite them in a common allegiance. In the new movement, at the same time that
reason was being encouraged by scientific method to rise up in
revolt against tradition, imagination was being fascinated and
drawn to the naturalistic level by scientific discovery and the
vista of an endless advance that it opened up. A main problem,
therefore, for the student of this movement is to determine
what forms of imaginative activity are possible on the naturalistic level. A sort of understanding was reached on this point
by different types of naturalists in the course of the eighteenth
century. One form of imagination, it was agreed, should be
displayed in science, another form in art and literature.[3] The
scientific imagination should be controlled by judgment and
work in strict subordination to the facts. In art and literature,
on the other hand, the imagination should be free. Genius and
originality are indeed in strict ratio to this freedom. "In the
fairy land of fancy," says Young, "genius may wander wild;
there it has a creative power, and may reign arbitrarily over
its own empire of chimeras." (The empire of chimeras was
later to become the tower of ivory.) This sheer indiscipline of
the literary imagination might seem in contrast with the discipline of the scientific imagination an inferiority; but such was
not the view of the partisans of original genius. Kant, indeed,
who was strongly influenced in his "Critique of Æsthetic Judgment" by these English theorists,[4] inclined to deny genius to
the man of science for the very reason that his imagination is
so strictly controlled. The fact would seem to be that a great
scientist, a Newton let us say, has as much right to be accounted a genius as Shakespeare. The inferiority of the genius
of a Newton compared with that of a Shakespeare lies in a
certain coldness. Scientific genius is thus cold because it oper-
ates in a region less relevant to man than poetic genius; it is,

in Bagehot's phrase, more remote from the "hearth of the soul."

The scientific and the literary imagination are indeed not quite so sharply contrasted by most of the theorists as might be inferred from what I have said; most of them do not admit that the literary imagination should be entirely free to wander in its own "empire of chimeras." Even literary imagination, they maintain, should in some measure be under the surveillance of judgment or taste. One should observe, however, that the judgment or taste that is supposed to control or restrict genius is not associated with the imagination. On the contrary, imagination is associated entirely with the element of novelty in things, which means, in the literary domain, with the expansive eagerness of a man to get his own uniqueness uttered. The genius for the Greek, let us remind ourselves, was not the man who was in this sense unique, but the man who perceived the universal; and as the universal can be perceived only with the aid of the imagination, it follows that genius may be defined as imaginative perception of the universal. The universal thus conceived not only gives a centre and purpose to the activity of the imagination, but sets bounds to the free expansion of temperament and impulse, to what came to be known in the eighteenth century as nature.

Kant, who denies genius to the man of science on grounds I have already mentioned, is unable to associate genius in art or literature with this strict discipline of the imagination to a purpose. The imagination must be free and must, he holds, show this freedom not by working but by playing. At the same time Kant had the cool temper of a man of the Enlightenment, and looked with the utmost disapproval on the aberrations that had marked in Germany the age of original genius (die Genie-zeit). He was not in the new sense of the word, nor indeed in any sense, an enthusiast. And so he wished the reason, or judgment, to keep control over the imagination without disturbing its free play; art is to have a purpose which is at the same time not a purpose. The distinctions by which he works out the supposed relationship between judgment and imagination are at once difficult and unreal. One can indeed put one's finger here more readily perhaps than elsewhere on the central impotence of the whole Kantian system. Once discredit tradition and outer authority and then set up as a substitute a reason that is divorced from the imagination and so lacks the support of supersensuous insight, and reason will prove unable to maintain its hegemony. When the imagination has ceased to pull in accord with the reason in the service of a reality that is set above them both, it is sure to become the accomplice of expansive impulse, and mere reason is not strong enough to prevail over this union of imagination and desire. Reason needs some driving power behind it, a driving power that, when working in alliance with the imagination, it gets from insight. To suppose that man will long rest content with mere naked reason as his guide is to forget that "illusion is the queen of the human heart"; it is to revive the stoical error. Schiller, himself a Kantian, felt this rationalistic rigor and coldness of his master, and so sought, while retaining the play theory of art, to put behind the cold reason of Kant the driving power it lacked; for this driving power he looked not to a supersensuous reality, not to insight in short, but to emotion. He takes appropriately the motto for his "Æsthetic Letters" from Rousseau: *Si c'est la raison qui fait l'homme, c'est le sentiment qui le conduit.* He retains Kant's play theory of art without even so much offset to this play as is implied in Kant's "purposiveness without purpose." The nobility of Schiller's intentions is beyond question. At the same time, by encouraging the notion that it is possible to escape from neo-classical didacticism only by eliminating masculine purpose from art, he opens the way for the worst perversions of the æsthete, above all for the divorce of art from ethical reality. In art, according to Schiller, both imagination and feeling should be free and spontaneous, and the result of all this freedom, as he sees it, will be perfectly "ideal." His suspicion of a purpose is invincible. As soon as anything has a purpose it ceases to be æsthetic and in the same measure suffers a loss of dignity. Thus the æsthetic moment of the lion, he says, is when he roars not with any definite design, but out of sheer lustiness, and for the pure pleasure of roaring.

One may assume safely the æsthetic attitude, or what amounts to the same thing, allow one's self to be guided by feeling, only on the assumption that feeling is worthy of trust. As appears in the very motto he took for his "Æsthetic Letters" Schiller was helped to this faith in man's native goodness by Rousseau. We need to pause for a moment at this point and consider the background of this belief which finds not only in Schiller but in Rousseau himself, with whom it is usually associated, a rather late expression. The movement that took its rise in the eighteenth century involves, we should recollect, a break not with one but with two traditions—the classical and the Christian. If the plea for genius and originality is to be largely explained as a protest against the mechanical imitation and artificial decorum of a certain type of classicist, the assertion of man's natural goodness is to be understood rather as a rebound from the doctrine of total depravity that was held by the more austere type of Christian. This doctrine had even in the early centuries of the faith awakened certain protests like that of Pelagius, but for an understanding of the Rousseauistic protest one does not need to go behind the great deistic movement of the early eighteenth century. God, instead of being opposed to nature, is conceived by the deist as a power that expresses his goodness and loveliness through nature. The oppressive weight of fear that the older theology had laid upon the human spirit is thus gradually lifted. Man begins to discover harmonies instead of discords in himself and outer nature. He not only sees virtue in instinct but inclines to turn virtue itself into a "sense," or instinct. And this means in practice to put emotional expansion in the place of spiritual concentration at the basis of life and morals. In studying this drift towards an æsthetic or sentimental morality one may most conveniently take one's point of departure in certain English writers of deistic tendency, especially in Shaftesbury and his disciple Hutcheson. Considered purely as an initiator, Shaftesbury is probably more important than Rousseau. His influence ramifies out in every direction, notably into Germany.

The central achievement of Shaftesbury from a purely psychological point of view may be said to be his transformation of conscience from an inner check into an expansive emotion. He is thus enabled to set up an æsthetic substitute not merely for traditional religion but for traditional humanism. He undermines insidiously decorum, the central doctrine of the classicist, at the very time that he seems to be defending it. For decorum also implies a control upon the expansive instincts of human nature, and Shaftesbury is actually engaged in rehabilitating "nature," and insinuating that it does not need any control. He attains this expansiveness by putting æsthetic in the place of spiritual perception, and so merging more or less completely the good and the true with the beautiful. He thus points the way very directly to Rousseau's rejection of both inner and outer control in the name of man's natural goodness. Once accept Shaftesbury's transformation of conscience and one is led almost inevitably to look on everything that is expansive as natural or vital and on everything that restricts expansion as conventional or artificial. Villers wrote to Madame de Staël (4 May, 1803): "The fundamental and creative idea of all your work has been to show primitive, incorruptible, naïve, passionate nature in conflict with the barriers and shackles of conventional life. . . . Note that this is also the guiding idea of the author of 'Werther.' " This contrast between nature and convention is indeed almost the whole of Rousseauism. In permitting his expansive impulses to be disciplined by either humanism or religion man has fallen away from nature much as in the old theology he has fallen away from God, and the famous "return to nature" means in practice the emancipation of the ordinary or temperamental self that had been thus artificially controlled. This throwing off of the yoke of both Christian and classical discipline in the name of temperament is the essential aspect of the movement in favor of original genius. The genius does not look to any pattern that is set above his ordinary spontaneous ego and imitate it. On the contrary, he attains to the self-expression that other men, intimidated by convention, weakly forego.

In thus taking a stand for self-expression, the original genius is in a sense on firm ground—at least so far as the mere rationalist or the late and degenerate classicist is concerned. No conventions are final, no rules can set arbitrary limits to creation. Reality cannot be locked up in any set of formulæ. The element of change and novelty in things, as the romanticists are never tired of repeating, is at once vital and inexhaustible.

Wherever we turn, we encounter, as a romantic authority, Jacob Boehme, declares, "abysmal, unsearchable and infinite multiplicity." Perhaps not since the beginning of the world have two men or indeed two leaves or two blades of grass been exactly alike. Out of a thousand men shaving, as Dr. Johnson himself remarked, no two will shave in just the same way. A person carries his uniqueness even into his thumbprint—as a certain class in the community has learned to its cost. But though all things are ineffably different they are at the same time ineffably alike. And this oneness in things is, no less than the otherwiseness, a matter of immediate perception. This universal implication of the one in the many is found even more marked than elsewhere in the heart of the individual. Each man has his idiosyncrasy (literally his "private mixture"). But in addition to his complexion, his temperamental or private self, every man has a self that he possesses in common with other men. Even the man who is most filled with his own uniqueness, or "genius," a Rousseau, for example, assumes this universal self in every word he utters. "Jove nods to Jove behind us as we talk." The word character, one may note, is ambiguous, inasmuch as it may refer either to the idiosyncratic or to the universal human element in a man's dual nature. For example, an original genius like William Blake not only uses the word character in a different sense from Aristotle—he cannot even understand the Aristotelian usage. "Aristotle," he complains, "says characters are either good or bad; now Goodness or Badness has nothing to do with Character. An apple tree, a pear tree, a horse, a lion are Characters; but a good apple tree or a bad is an apple tree still, etc." But character as Aristotle uses the word implies something that man possesses and that a horse or tree does not possess—the power namely to deliberate and choose. A man has a good or bad character, he is ethical or unethical, as one may say from the Greek word for character in this sense ($\mathring{\eta}\theta os$), according to the quality of his choice as it appears in what he actually does. This distinction between a man's private, peculiar character ($\chi\alpha\rho\alpha\kappa\tau\mathring{\eta}\rho$) and the character he possesses when judged with reference to something more general than his own complexion is very similar to the

French distinction between the *sens propre* and the *sens commun*.

The general sense or norm that is opposed to mere temperament and impulse may rest upon the ethos of a particular time and country—the traditional habits and customs that the Rousseauist is wont to dismiss as "artificial"—or it may rest in varying degrees upon immediate perception. For example, the Ismene and Antigone of Sophocles are both ethical; but Ismene would abide by the law of the state, whereas Antigone opposes to this law something still more universal—the "unwritten laws of heaven." This insight of Antigone into a moral order that is set not only above her ordinary self but above the convention of her time and country is something very immediate, something achieved, as I shall try to show more fully later, with the aid of the imagination.

It is scarcely necessary to add that such a perfect example of the ethical imagination as one finds in Antigone—the imagination that works concentric with the human law—is rare. In actual life for one Antigone who obeys the "unwritten laws of heaven" there will be a thousand Ismenes who will be guided in their moral choices by the law of the community. This law, the convention of a particular place and time, is always but a very imperfect image, a mere shadow indeed of the unwritten law which being above the ordinary rational level is, in a sense to be explained later, infinite and incapable of final formulation. And yet men are forced if only on practical grounds to work out some approximation to this law as a barrier to the unchained appetites of the individual. The elements that enter into any particular attempt to circumscribe the individual in the interests of the community are very mixed and in no small measure relative. Yet the things that any group of men have come together about—their conventions in the literal meaning of the word—even the tabus of a savage tribe, are sure to reflect, however inadequately, the element of oneness in man, the element which is opposed to expansive impulse, and which is no less real, no less a matter of immediate experience, than the element of irreducible difference. The general sense therefore should never be sacrificed lightly to the sense of the individual. Tabu, however inferior it may be to insight, deserves to rank higher after all than mere temperament.[5]

The original genius proceeds upon the opposite assumption. Everything that limits temperamental expansion is dismissed as either artificial or mechanical; everything on the contrary that makes for the emancipation of temperament, and so for variety and difference, he welcomes as vital, dynamic, creative. Now, speaking not metaphysically but practically and experimentally, man may, as I have said, follow two main paths: he may develop his ethical self—the self that lays hold of unity—or he may put his main emphasis on the element within him and without him that is associated with novelty and change. In direct proportion as he turns his attention to the infinite manifoldness of things he experiences wonder; if on the other hand he attends to the unity that underlies the manifoldness and that likewise transcends him, he experiences awe. As a man grows religious, awe comes more and more to take the place in him of wonder. The humanist is less averse from the natural order and its perpetual gushing forth of novelties than the man who is religious, yet even the humanist refuses to put his final emphasis on wonder (his motto is rather *nil admirari*). To illustrate concretely, Dr. Johnson can scarcely conceal his disdain for the wonderful, but being a genuinely religious spirit, is very capable of awe. Commenting on Yalden's line

Awhile th' Almighty wondering stood,

Dr. Johnson remarks: "He ought to have remembered that Infinite Knowledge can never wonder. All wonder is the effect of novelty upon Ignorance." Granted the justness of the remark, Johnson seems inclined at times to forget how wide is the gap in this respect between us and the Almighty and therefore to be unduly hostile to the element of wonder. To take the opposite case, it is not easy to discover in either the personality or writings of Poe an atom of awe or reverence. On the other hand he both experiences wonder and seeks in his art to be a pure wondersmith. It is especially important to determine a man's attitude towards himself in this matter of awe and wonder, in other words to determine whether he is taken up first of all with that element in his own nature which makes him incomprehensibly like other men or with that element which makes him incomprehensibly different from them. A man, the wise have always insisted, should look with reverence but not with wonder on himself. Rousseau boasts that if not better than other men, he is at least different. By this gloating sense of his own otherwiseness he may be said to have set the tone for a whole epoch. Chateaubriand, for instance, is quite overcome by his own uniqueness and wonderfulness. At the most ordinary happenings he exclaims, as Sainte-Beuve points out, that such things happen only to him. Hugo again is positively stupefied at the immensity of his own genius. The theatricality that one feels in so much of the art of this period arises from the eagerness of the genius to communicate to others something of the amazement that he feels at himself. René's first concern is to inspire wonder even in the women who love him. "Céluta felt that she was going to fall upon the bosom of this man as one falls into an abyss."

In thus putting such an exclusive emphasis on wonder the Rousseauistic movement takes on a regressive character. For if life begins in wonder it culminates in awe. To put "the budding rose above the rose full-blown" may do very well for a mood, but as an habitual attitude it implies that one is more interested in origins than in ends; and this means in practice to look backward and downward instead of forward and up. The conscious analysis that is needed if one is to establish orderly sequences and relationships and so work out a kingdom of ends is repudiated by the Rousseauist because it diminishes wonder, because it interferes with the creative impulse of genius as it gushes up spontaneously from the depths of the unconscious. The whole movement is filled with the praise of ignorance and of those who still enjoy its inappreciable advantages—the savage, the peasant and above all the child. The Rousseauist may indeed be said to have discovered the poetry of childhood of which only traces can be found in the past, but at what would seem at times a rather heavy sacrifice of rationality. Rather than consent to have the bloom taken off things by analysis one should, as Coleridge tells us, *sink back* to the devout state of childlike wonder. However, to grow ethically is not to sink back but to struggle painfully forward.

To affirm the contrary is to set up the things that are below
the ordinary rational level as a substitute for the things that
are above it, and at the same time to proclaim one's inability
to mature. The romanticist, it is true, is wont to oppose to the
demand for maturity Christ's praise of the child. But Christ
evidently praises the child not because of his capacity for wonder but because of his freedom from sin, and it is of the essence of Rousseauism to deny the very existence of sin—at
least in the Christian sense of the word. One may also read in
the New Testament that when one has ceased to be a child
one should give up childish things, and this is a saying that no
primitivist, so far as I am aware, has ever quoted. On the contrary, he is ready to assert that what comes to the child spontaneously is superior to the deliberate moral effort of the mature
man. The speeches of all the sages are, according to
Maeterlinck, outweighed by the unconscious wisdom of the
passing child. Wordsworth hails a child of six as "Mighty
Prophet! Seer blest!" (It is only fair to Coleridge to say that he
refused to follow Wordsworth into this final abyss of absurd-
ity.[6]) In much the same way Hugo pushes his adoration of the
child to the verge of what has been termed "solemn silliness"
(*niaiserie solennelle*).

To set up the spontaneity of the child as a substitute for
insight, to identify wonder with awe, romance with religion,
is to confuse the very planes of being. There would appear to
be a confusion of this kind in what Carlyle takes to be his own
chief discovery, in his "natural supernaturalism." [7] The natural
order, we must grant Carlyle, is unfathomable, but it is not
therefore awful, only wonderful. A movement of charity belongs, as Pascal says, to an entirely different order.[8]

The spiritual order to which Pascal refers lifts a man so far
as he perceives it out of his ordinary self and draws him to an
ethical centre. But the Rousseauist tends, as I have said, to
repudiate the very idea of an ethical centre along with the
special forms in which it had got itself embedded. Every attempt, whether humanistic or religious, to set up some such
centre, to oppose a unifying and centralizing principle to expansive impulse, seems to him arbitrary and artificial. He does
not discriminate between the ethical norm or centre that a

Sophocles grasps intuitively and the centrality that the pseudo-classicist hopes to achieve by mechanical imitation. He argues from his underlying assumption that the principle of variation is alone vital, that one's genius and originality are in pretty direct ratio to one's eccentricity in the literal meaning of the word; and he is therefore ready to affirm his singularity or difference in the face of whatever happens to be established. This attitude, it is worth noting, is quite unlike that of the humorist in the old English sense of the word, who indulges his bent and is at the same time quite unconcerned with any central model that he should imitate and with reference to which he should discipline his oddities. The idiosyncrasy of the Rousseauist is not, like that of the humorist, genial, but defiant. He is strangely self-conscious in his return to the unconscious. In everything, from his vocabulary to the details of his dress, he is eager to emphasize his departure from the norm. Hence the persistent pose and theatricality in so many of the leaders of this movement, in Rousseau himself, for instance, or in Chateaubriand and Byron. As for the lesser figures in the movement their "genius" is often chiefly displayed in their devices for calling attention to themselves as the latest and most marvellous births of time; it is only one aspect in short of an art in which the past century, whatever its achievement in the other arts, has easily surpassed all its predecessors—the art of advertising.

One needs always to return, however, if one is to understand the romantic notion of genius, to a consideration of the pseudo-classic decorum against which it is a protest. The gentleman or man of the world (*honnête homme*) was not, like the original genius, anxious to advertise himself, to call attention to his own special note of originality, since his primary concern was with an entirely different problem, with the problem, namely, not of expressing but of humanizing himself; and he could humanize himself, he felt, only by constant reference to the accepted standard of what the normal man should be. He refused to "pride himself on anything"; he was fearful of overemphasis, because the first of virtues in his eyes was a sense of proportion. The total symmetry of life to which the best type of classicist refers back his every impulse, he ap-

prehends intuitively with the aid of his imagination. The symmetry to which the pseudo-classicist refers back his impulses
has ceased to be imaginative and has become a mere conformity to an outer code or even to the rules of etiquette; and so,
instead of a deep imaginative insight, he gets mere elegance
or polish. The unity that a purely external decorum of this
kind imposes on life degenerates into a tiresome sameness. It
seems an unwarranted denial of the element of wonder and
surprise. "Boredom was born one day of uniformity," said La
Motte Houdard, who was himself a pseudo-classicist; whereas
variety as everybody knows is the spice of life. The romanticist
would break up the smooth and tiresome surface of artificial
decorum by the pursuit of strangeness. If he can only get his
thrill he cares little whether it is probable, whether it bears
any relation, that is, to normal human experience. This sacrifice
of the probable to the surprising appears, as I said at the outset,
in all types of romanticism—whether of action or thought or
feeling. The genuine classicist always puts his main stress on
design or structure; whereas the main quest of every type of
romanticist is rather for the intense and vivid and arresting
detail. Take, for instance, the intellectual romanticism that prevailed especially in the late sixteenth and early seventeenth centuries. In the "witty and conceited" poets of this period the
intellect is engaged in a more or less irresponsible vagabondage
with the imagination as its free accomplice. The conceits by
which a poet of this type displays his "ingenuity" (genius) are
not structural, are not, that is, referred back to any centre.
They stand forth each separately and sharply from the surface
of the style (hence known to the French as "points"), and
so arrest the reader by their novelty. Their rareness and pre-
ciousness, however, are intended to startle the intellect alone.
They do not have and are not intended to have any power of
sensuous suggestion. The Rousseauistic romanticist, on the
other hand, so far from being "metaphysical," strives to be
concrete even at the risk of a certain materialism of style, of
turning his metaphors into mere images. Like the intellectual
romanticist, though in a different way, he wishes to break up
the smooth and monotonous surface of life and style, and so
he sets up the cult of the picturesque. To understand this cult

one needs to remember the opposite extreme of artificial symmetry. One needs to recall, for example, the neo-classicist who complained of the stars in heaven because they were not arranged in symmetrical patterns, or various other neo-classicists who attacked mountains because of their rough and irregular shapes, because of their refusal to submit to the rule and compass. When beauty is conceived in so mechanical a fashion some one is almost certain to wish to "add strangeness" to it.

The cult of the picturesque is closely associated with the cult of local color. Here as elsewhere romantic genius is, in contradistinction to classical genius which aims at the "grandeur of generality," the genius of wonder and surprise. According to Buffon, who offers the rare spectacle of a man of science who is at the same time a theorist of the grand manner, genius is shown in the architectonic gift—in the power so to unify a subject as to keep its every detail in proper subordination to the whole. Any mere wantoning of the imagination in the pursuit of either the precious or the picturesque is to be severely repressed if one is to attain to the grandeur of generality. Buffon is truly classic in relating genius to design. Unfortunately he verges towards the pseudo-classic in his distrust of color, of the precise word and the vivid descriptive epithet. The growing verbal squeamishness that so strikes one towards the end of the neo-classic period is one outcome of artificial decorum, of confusing nobility of language with the language of the nobility. There was an increasing fear of the trivial word that might destroy the illusion of the grand manner, and also of the technical term that should be too suggestive of specialization. All terms were to be avoided that were not readily intelligible to a lady or gentleman in the drawing-room. And so it came to pass that by the end of the eighteenth century the grand manner, or elevated style, had come to be largely an art of ingenious circumlocution, and Buffon gives some countenance to this conception of classic dignity and representativeness when he declares that one should describe objects "only by the most general terms." At all events the reply of the romantic genius to this doctrine is the demand for local color, for the concrete and picturesque phrase. The general truth at which the classicist aims the Rousseauist dismisses as identical with the gray and the academic, and bends all his efforts to the rendering of the vivid and unique detail. Of the readiness of the romantic genius to show (or one is tempted to say) to advertise his originality by trampling verbal decorum under foot along with every other kind of decorum, I shall have more to say later. He is ready to employ not only the homely and familiar word that the pseudo-classicist had eschewed as "low," but words so local and technical as to be unintelligible to ordinary readers. Chateaubriand deals so specifically with the North American Indian and his environment that the result, according to Sainte-Beuve, is a sort of "tattooing" of his style. Hugo bestows a whole dictionary of architectural terms upon the reader in his "Notre Dame," and of nautical terms in his "Toilers of the Sea." In order to follow some of the passages in Balzac's "César Birotteau," one needs to be a lawyer or a professional accountant, and it has been said that in order to do justice to a certain description in Zola one would need to be a pork-butcher. In this movement towards a highly specialized vocabulary one should note a coöperation, as so often elsewhere, between the two wings of the naturalistic movement— the scientific and the emotional. The Rousseauist is, like the scientist, a specialist—he specializes in his own sensations. He goes in quest of emotional thrills for their own sake, just as Napoleon's generals, according to Sainte-Beuve, waged war without any ulterior aim but for the sheer lust of conquest. The vivid images and picturesque details are therefore not sufficiently structural; each one tends to thrust itself forward without reference to the whole and to demand attention for its own sake.

The pursuit of the unrelated thrill without reference to its motivation or probability leads in the romantic movement to a sort of descent—often, it is true, a rapturous and lyrical descent—from the dramatic to the melodramatic. It is possible to trace this one-sided emphasis on wonder not merely in vocabulary but in the increasing resort to the principle of contrast. One suspects, for example, that Rousseau exaggerates the grotesqueness of his youthful failure as a musical composer at Lausanne in order that his success in the same rôle before the king and all the ladies of the court at Versailles may "stick more fiery off." The contrast that Chateaubriand establishes between the two banks of the Mississippi at the beginning of his "Atala" is so complete as to put some strain on verisimilitude. One may note in this same description, as a somewhat different way of sacrificing the probable to the picturesque, the bears drunk on wild grapes and reeling on the branches of the elms. To prove that it was possible on some particular occasion to look down the vista of a forest glade on the lower Mississippi and see it closed by a drunken bear does not meet the difficulty at all. For art has to do, as was remarked long ago, not with the possible but the probable; and a bear in this posture is a possible but scarcely a probable bear.

To return to the principle of contrast: Hugo dilates upon his puniness as an infant ("abandoned by everybody, even by his mother") in order to make his later achievement seem still more stupendous.[9] The use of the antithesis as the auxiliary of surprise, the abrupt and thrilling passage from light to shade or the contrary, finds perhaps its culminating expression in Hugo. A study of this one figure as it appears in his words and ideas, in his characters and situations and subjects, would show that he is the most melodramatic genius for whom high rank has ever been claimed in literature. The suddenness of Jean Valjean's transformation from a convict into a saint may serve as a single instance of Hugo's readiness to sacrifice verisimilitude to surprise in his treatment of character.

Closely allied to the desire to break up the monotonous surface of "good form" by the pointed and picturesque style in writing is the rise of the pointed and picturesque style in dress. A man may advertise his genius and originality (in the romantic sense of these terms) by departing from the accepted modes of costume as well as from the accepted modes of speech. Gautier's scarlet waistcoat at the first performance of "Hernani" is of the same order as his flamboyant epithets, his riot of local color, and was at least as effective in achieving the main end of his life—to be, in his own phrase, the "terror of the sleek, baldheaded bourgeois." In assuming the Armenian garb to the astonishment of the rustics of Motiers-Travers, Rousseau anticipates not merely Gautier but innumerable other violators of conventional correctness: here as elsewhere he deserves to rank as the classic instance, one is tempted to say, of romantic eccentricity. La Bruyère, an exponent of the traditional good-breeding against which Rousseauism is a protest, says that the gentleman allows himself to be dressed by his tailor. He wishes to be neither ahead of the mode nor behind it, being reluctant as he is in all things to oppose his private sense to the general sense. His point of view in the matter of dress is not so very remote from that of a genuine classicism, whereas the enthusiast who recently went about the streets of New York (until taken in by the police) garbed as a contemporary of Pericles is no less plainly a product of Rousseauistic revolt.

Chateaubriand's relation to Rousseauism in this matter calls for special comment. He encouraged, and to some extent held, the belief that to show genius and originality one must be irregular and tempestuous in all things, even in the arrangement of one's hair. At the same time he preached reason. His heart, in short, was romantic, his head classical. Both as a classicist and a romanticist he was ready to repudiate on the one hand his master Rousseau, and on the other his own disciples. As a romantic genius he wished to regard himself as unique and so unrelated to Rousseau. At the same time he also looked upon it as a sort of insolence for any of his own followers to aspire to such a lonely preëminence in grief as René. As a classicist he saw that great art aims at the normal and the representative, and that it is therefore absurd for people to pattern themselves on such morbid and exceptional characters as René and Childe Harold. Most of the romanticists indeed showed themselves very imitative even in their attempts at uniqueness, and the result was a second or third hand, or as one is tempted to say, a stale eccentricity. In their mere following of the mode many of the French romanticists of 1830 were ready to impose a painful discipline upon themselves[10] in order to appear abnormal, in order, for instance, to acquire a livid Byronic complexion. Some of those who wished to seem elegiac like Lamartine rather than to emulate the violent and histrionic revolt of the Conrads and Laras actually succeeded, we are told, in giving themselves consumption (hence the epithet *école poitrinaire*).

In outer and visible freakishness the French romanticists of 1830 probably bore away the palm, though in inner and spiritual remoteness from normal human experience they can scarcely vie with the early German romanticists. And this is doubtless due to the fact that in France there was a more definite outer standard from which to advertise their departure, and also to the fact that the revolt against this standard was so largely participated in by the painters and by writers like Gautier who were also interested in painting. Chateaubriand writes of the romantic painters (and the passage will also serve to illustrate his attitude towards his own disciples): "[These artists] rig themselves up as comic sketches, as grotesques, as caricatures. Some of them wear frightful mustaches, one would suppose that they are going forth to conquer the world —their brushes are halberds, their paint-scratchers sabres; others have enormous beards and hair that puffs out or hangs down their shoulders; they smoke a cigar volcanically. These cousins of the rainbow, to use a phrase of our old Régnier, have their heads filled with deluges, seas, rivers, forests, cataracts, tempests, or it may be with slaughters, tortures and scaffolds. One finds among them human skulls, foils, mandolins, helmets and dolmans. . . . They aim to form a separate species between the ape and the satyr; they give you to understand that the secrecy of the studio has its dangers and that there is no safety for the models."

These purely personal eccentricities that so marked the early stages in the warfare between the Bohemian and the philistine have as a matter of fact diminished in our own time. Nowadays a man of the distinction of Disraeli or even of Bulwer-Lytton[11] would scarcely affect, as they did, the flamboyant style in dress. But the underlying failure to discriminate between the odd and the original has persisted and has worked out into even extremer consequences. One may note, as I have said, even in the early figures in the movement a tendency to play to the gallery, a something that suggests the approach of the era of the lime-light and the big headline. Rousseau himself has been called the father of yellow journalists. There is an unbroken development from the early exponents of original genius down to cubists, futurists and post-impressionists and the corresponding schools in literature. The partisans of expression as opposed to form in the eighteenth century led to the fanatics of expression in the nineteenth and these have led to the maniacs of expression of the twentieth. The extremists in painting have got so far beyond Cézanne, who was regarded not long ago as one of the wildest of innovators, that Cézanne is, we are told, "in a fair way to achieve the unhappy fate of becoming a classic." Poe was fond of quoting a saying of Bacon's that "there is no excellent beauty that hath not some strangeness in the proportion." This saying became known in France through Baudelaire's rendering of Poe and was often ascribed to Poe himself. It was taken to mean that the stranger one became the nearer one was getting to perfect beauty. And if we grant this view of beauty we must admit that some of the decadents succeeded in becoming very beautiful indeed. But the more element of proportion in beauty is sacrificed to strangeness the more the result will seem to the normal man to be, not beauty at all, but rather an esoteric cult of ugliness. The romantic genius therefore denounces the normal man as a philistine and at the same time, since he cannot please him, seeks at least to shock him and so capture his attention by the very violence of eccentricity.

The saying I have quoted from Bacon is perhaps an early example of the inner alliance between things that superficially often seem remote—the scientific spirit and the spirit of romance. Scientific discovery has given a tremendous stimulus to wonder and curiosity, has encouraged a purely exploratory attitude towards life and raised an overwhelming prepossession in favor of the new as compared with the old. Baconian and Rousseauist evidently come together by their primary emphasis on novelty. The movement towards a more and more eccentric conception of art and literature has been closely allied in practice with the doctrine of progress—and that from the very dawn of the so-called Quarrel of Ancients and Moderns. It is scarcely possible to exaggerate the havoc that has been wrought by the transfer of the belief that the latest thing is the best—a belief that is approximately true of automobiles—from the material order to an entirely different realm.[12] The very heart of the classical message, one cannot repeat too often, is that one should aim first of all not to be original, but to be human, and that to be human one needs to look up to a sound model and imitate it. The imposition of form and proportion upon one's expansive impulses which results from this process of imitation is, in the true sense of that much abused word, culture. Genuine culture is difficult and disciplinary. The mediation that it involves between the conflicting claims of form and expression requires the utmost contention of spirit. We have here a clue to the boundless success of the Rousseauistic doctrine of spontaneity, of the assertion that genius resides in the region of the primitive and unconscious and is hindered rather than helped by culture. It is easier to be a genius on Rousseauistic lines than to be a man on the terms imposed by the classicist. There is a fatal facility about creation when its quality is not tested by some standard set above the creator's temperament; and the same fatal facility appears in criticism when the critic does not test creation by some standard set above both his own temperament and that of the creator. The romantic critic as a matter of fact confines his ambition to receiving so keen an impression from genius, conceived as something purely temperamental, that when this creative expression is passed through his temperament it will issue forth as a fresh expression. Taste, he holds, will thus tend to become one with genius, and criticism, instead of being cold and negative like that of the neo-classicist, will itself grow creative.[13] But the critic who does not get beyond this stage will have gusto, zest, relish, what you will, he will not have taste. For taste involves a difficult mediation between the element of uniqueness in both critic and creator and that which is representative and human. Once eliminate this human standard that is set above the temperament of the creator and make of the critic in turn a mere pander to "genius" and it is hard to see what measure of a man's excellence is left save his intoxication with himself; and this measure would scarcely seem to be trustworthy. "Every ass that's romantic," says Wolseley in his Preface to "Valentinian" (1686) "believes he's inspired."

An important aspect of the romantic theory of genius remains to be considered. This theory is closely associated in its rise and growth with the theory of the master faculty or ruling passion. A man can do that for which he has a genius without effort, whereas no amount of effort can avail to give a man that for which he has no native aptitude.[14] Buffon affirmed in opposition to this view that genius is only a capacity for taking pains or, as an American recently put it, is ten per cent inspiration and ninety per cent perspiration. This notion of genius not only risks running counter to the observed facts as to the importance of the native gift but it does not bring out as clearly as it might the real point at issue. Even though genius were shown to be ninety per cent inspiration a man should still, the classicist would insist, fix his attention on the fraction that is within his power. Thus Boileau says in substance at the outset of his "Art of Poetry" that a poet needs to be born under a propitious star. Genius is indispensable, and not merely genius in general but genius for the special kind of poetry in which he is to excel. Yet granting all this, he says to the poetical aspirant, bestir yourself! The mystery of grace will always be recognized in any view of life that gets at all beneath the surface. Yet it is still the better part to turn to the feasibility of works. The view of genius as merely a temperamental overflow is as a matter of fact only a caricature of the doctrine of grace. It suits the spiritual indolence of the creator who seeks to evade the more difficult half of his problem—which is not merely to create but to humanize his creation. Hawthorne, for example, is according to Mr. Brownell, too prone (except in the "Scarlet Letter") to get away from the clear sunlight of normal human experience into a region of somewhat crepuscular symbolism, and this is because he yielded too complacently and fatalistically to what he conceived to be his genius. The theory of genius is perhaps the chief inheritance of the New England transcendentalists from romanticism. Hawthorne was more on his guard against the extreme implications of the theory than most other members of this group. It remains to be seen how much the exaltation of genius and depreciation of culture that marks one whole side of Emerson will in the long run tell against his reputation. The lesser New England men showed a rare incapacity to distinguish between originality and mere freakishness either in themselves or in others.

It is fair to say that in lieu of the discipline of culture the romantic genius has often insisted on the discipline of technique; and this has been especially true in a country like

France with its persistent tradition of careful workmanship. Gautier, for example, would have one's "floating dream sealed" [15] in the hardest and most resisting material, that can only be mastered by the perfect craftsman; and he himself, falling into a confusion of the arts, tries to display such a craftsmanship by painting and carving with words. Flaubert, again, refines upon the technique of writing to a point where it becomes not merely a discipline but a torture. But if a man is to be a romantic genius in the fullest sense he must, it should seem, repudiate even the discipline of technique as well as the discipline of culture in favor of an artless spontaneity. For after all the genius is only the man who retains the virtues of the child, and technical proficiency is scarcely to be numbered among these virtues. The German romanticists already prefer the early Italian painters because of their naïveté and divine awkwardness to the later artists who had a more conscious mastery of their material. The whole Pre-Raphaelite movement is therefore only one aspect of Rousseau's return to nature. To later primitivists the early Italians themselves seem far too deliberate. They would recover the spontaneity displayed in the markings on Alaskan totem poles or in the scratchings of the caveman on the flint. A prerequisite to pure genius, if we are to judge by their own productions, is an inability to draw. The futurists in their endeavor to convey symbolically their own "soul" or "vision"—a vision be it noted of pure flux and motion —deny the very conditions of time and space that determine the special technique of painting; and inasmuch as to express one's "soul" means for these moderns, as it did for the "genius" of the eighteenth century, to express the ineffable difference between themselves and others, the symbolizing of this soul to which they have sacrificed both culture and technique remains a dark mystery.

An eccentricity so extreme as to be almost or quite indistinguishable from madness is then the final outcome of the revolt of the original genius from the regularity of the eighteenth century. The eighteenth century had, one must confess, become too much like the Happy Valley from which Rasselas, Prince of Abyssinia, sought an egress. It was fair to the eye and satisfied all man's ordinary needs, but it seemed at the same time to hem him in oppressively, and limit unduly his horizons. For the modern man, as for the prince in Johnson's tale, a regular round of assured felicities has counted for nought as compared with the passion for the open; though now that he has tasted strange adventures, the modern man will scarcely decide at the end, like the prince, to "return to Abyssinia." I have already spoken of the rationalistic and pseudo-classic elements in the eighteenth century that the romantic rebels found so intolerable. It is impossible to follow "reason," they said in substance, and also to slake one's thirst for the "infinite"; it is impossible to conform and imitate and at the same time to be free and original and spontaneous. Above all it is impossible to submit to the yoke of either reason or imitation and at the same time to be imaginative. This last assertion will always be the main point at issue in any genuine debate between classicist and romanticist. The supreme thing in life, the romanticist declares, is the creative imagination, and it can be restored to its rights only be repudiating imitation. The imagination is supreme the classicist grants but adds that to imitate rightly is to make the highest use of the imagination. To understand all that is implied in this central divergence between classicist and romanticist we shall need to study in more detail the kind of imaginative activity that has been encouraged in the whole movement extending from the rise of the original genius in the eighteenth century to the present day.

CHAPTER THREE

ROMANTIC IMAGINATION

I have already spoken of the contrast established by the theorists of original genius in the eighteenth century between the different types of imagination—especially between the literary and the scientific imagination. According to these theorists, it will be remembered, the scientific imagination should be strictly subordinated to judgment, whereas the literary imagination, freed from the shackles of imitation, should be at liberty to wander wild in its own empire of chimeras, or, at all events, should be far less sharply checked by judgment. It is easy to follow the extension of these English views of genius and imagination into the France of Rousseau and Diderot, and then the elaboration of these same views, under the combined influence of both France and England, in Germany. I have tried to show that Kant, especially in his "Critique of Judgment," and Schiller in his "Æsthetic Letters" (1795) prepare the way for the conception of the creative imagination that is at the very heart of the romantic movement. According to this romantic conception, as we have seen, the imagination is to be free, not merely from outer formalistic constraint, but from all constraint whatever. This extreme romantic emancipation of the imagination was accompanied by an equally extreme emancipation of the emotions. Both kinds of emancipation are, as

I have tried to show, a recoil partly from neo-classical judgment—a type of judgment which seemed to oppress all that is
creative and spontaneous in man under a weight of outer convention; partly, from the reason of the Enlightenment, a type
of reason that was so logical and abstract that it seemed to
mechanize the human spirit, and to be a denial of all that is
immediate and intuitive. The neo-classical judgment, with its
undue unfriendliness to the imagination, is itself a recoil, let us
remember, from the imaginative extravagance of the "metaphysicals," the intellectual romanticists of the sixteenth and
seventeenth centuries, and also, if we take a sufficiently wide
view, from the Quixotic type of romanticism, the romanticism
of action, that we associate with the Middle Ages.

Now not only are men governed by their imaginations (the
imagination, as Pascal says, disposes of everything), but the
type of imagination by which most men are governed may be
defined in the widest sense of the word as romantic. Nearly
every man cherishes his dream, his conceit of himself as he
would like to be, a sort of "ideal" projection of his own desires,
in comparison with which his actual life seems a hard and
cramping routine. "Man must conceive himself what he is
not," as Dr. Johnson says, "for who is pleased with what he
is?" The ample habitation that a man rears for his fictitious or
"ideal" self often has some slight foundation in fact, but the
higher he rears it the more insecure it becomes, until finally,
like Perrette in the fable, he brings the whole structure down
about his ears by the very gesture of his dream. "We all of
us," La Fontaine concludes in perhaps the most delightful account of the romantic imagination in literature, "wise as well
as foolish, indulge in day-dreams. There is nothing sweeter. A
flattering illusion carries away our spirits. All the wealth in the
world is ours, all honors and all women," [1] etc. When Johnson
descants on the "dangerous prevalence of imagination," [2] and
warns us to stick to "sober probability," what he means is the
dangerous prevalence of day-dreaming. The retreat of the
Rousseauist into some "land of chimeras" or tower of ivory assumes forms almost incredibly complex and subtle, but at bottom the ivory tower is only one form of man's ineradicable
longing to escape from the oppression of the actual into some

land of heart's desire, some golden age of fancy. As a matter of fact, Rousseau's imaginative activity often approaches very closely to the delights of day-dreaming as described by La Fontaine. He was never more imaginative, he tells us, than when on a walking-trip—especially when the trip had no definite goal, or at least when he could take his time in reaching it. The *Wanderlust* of body and spirit could then be satisfied together. Actual vagabondage seemed to be an aid to the imagination in its escape from verisimilitude. One should note especially Rousseau's account of his early wandering from Lyons to Paris and the airy structures that he raised on his anticipations of what he might find there. Inasmuch as he was to be attached at Paris to the Swiss Colonel Godard, he already traced for himself in fancy, in spite of his short-sightedness, a career of military glory. "I had read that Marshal Schomberg was short-sighted, why shouldn't Marshal Rousseau be so too?" In the meanwhile, touched by the sight of the groves and brooks, "I felt in the midst of my glory that my heart was not made for so much turmoil, and soon without knowing how, I found myself once more among my beloved pastorals, renouncing forever the toils of Mars."

Thus alongside the real world and in more or less sharp opposition to it, Rousseau builds up a fictitious world, that *pays des chimères,* which is alone, as he tells us, worthy of habitation. To study his imaginative activity is simply to study the new forms that he gives to what I have called man's ineradicable longing for some Arcadia, some land of heart's desire. Goethe compares the illusions that man nourishes in his breast to the population of statues in ancient Rome which were almost as numerous as the population of living men. The important thing from the point of view of sanity is that a man should not blur the boundaries between the two populations, that he should not cease to discriminate between his fact and his fiction. If he confuses what he dreams himself to be with what he actually is, he has already entered upon the pathway of madness. It was, for example, natural for a youth like Rousseau who was at once romantic and musical, to dream that he was a great composer; but actually to set up as a great composer and to give the concert at Lausanne shows an unwillingness to discriminate between his fictitious and his real world that is plainly pathological. If not already a megalomaniac, he was even then on the way to megalomania.

To wander through the world as though it were an Arcadia or enchanted vision contrived for one's especial benefit is an attitude of childhood—especially of imaginative childhood. "Wherever children are," says Novalis, "there is the golden age." As the child grows and matures there is a more or less painful process of adjustment between his "vision" and the particular reality in which he is placed. A little sense gets knocked into his head, and often, it must be confessed, a good deal of the imagination gets knocked out. As Wordsworth complains, the vision fades into the light of common day. The striking fact about Rousseau is that, far more than Wordsworth, he held fast to his vision. He refused to adjust it to an unpalatable reality. During the very years when the ordinary youth is forced to subordinate his luxurious imaginings to some definite discipline he fell under the influence of Madame de Warens who encouraged rather than thwarted his Arcadian bent. Later, when almost incurably confirmed in his penchant for revery, he came into contact with the refined society of Paris, an environment requiring so difficult an adjustment that no one we are told could accomplish the feat unless he had been disciplined into the appropriate habits from the age of six. He is indeed the supreme example of the unadjusted man, of the original genius whose imagination has never suffered either inner or outer constraint, who is more of an Arcadian dreamer at sixty perhaps than he was at sixteen. He writes to the Bailli de Mirabeau (31 January, 1767):

"The fatigue of thinking becomes every day more painful to me. I love to dream, but freely, allowing my mind to wander without enslaving myself to any subject. . . . This idle and contemplative life which you do not approve and which I do not excuse, becomes to me daily more delicious; to wander alone endlessly and ceaselessly among the trees and rocks about my dwelling, to muse or rather to be as irresponsible as I please, and as you say, to go wool-gathering; . . . finally to give myself up unconstrainedly to my fantasies which, thank heaven, are all within my power: that, sir, is for me the supreme enjoyment,

*than which I can imagine nothing superior in this world for a
man at my age and in my condition."*

Rousseau, then, owes his significance not only to the fact
that he was supremely imaginative in an age that was disposed
to deny the supremacy of the imagination, but to the fact that
he was imaginative in a particular way. A great multitude
since his time must be reckoned among his followers, not because they have held certain ideas but because they have ex-
hibited a similar quality of imagination. In seeking to define
this quality of imagination we are therefore at the very heart
of our subject.

It is clear from what has already been said that Rousseau's
imagination was in a general way Arcadian, and this, if not
the highest, is perhaps the most prevalent type of imagination.
In surveying the literature of the world one is struck not only
by the universality of the pastoral or idyllic element, but by
the number of forms it has assumed—forms ranging from the
extreme of artificiality and conventionalism to the purest poetry. The very society against the artificiality of which Rousseau's whole work is a protest is itself in no small degree a
pastoral creation. Various elements indeed entered into the life
of the drawing-room as it came to be conceived towards the
beginning of the seventeenth century. The Marquise de Ram-
bouillet and others who set out at this time to live in the grand
manner were in so far governed either by genuine or by artificial decorum. But at the same time that the creators of *le
grand monde* were aiming to be more "decent" than the men
and women of the sixteenth century, they were patterning
themselves upon the shepherds and shepherdesses of D'Urfé's
interminable pastoral "l'Astrée." They were seeking to create a
sort of enchanted world from which the harsh cares of ordinary life were banished and where they might be free, like true
Arcadians, to discourse of love. This discourse of love was associated with what I have defined as intellectual romanticism.
In spite of the attacks by the exponents of humanistic good
sense (Molière, Boileau, etc.) on this drawing-room affectation,
it lingered on and still led in the eighteenth century, as Rousseau complained, to "inconceivable refinements." [3] At the same

time we should recollect that there is a secret bond between all forms of Arcadian dreaming. Not only was Rousseau fascinated, like the early *precieux* and *précieuses,* by D'Urfé's pastoral, but he himself appealed by his renewal of the main pastoral theme of love to the descendants of these former Arcadians in the polite society of his time. The love of Rousseau is associated not, like that of the *précieux,* with the intellect, but with the emotions, and so he substitutes for a "wire-drawn and supersubtilized gallantry" the ground-swell of elemental passion.[4] Moreover, the definitely primitivistic coloring that he gave to his imaginative renewal of the pastoral dream appealed to an age that was reaching the last stages of over-refinement. Primitivism is, strictly speaking, nothing new in the world. It always tends to appear in periods of complex civilization. The charms of the simple life and of a return to nature were celebrated especially during the Alexandrian period of Greek literature for the special delectation no doubt of the most sophisticated members of this very sophisticated society. "Nothing," as Dr. Santayana says, "is farther from the common people than the corrupt desire to be primitive." Primitivistic dreaming was also popular in ancient Rome at its most artificial moment. The great ancients, however, though enjoying the poetry of the primitivistic dream, were not the dupes of this dream. Horace, for example, lived at the most artificial moment of Rome when primitivistic dreaming was popular as it had been at Alexandria. He descants on the joys of the simple life in a well-known ode. One should not therefore hail him, like Schiller, as the founder of the sentimental school "of which he has remained the unsurpassed model." [5] For the person who plans to return to nature in Horace's poem is the old usurer Alfius, who changes his mind at the last moment and puts out his mortgages again. In short, the final attitude of the urbane Horace towards the primitivistic dream—it could hardly be otherwise—is ironical.

Rousseau seems destined to remain the supreme example, at least in the Occident, of the man who takes the primitivistic dream seriously, who attempts to set up primitivism as a philosophy and even as a religion. Rousseau's account of his sudden illumination on the road from Paris to Vincennes is famous: the scales, he tells us, fell from his eyes even as they had from the eyes of Paul on the road to Damascus, and he saw how man had fallen from the felicity of his primitive estate; how the blissful ignorance in which he had lived at one with himself and harmless to his fellows had been broken by the rise of intellectual self-consciousness and the resulting progress in the sciences and arts. Modern students of Rousseau have, under the influence of James, taken this experience on the road to Vincennes to be an authentic case of conversion,[6] but this is merely one instance of our modern tendency to confound the subrational with the superrational. What one finds in this alleged conversion when one looks into it, is a sort of "subliminal uprush" of the Arcadian memories of his youth, especially of his life at Annecy and Les Charmettes, and at the same time the contrast between these Arcadian memories and the hateful constraints he had suffered at Paris in his attempts to adjust himself to an uncongenial environment.

We can trace even more clearly perhaps the process by which the Arcadian dreamer comes to set up as a seer in Rousseau's relation of the circumstances under which he came to compose his "Discourse on the Origins of Inequality." He goes off on a sort of picnic with Thérèse into the forest of St. Germain and gives himself up to imagining the state of primitive man. "Plunged in the forest," he says, "I sought and found there the image of primitive times of which I proudly drew the history; I swooped down on the little falsehoods of men; I ventured to lay bare their nature, to follow the progress of time and of circumstances which have disfigured it, and comparing artificial man (*l'homme de l'homme*) with natural man, to show in his alleged improvement the true source of his miseries. My soul, exalted by these sublime contemplations, rose into the presence of the Divinity. Seeing from this vantage point that the blind pathway of prejudices followed by my fellows was also that of their errors, misfortunes and crimes, I cried out to them in a feeble voice that they could not hear: Madmen, who are always complaining of nature, know that all your evils come from yourselves alone."

The golden age for which the human heart has an ineradicable longing is here presented not as poetical, which it certainly is, but as a "state of nature" from which man has actually fallen. The more or less innocent Arcadian dreamer is being transformed into the dangerous Utopist. He puts the blame of the conflict and division of which he is conscious in himself upon the social conventions that set bounds to his temperament and impulses; once get rid of these purely artificial restrictions and he feels that he will again be at one with himself and "nature." With such a vision of nature as this it is not surprising that every constraint is unendurable to Rousseau, that he likes, as Berlioz was to say of himself later, to "make all barriers crack." He is ready to shatter all the forms of civilized life in favor of something that never existed, of a state of nature that is only the projection of his own temperament and its dominant desires upon the void. His programme amounts in practice to the indulgence of infinite indeterminate desire, to an endless and aimless vagabondage of the emotions with the imagination as their free accomplice.

This longing of the highly sophisticated person to get back to the primitive and naïve and unconscious, or what amounts to the same thing, to shake off the trammels of tradition and reason in favor of free and passionate self-expression, underlies, as I have pointed out, the conception of original genius which itself underlies the whole modern movement. A book reflecting the primitivistic trend of the eighteenth century, and at the same time pointing the way, as we shall see presently, to the working out of the fundamental primitivistic contrast between the natural and the artificial in the romanticism of the early nineteenth century, is Schiller's "Essay on Simple and Sentimental Poetry." The poetry that does not "look before or after," that is free from self-questioning and self-consciousness, and has a child-like spontaneity, Schiller calls simple or naïve. The poet, on the other hand, who is conscious of his fall from nature and who, from the midst of his sophistication, longs to be back once more at his mother's bosom, is sentimental. Homer and his heroes, for example, are naïve; Werther, who yearns in a drawing-room for the Homeric simplicity, is sentimental. The longing of the modern man for nature, says Schiller, is that of the sick man for health. It is hard to see in Schiller's "nature" anything more than a development of Rousseau's primitivistic Arcadia. To be sure, Schiller warns us that, in order to recover the childlike and primitive virtues still visible in the man of genius, we must not renounce culture. We must not seek to revert lazily to an Arcadia, but must struggle forward to an Elysium. Unfortunately Schiller's Elysium has a strange likeness to Rousseau's Arcadia; and that is because Schiller's own conception of life is, in the last analysis, overwhelmingly sentimental. His most Elysian conception, that of a purely æsthetic Greece, a wonderland of unalloyed beauty, is also a bit of Arcadian sentimentalizing. Inasmuch as Rousseau's state of nature never existed outside of dreamland, the Greek who is simple or naïve in this sense is likewise a myth. He has no real counterpart either in the Homeric age or any other age of Greece. It is hard to say which is more absurd, to make the Greeks naïve, or to turn Horace into a sentimentalist. One should note how this romantic perversion of the Greeks for which Schiller is largely responsible is related to his general view of the imagination. We have seen that in the "Æsthetic Letters" he maintains that if the imagination is to conceive the ideal it must be free; and that to be free it must be emancipated from purpose and engage in a sort of play. If the imagination has to subordinate itself to a real object it ceases in so far to be free. Hence the more ideal the imagination the farther it gets away from a real object. By his theory of the imagination, Schiller thus encourages that opposition between the ideal and the real which figures so largely in romantic psychology. A man may consent to adjust a mere dream to the requirements of the real, but when his dream is promoted to the dignity of an ideal it is plain that he will be less ready to make the sacrifice. Schiller's Greece is very ideal in the sense I have just defined. It hovers before the imagination as a sort of Golden Age of pure beauty, a land of chimeras that is alone worthy of the æsthete's habitation. As an extreme type of the romantic Hellenist, one may take Hölderlin, who was a disciple at once of Schiller and of Rousseau. He begins by urging emancipation from every form of outer and traditional control in the name of spontaneity. "Boldly forget," he cries in the very accents of Rousseau, "what you have inherited and won— all laws and customs—and like new-born babes lift up your eyes to godlike nature." Hölderlin has been called a "Hellenizing Werther," and Werther, one should recollect, is only a German Saint-Preux, who is in turn, according to Rousseau's own avowal, only an idealized image of Rousseau. The nature that Hölderlin worships and which is, like the nature of Rousseau, only an Arcadian intoxication of the imagination, he associates with a Greece which is, like the Grece of Schiller, a dreamland of pure beauty. He longs to escape into this dreamland from an actual world that seems to him intolerably artificial. The contrast between his "ideal" Greece and reality is so acute as to make all attempt at adjustment out of the question. As a result of this maladjustment his whole being finally gave way and he lingered on for many years in madness.

The acuteness of the opposition between the ideal and the real in Hölderlin recalls Shelley, who was also a romantic Hellenist, and at the same time perhaps the most purely Rousseauistic of the English romantic poets. But Shelley was also a political dreamer, and here one should note two distinct phases in his dream: a first phase that is filled with the hope of transforming the real world into an Arcadia[7] through revolutionary reform; and then a phase of elegiac disillusion when the gap between reality and his ideal refuses to be bridged.[8] Something of the same radiant political hope and the same disillusion is found in Wordsworth. In the first flush of his revolutionary enthusiasm, France seemed to him to be "standing on the top of golden hours" and pointing the way to a new birth of human nature:

> *Bliss was it in that dawn to be alive,*
> *But to be young was very heaven! O times,*
> *In which the meagre stale forbidding ways*
> *Of custom, law and statute, took at once*
> *The attraction of a country in romance!*

When it became evident that the actual world and Utopia did not coincide after all, when the hard sequences of cause and effect that bind the present inexorably to the past refused to yield to the creations of the romantic imagination, what ensued in Wordsworth was not so much an awakening to true wisdom as a transformation of the pastoral dream. The English Lake Country became for him in some measure, as it was later to be for Ruskin, the ivory tower into which he retreated from the oppression of the real. He still continued to see, if not the general order of society, at least the denizens of his chosen retreat through the Arcadian mist, and contrasted their pastoral felicity with the misery of men "barricadoed in the walls of cities." I do not mean to disparage the poetry of humble life or to deny that many passages may be cited from Wordsworth that justify his reputation as an inspired teacher: I wish merely to point out here and elsewhere what is specifically romantic in the quality of his imagination.

After all it is to Rousseau himself even more than to his German or English followers that one needs to turn for the best examples of the all-pervasive conflict between the ideal and the actual. The psychology of this conflict is revealed with special clearness in the four letters that he wrote to M. de Malesherbes, and into which he has perhaps put more of himself than into any other similar amount of his writing. His natural indolence and impatience at the obligations and constraints of life were, he avows to M. de Malesherbes, increased by his early reading. At the age of eight he already knew Plutarch by heart and had read "all novels" and shed tears over them, he adds, "by the pailful." Hence was formed his "heroic and romantic taste" which filled him with aversion for everything that did not resemble his dreams. He had hoped at first to find the equivalent of these dreams among actual men, but after painful disillusions he had come to look with disdain on his age and his contemporaries. "I withdrew more and more from human society and created for myself a society in my imagination, a society that charmed me all the more in that I could cultivate it without peril or effort and that it was always at my call and such as I required it." He associated this dream society with the forms of outer nature. The long walks in particular that he took during his stay at the Hermitage were, he tells us, filled with a "continual delirium" of this kind. "I peopled nature with beings according to my heart. . . . I created for myself a golden age to suit my fancy." It is not unusual for a man thus to console himself for his poverty in the real relations of life by accumulating a huge hoard of fairy gold. Where the Rousseauist goes beyond the ordinary dreamer is in his proneness to regard his retirement into some land of chimeras as a proof of his nobility and distinction. Poetry and life he feels are irreconcilably opposed to each other, and he for his part is on the side of poetry and the "ideal." Goethe symbolized the hopelessness of this conflict in the suicide of the young Werther. But though Werther died, his creator continued to live, and more perhaps than any other figure in the whole Rousseauistic movement perceived the peril of this conception of poetry and the ideal. He saw phantasts all about him who refused to be reconciled to the gap between the infinitude of their longing and the platitude of their actual lot. Perhaps no country and time ever produced more such phantasts than Germany of the Storm and Stress and romantic periods—partly no doubt because it did not offer any proper outlet for the activity of generous youths. Goethe himself had been a phantast, and so it was natural in works like his "Tasso" that he should show himself specially preoccupied with the problem of the poet and his adjustment to life. About the time that he wrote this play, he was, as he tells us, very much taken up with thoughts of "Rousseau and his hypochondriac misery." Rousseau for his part felt a kinship between himself and Tasso, and Goethe's Tasso certainly reminds us very strongly of Rousseau. Carried away by his Arcadian imaginings, Tasso violates the decorum that separates him from the princess with whom he has fallen in love. As a result of the rebuffs that follow, his dream changes into a nightmare, until he finally falls like Rousseau into wild and random suspicion and looks on himself as the victim of a conspiracy. In opposition to Tasso is the figure of Antonio, the man of the world, whose imagination does not run away with his sense of fact, and who is therefore equal to the "demands of the day." The final reconciliation between Tasso and Antonio, if not very convincing dramatically, symbolizes at least what Goethe achieved in some measure in his own life. There were moments, he declares, when he might properly look upon himself as mad, like Rousseau. He escaped from this world of morbid brooding, this giddy downward gazing into the bottomless pit of the romantic heart against which he utters a warning in "Tasso," by his activity at the court of Weimar, by classical culture, by scientific research. Goethe carries the same problem of reconciling the ideal to the real a stage further in his "Wilhelm Meister." The more or less irresponsible and Bohemian youth that we see at the beginning learns by renunciation and self-limitation to fit into a life of wholesome activity. Goethe saw that the remedy for romantic dreaming is work, though he is open to grave criticism, as I shall try to show elsewhere, for his unduly naturalistic conception of work. But the romanticists as a rule did not wish work in any sense and so, attracted as they were by the free artistic life of Meister at the beginning, they looked upon his final adjustment to the real as a base capitulation to philistinism. Novalis described the book as a "Candide directed against poetry," and set out to write a counterblast in "Heinrich von Ofterdingen." This apotheosis of pure poetry, as he meant it to be, is above all an apotheosis of the wildest vagabondage of the imagination. Novalis did not, however, as a result of the conflict between the ideal and the real, show any signs of going mad like Hölderlin, or of simply fading from life like his friend Wackenroder. Like E.T.A. Hoffmann and a certain number of other phantasts he had a distinct gift for leading a dual life—for dividing himself into a prosaic self which went one way, and a poetical self which went another.

This necessary and fatal opposition between poetry and prose the romanticist saw typified in "Don Quixote," and of course he sided with the idealism of the knight against the philistine good sense of Sancho Panza; and so for the early romanticists as well as for those who were of their spiritual posterity,— Heine, for example, and Flaubert,—"Don Quixote" was a book to evoke not laughter but tears.

To the romantic conception of the ideal can be traced the increasing lack of understanding between the poet, or in general the creator, and the public during the past century. Many neo-classical writers may, like Boileau, have shown an undue reverence for what they conceived to be the general sense of their time, but to measure one's inspiration by one's remoteness from this general sense is surely a far more dangerous error; and yet one was encouraged to do this very thing by the views of original genius that were held in the eighteenth century. Certain late neo-classicists lacked imagination and were at the

same time always harping on good sense. It was therefore assumed that to insist on good sense was necessarily proof of a
lack of imagination. Because the attempt to achieve the universal had led to a stale and lifeless imitation it was assumed
that a man's genius consists in his uniqueness, in his unlikeness
to other men. Now nothing is more private and distinctive in
a man than his feelings, so that to be unique meant practically
for Rousseau and his followers to be unique in feeling. Feeling
alone they held was vital and immediate. As a matter of fact
the element in a man's nature that he possesses in common
with other men is also something that he *senses*, something
that is in short intuitive and immediate. But good sense the
genius identifies with lifeless convention and so measures his
originality by the distance of his emotional and imaginative recoil from it. Of this warfare between sense and sensibility that
begins in the eighteenth century, the romantic war between
the poet and the philistine is only the continuation. This war
has been bad for both artist and public. If the artist has become more and more eccentric, it must be confessed that the
good sense of the public against which he has protested has
been too flatly utilitarian. The poet who reduces poetry to the
imaginative quest of strange emotional adventure, and the
plain citizen who does not aspire beyond a reality that is too
literal and prosaic, both suffer; but the æsthete suffers the more
severely—so much so that I shall need to revert to this conception of poetry in my treatment of romantic melancholy. It leads
at last to a contrast between the ideal and the real such as is
described by Anatole France in his account of Villiers de l'Isle
Adam. "For thirty years," says M. France, "Villiers wandered
around in cafés at night, fading away like a shadow at the first
glimmer of dawn. . . . His poverty, the frightful poverty of
cities, had so put its stamp on him and fashioned him so thoroughly that he resembled those vagabonds, who, dressed in
black, sleep on park benches. He had the livid complexion with
red blotches, the glassy eye, the bowed back of the poor; and
yet I am not sure we should call him unhappy, for he lived in
a perpetual dream and that dream was radiantly golden. . . .
His dull eyes contemplated within himself dazzling spectacles.
He passed through the world like a somnambulist seeing

nothing of what we see and seeing things that it is not given us to behold. Out of the commonplace spectacle of life he succeeded in creating an ever fresh ecstacy. On those ignoble café tables in the midst of the odor of beer and tobacco, he poured forth floods of purple and gold."

This notion that literal failure is ideal success, and conversely, has been developed in a somewhat different form by Rostand in his "Cyrano de Bergerac." By his refusal to compromise or adjust himself to things as they are, Cyrano's real life has become a series of defeats. He is finally forced from life by a league of all the mediocrities whom his idealism affronts. His discomfiture is taken to show, not that he is a Quixotic extremist, but that he is the superior of the successful Guise, the man who has stooped to compromise, the French equivalent of the Antonio whom Goethe finally came to prefer to Tasso. Rostand's "Chanticleer" is also an interesting study of romantic idealism and of the two main stages through which it passes —the first stage when one relates one's ideal to the real; the second, when one discovers that the ideal and the real are more or less hopelessly dissevered. Chanticleer still maintains his idealistic pose even after he has discovered that the sun is not actually made to rise by his crowing. In this hugging of his illusion in defiance of reality Chanticleer is at the opposite pole from Johnson's astronomer in "Rasselas" who thinks that he has control of the weather, but when disillusioned is humbly thankful at having escaped from this "dangerous prevalence of imagination," and entered once more into the domain of "sober probability."

The problem, then, of the genius or the artist versus the philistine has persisted without essential modification from the eighteenth century to the present day—from the suicide of Chatterton, let us say, to the suicide of John Davidson. The man of imagination spurns in the name of his "ideal" the limits imposed upon it by a dull respectability, and then his ideal turns out only too often to lack positive content and to amount in practice to the expansion of infinite indeterminate desire. What the idealist opposes to the real is not only something that does not exist, but something that never can exist. The Arcadian revery which should be allowed at most as an occasional solace from the serious business of living is set up as a substitute for living. The imaginative and emotional dalliance of the Rousseauistic romanticist may assume a bewildering variety of forms. We have already seen in the case of Hölderlin how easily Rousseau's dream of a state of nature passes over—and that in spite of Rousseau's attacks on the arts—into the dream of a paradise of pure beauty. The momentous matter is not that a man's imagination and emotions go out towards this or that particular haven of refuge in the future or in the past, in the East or in the West, but that his primary demand on life is for some haven or refuge; that he longs to be away from the here and now and their positive demands on his character and will. Poe may sing of "the glory that was Greece and the grandeur that was Rome," but he is not therefore a classicist. With the same wistfulness innumerable romanticists have looked towards the Middle Ages. So C. E. Norton says that Ruskin was a white-winged anachronism,[9] that he should have been born in the thirteenth century. But one may surmise that a man with Ruskin's special quality of imagination would have failed to adjust himself to the actual life of the thirteenth or any other century. Those who put their Arcadia in the Middle Ages or some other period of the past have at least this advantage over those who put it in the present, they are better protected against disillusion. The man whose Arcadia is distant from him merely in space may decide to go and see for himself, and the results of this overtaking of one's dream are somewhat uncertain. The Austrian poet Lenau, for example, actually took a trip to his primitive paradise that he had imagined somewhere in the neighborhood of Pittsburgh. Perhaps it is not surprising that he finally died mad. The disenchantment of Chateaubriand in his quest for a Rousseauistic Arcadia in America and for Arcadian savages I describe later. In his journey into the wilderness Chateaubriand reveals himself as a spiritual lotos-eater no less surely than the man who takes flight into what is superficially most remote from the virgin forest—into some palace of art. His attitude towards America does not differ psychically from that of many early romanticists towards Italy. Italy was their land of heart's desire, the land that filled them with ineffable longing (*Sehnsucht nach Italien*), a palace of art that, like the Latin Quarter of later Bohemians, had some points of contact with Mohammed's paradise. A man may even develop a romantic longing for the very period against which romanticism was originally a protest and be ready to "fling his cap for polish and for Pope." One should add that the romantic Eldorado is not necessarily rural. Lamb's attitude towards London is almost as romantic as that of Wordsworth towards the country. Dr. Johnson cherished urban life because of its centrality. Lamb's imaginative dalliance, on the other hand, is stimulated by the sheer variety and wonder of the London streets as another's might be by the mountains or the sea.[10] Lamb could also find an Elysium of unmixed æsthetic solace in the literature of the past—especially in Restoration Comedy.

The essence of the mood is always the straining of the imagination away from the here and now, from an actuality that seems paltry and faded compared to the radiant hues of one's dream. The classicist, according to A. W. Schlegel,[11] is for making the most of the present, whereas the romanticist hovers between recollection and hope. In Shelleyan phrase he "looks before and after and pines for what is not." He inclines like the Byronic dandy, Barbey d'Aurevilly, to take for his mottoes the words "Too late" and "Nevermore."

Nostalgia, the term that has come to be applied to the infinite indeterminate longing of the romanticist—his never-ending quest after the ever-fleeting object of desire—is not, from the point of view of strict etymology, well-chosen. Romantic nostalgia is not "homesickness," accurately speaking, but desire to get away from home. Odysseus in Homer suffers from true nostalgia. The Ulysses of Tennyson, on the other hand, is nostalgic in the romantic sense when he leaves home "to sail beyond the sunset." Ovid, as Goethe points out, is highly classical even in his melancholy. The longing from which he suffers in his exile is very determinate; he longs to get back to Rome, the centre of the world. Ovid indeed sums up the classic point of view when he says that one cannot desire the unknown (*ignoti nulla cupido*).[12] The essence of nostalgia is the desire for the unknown. "I was burning with desire," says Rousseau, "without any definite object." One is filled with a desire to fly one knows not whither, to be off on a journey into the blue distance.[13] Music is exalted by the romanticists above all other arts because it is the most nostalgic, the art that is most suggestive of the hopeless gap between the "ideal" and the "real." "Music," in Emerson's phrase, "pours on mortals its beautiful disdain." "Away! away!" cries Jean Paul to Music. "Thou speakest of things which throughout my endless life I have found not, and shall not find." In musical and other nostalgia, the feelings receive a sort of infinitude from the coöperation of the imagination; and this infinitude, this quest of something that must ever elude one, is at the same time taken to be the measure of one's idealism. The symmetry and form that the classicist gains from working within bounds are no doubt excellent, but then the willingness to work within bounds betokens a lack of aspiration. If the primitivist is ready, as some one has complained, to turn his back on the bright forms of Olympus and return to the ancient gods of chaos and of night, the explanation is to be sought in this idea of the infinite. It finally becomes a sort of Moloch to which he is prepared to sacrifice most of the values of civilized life. The chief fear of the classicist is to be thought monstrous. The primitivist on the contrary is inclined to see a proof of superior amplitude of spirit in mere grotesqueness and disproportion. The creation of monsters is, as Hugo says, a "satisfaction due to the infinite." [14]

The breaking down by the emotional romanticist of the barriers that separate not merely the different literary genres but the different arts is only another aspect of his readiness to follow the lure of the infinite. The title of a recent bit of French decadent verse—"Nostalgia in Blue Minor"—would already have been perfectly intelligible to a Tieck or a Novalis. The Rousseauist—and that from a very early stage in the movement—does not hesitate to pursue his ever receding dream across all frontiers, not merely those that separate art from art, but those that divide flesh from spirit and even good from evil, until finally he arrives like Blake at a sort of "Marriage of Heaven and Hell." When he is not breaking down barriers in the name of the freedom of the imagination he is doing so in the name of what he is pleased to term love.

"The ancient art and poetry," says A. W. Schlegel, "rigorously separate things which are dissimilar; the romantic delights in indissoluble mixtures. All contrarieties: nature and art, poetry and prose, seriousness and mirth, recollection and anticipation, spirituality and sensuality, terrestrial and celestial, life and death, are by it blended together in the most intimate combination. As the oldest lawgivers delivered their mandatory instructions and prescriptions in measured melodies; as this is fabulously ascribed to Orpheus, the first softener of the yet untamed race of mortals; in like manner the whole of the ancient poetry and art is, as it were a *rhythmical nomos* (law), an harmonious promulgation of the permanently established legislation of a world submitted to a beautiful order, and reflecting in itself the eternal images of things. Romantic poetry, on the other hand, is the expression of the secret attraction to a chaos which lies concealed in the very bosom of the ordered universe, and is perpetually striving after new and marvellous births; the life-giving spirit of primal love broods here anew on the face of the waters. The former is more simple, clear, and like to nature in the self-existent perfection of her separate works; the latter, notwithstanding its fragmentary appearance, approaches more to the secret of the universe. For Conception can only comprise each object separately, but nothing in truth can ever exist separately and by itself; Feeling perceives all in all at one and the same time." [15]

Note the assumption here that the clear-cut distinctions of classicism are merely abstract and intellectual, and that the only true unity is the unity of feeling.

In passages of this kind A. W. Schlegel is little more than the popularizer of the ideas of his brother Friedrich. Perhaps no one in the whole romantic movement showed a greater genius for confusion than Friedrich Schlegel; no one, in Nietzsche's phrase, had a more intimate knowledge of all the by-paths to chaos. Now it is from the German group of which Friedrich Schlegel was the chief theorist that romanticism as a distinct and separate movement takes its rise. We may therefore pause appropriately at this point to consider briefly how the epithet romantic of which I have already sketched the early history came to be applied to a distinct school. In the latter part of the eighteenth century, it will be remembered, romantic had become a fairly frequent word in English and also (under English influence) a less frequent, though not rare word, in French and German; it was often used favorably in all these countries as applied to nature, and usually indeed in this sense in France and Germany; but in England, when applied to human nature and as the equivalent of the French *romanesque*, it had ordinarily an unfavorable connotation; it signified the "dangerous prevalence of imagination" over "sober probability," as may be seen in Foster's essay "On the Epithet Romantic." One may best preface a discussion of the next step—the transference of the word to a distinct movement—by a quotation from Goethe's "Conversations with Eckermann" (21 March, 1830):

> *This division of poetry into classic and romantic [says Goethe] which is to-day diffused throughout the whole world and has caused so much argument and discord, comes originally from Schiller and me. It was my principle in poetry always to work objectively. Schiller on the contrary wrote nothing that was not subjective; he thought his manner good, and to defend it he wrote his article on naïve and sentimental poetry. . . . The Schlegels got hold of this idea, developed it and little by little it has spread throughout the whole world. Everybody is talking of romanticism and classicism. Fifty years ago nobody gave the matter a thought.*

One statement in this passage of Goethe's is perhaps open to question—that concerning the obligation of the Schlegels, or rather Friedrich Schlegel, to Schiller's treatise. A comparison of the date of publication of the treatise on "Naïve and Sentimental Poetry" with the date of composition of Schlegel's early writings would seem to show that some of Schlegel's distinctions, though closely related to those of Schiller, do not derive from them so immediately as Goethe seems to imply.[16] Both sets of views grow rather inevitably out of a primitivistic or Rousseauistic conception of "nature" that had been epidemic in Germany ever since the Age of Genius. We need also to keep in mind certain personal traits of Schlegel if we are to understand the development of his theories about literature and art. He was romantic, not only by his genius for confusion, but also one should add, by his tendency to oscillate violently be-

tween extremes. For him as for Rousseau there was "no intermediary term between everything and nothing." One should
note here another meaning that certain romanticists give to the
word "ideal"—Hazlitt, for example, when he says that the
"ideal is always to be found in extremes." Every imaginable extreme, the extreme of reaction as well as the extreme of radi-
calism, goes with romanticism; every genuine mediation between extremes is just as surely unromantic. Schlegel then was
very idealistic in the sense I have just defined. Having begun as
an extreme partisan of the Greeks, conceived in Schiller's fashion as a people that was at once harmonious and instinctive, he
passes over abruptly to the extreme of revolt against every form
of classicism, and then after having posed in works like his
"Lucinde" as a heaven-storming Titan who does not shrink at
the wildest excess of emotional unrestraint, he passes over no
less abruptly to Catholicism and its rigid outer discipline. This
last phase of Schlegel has at least this much in common with
his phase of revolt, that it carried with it a cult of the Middle
Ages. The delicate point to determine about Friedrich Schlegel
and many other romanticists is why they finally came to place
their land of heart's desire in the Middle Ages rather than in
Greece. In treating this question one needs to take at least a
glance at the modification that Herder (whose influence on
German romanticism is very great) gave to the primitivism of
Rousseau. Cultivate your genius, Rousseau said in substance,
your ineffable difference from other men, and look back with
longing to the ideal moment of this genius—the age of childhood, when your spontaneous self was not as yet cramped by
conventions or "sicklied o'er by the pale cast of thought." Cultivate your national genius, Herder said in substance, and look
back wistfully at the golden beginnings of your nationality
when it was still naïve and "natural," when poetry instead of
being concocted painfully by individuals was still the unconscious emanation of the folk. Herder indeed expands primitivism along these lines into a whole philosophy of history. The
romantic notion of the origin of the epic springs out of this
soil, a notion that is probably at least as remote from the facts
as the neo-classical notion—and that is saying a great deal. Any
German who followed Herder in the extension that he gave to

Rousseau's views about genius and spontaneity could not only see the folk soul mirrored at least as naïvely in the "Nibelungenlied" as in the "Iliad," but by becoming a mediæval enthusiast he could have the superadded pleasure of indulging not merely personal but racial and national idiosyncrasy. Primitivistic mediævalism is therefore an important ingredient, especially in the case of Germany, in romantic nationalism— the type that has flourished beyond all measure during the past century. Again, though one might, like Hölderlin, cherish an infinite longing for the Greeks, the Greeks themselves, at least the Greeks of Schiller, did not experience longing; but this fact came to be felt more and more by F. Schlegel and other romanticists as an inferiority, showing as it did that they were content with the finite. As for the neo-classicists who were supposed to be the followers of the Greeks, their case was even worse; they not only lacked aspiration and infinitude, but were sunk in artificiality, and had moreover become so analytical that they must perforce see things in "disconnection dead and spiritless." The men of the Middle Ages, on the other hand, as F. Schlegel saw them, were superior to the neo-classicists in being naïve; their spontaneity and unity of feeling had not yet suffered from artificiality, or been disintegrated by analysis.[17] At the same time they were superior to the Greeks in having aspiration and the sense of the infinite. The very irregularity of their art testified to this infinitude. It is not uncommon in the romantic movement thus to assume that because one has very little form one must therefore have a great deal of "soul." F. Schlegel so extended his definition of the mediæval spirit as to make it include writers like Shakespeare and Cervantes, who seemed to him to be vital and free from formalism. The new nationalism was also made to turn to the profit of the Middle Ages. Each nation in shaking off the yoke of classical imitation and getting back to its mediæval past was recovering what was primitive in its own genius, was substituting what was indigenous for what was alien to it.

The person who did more than any one else to give international currency to the views of the Schlegels about classic and romantic and to their primitivistic mediævalism was Madame de Staël in her book on Germany. It was with special reference

to Madame de Staël and her influence that Daunou wrote the
following passage in his introduction to La Harpe. a passage
that gives curious evidence of the early attitude of French literary conservatives towards the new school:

> *One of the services that he [La Harpe] should render now-*
> *adays is to fortify young people against vain and gothic doc-*
> *trines which would reduce the fine arts to childhood if they*
> *could ever gain credit in the land of Racine and Voltaire. La*
> *Harpe uttered a warning against these doctrines when he dis-*
> *covered the first germs of them in the books to Diderot, Mercier*
> *and some other innovators. Yet these writers were far from*
> *having professed fully the barbaric or childish system which has*
> *been taught and developed among us for a few years past; it is*
> *of foreign origin; it had no name in our language and the name*
> *that has been given to it is susceptible in fact of no precise*
> *meaning. Romanticism, for thus it is called, was imported into*
> *our midst along with Kantism, with mysticism and other doc-*
> *trines of the same stamp which collectively might be named*
> *obscurantism. These are words which La Harpe was happy*
> *enough not to hear. He was accustomed to too much clearness*
> *in his ideas and expression to use such words or even to under-*
> *stand them. He did not distinguish two literatures. The litera-*
> *ture that nature and society have created for us and which for*
> *three thousand years past has been established and preserved*
> *and reproduced by masterpieces appeared to him alone worthy*
> *of a Frenchman of the eighteenth century. He did not foresee*
> *that it would be reduced some day to being only a particular*
> *kind of literature, tolerated or reproved under the name of*
> *classic, and that its noblest productions would be put on the*
> *same level as the formless sketches of uncultivated genius and*
> *untried talents. Yet more than once decadence has thus been*
> *taken for an advance, and a retrograde movement for progress.*
> *Art is so difficult. It is quicker to abandon it and to owe every-*
> *thing to your genius. . . . Because perfection calls for austere*
> *toil you maintain that it is contrary to nature. This is a system*
> *that suits at once indolence and vanity. Is anything more*
> *needed to make it popular, especially when it has as auxiliary*
> *an obscure philosophy which is termed transcendent or trans-*
> *cendental? That is just the way sound literature fell into decline*
> *beginning with the end of the first century of the Christian era.*
> *It became extinct only to revive after a long period of darkness*
> *and barbarism; and that is how it will fall into decline again if*

great examples and sage lessons should ever lose their au-
thority.

The general public in England became at least vaguely aware
of the new movement with the translation of Madame de
Staël's "Germany" (1813) and A. W. Schlegel's "Dramatic Art
and Literature" (1815). Byron wrote in his reply to Bowles
(1821): "Schlegel and Madame de Staël have endeavored to
reduce poetry to *two* systems, classical and romantic. The effect is only beginning."

The distinction between classic and romantic worked out by
the Schlegels and spread abroad by Madame de Staël was, then,
largely associated with a certain type of mediævalism. Nevertheless one cannot insist too strongly that the new school deserved
to be called romantic, not because it was mediæval, but because
it displayed a certain quality of imagination in its mediævalism.
The longing for the Middle Ages is merely a very frequent
form of nostalgia, and nostalgia I have defined as the pursuit of
pure illusion. No doubt a man may be mediæval in his leanings
and yet very free from nostalgia. He may, for example, prefer
St. Thomas Aquinas to any modern philosopher on grounds
that are the very reverse of romantic; and in the attitude of
any particular person towards the Middle Ages, romantic and
unromantic elements may be mingled in almost any conceivable
proportion; and the same may be said of any past epoch that
one prefers to the present. Goethe, for instance, as has been remarked, took flight from his own reality, but he did not, like
the romanticists, take flight from all reality. The classical world
in which Goethe dwelt in imagination during his latter years,
in the midst of a very unclassical environment, was to some extent at least real, though one can discern even in the case of
Goethe the danger of a classicism that is too aloof from the
here and now. But the mediævalist, in so far as he is romantic,
does not turn to a mediæval reality from a real but distasteful
present. Here as elsewhere his first requirement is not that his
"vision" should be true, but that it should be rich and radiant;
and the more "ideal" the vision becomes in this sense, the
wider the gap that opens between poetry and life.

We are thus brought back to the problem of the romantic

imagination or, one may term it, the eccentric imagination. The classical imagination, I have said, is not free thus to fly off at a tangent, to wander wild in some empire of chimeras. It has a centre, it is at work in the service of reality. With reference to this real centre, it is seeking to disengage what is normal and representative from the welter of the actual. It does not evade the actual, but does select from it and seek to impose upon it something of the proportion and symmetry of the model to which it is looking up and which it is imitating. To say that the classicist (and I am speaking of the classicist at his best) gets at his reality with the aid of the imagination is but another way of saying that he perceives his reality only through a veil of illusion. The creator of this type achieves work in which illusion and reality are inseparably blended, work which gives the "illusion of a higher reality."

Proportionate and decorous in this sense æsthetic romanticism can in no wise be, but it does not follow that the only art of which the Rousseauist is capable is an art of idyllic dreaming. Schiller makes a remark about Rousseau that goes very nearly to the heart of the matter: he is either, says Schiller, dwelling on the delights of nature or else avenging her. He is either, that is, idyllic or satirical. Now Rousseau himself says that he was not inclined to satire and in a sense this is true. He would have been incapable of lampooning Voltaire in the same way that Voltaire lampooned him, though one might indeed wish to be lampooned by Voltaire rather than to be presented as Rousseau has presented certain persons in his "Confessions." In all that large portion of Rousseau's writing, however, in which he portrays the polite society of his time and shows how colorless and corrupt it is compared with his pastoral dream (for his "nature," as I have said, is only a pastoral dream) he is highly satirical. In general, he is not restrained, at least in the "Confessions," from the trivial and even the ignoble detail by any weak regard for decorum. At best decorum seems to him a hollow convention, at worst the "varnish of vice" and the "mask of hypocrisy." Every reader of the "Confessions" must be struck by the presence, occasionally on the same page, of passages that look forward to Lamartine, and of other passages that seem an anticipation rather of Zola. The passage in which Rousseau relates how he was abruptly brought to earth from his "angelic loves" [18] is typical. In short Rousseau oscillates between an Arcadian vision that is radiant but unreal, and a photographic and literal and often sordid reality. He does not so use his imagination as to disengage the real from the welter of the actual and so achieve something that strikes one still as nature but a selected and ennobled nature.[19] "It is a very odd circumstance," says Rousseau, "that my imagination is never more agreeably active than when my outer conditions are the least agreeable, and that, on the contrary, it is less cheerful when everything is cheerful about me. My poor head cannot subordinate itself to things. It cannot embellish, it wishes to create. Real objects are reflected in it at best such as they are; it can adorn only imaginary objects. If I wish to paint the springtime I must be in winter," etc.

This passage may be said to foreshadow the two types of art and literature that have been prevalent since Rousseau—romantic art and the so-called realistic art that tended to supplant it towards the middle of the nineteenth century.[20] This so-called realism does not represent any fundamental change of direction as compared with the earlier romanticism; it is simply, as some one has put it, romanticism going on all fours. The extreme of romantic unreality has always tended to produce a sharp recoil. As the result of the wandering of the imagination in its own realm of chimeras, one finally comes to feel the need of refreshing one's sense of fact; and the more trivial the fact, the more certain one is that one's feet are once more planted on *terra firma*. Don Quixote is working for the triumph of Sancho Panza. Besides this tendency of one extreme to produce the other, there are special reasons that I shall point out more fully later for the close relationship of the romanticism and the so-called realism of the nineteenth century. They are both merely different aspects of naturalism. What binds together realism and romanticism is their common repudiation of decorum as something external and artificial. Once get rid of decorum, or what amounts to the same thing, the whole body of "artificial" conventions, and what will result is, according to the romanticist, Arcadia. But what actually emerges with the progressive weakening of the principle of restraint is *la bête humaine*. The

Rousseauist begins by walking through the world as though it were an enchanted garden, and then with the inevitable clash between his ideal and the real he becomes morose and embittered. Since men have turned out not to be indiscriminately good he inclines to look upon them as indiscriminately bad and to portray them as such. At the bottom of much so-called realism therefore is a special type of satire, a satire that is the product of violent emotional disillusion. The collapse of the Revolution of 1848 produced a plentiful crop of disillusion of this kind. No men had ever been more convinced of the loftiness of their idealism than the Utopists of this period, or failed more ignominiously when put to the test. All that remained, many argued, was to turn from an ideal that had proved so disappointing to the real, and instead of dreaming about human nature to observe men as coolly, in Flaubert's phrase, as though they were mastodons or crocodiles. But what lurks most often behind this pretence to a cold scientific impassiveness in observing human nature is a soured and cynical emotionalism and a distinctly romantic type of imagination. The imagination is still idealistic, still straining, that is, away from the real, only its idealism has undergone a strange inversion; instead of exaggerating the loveliness it exaggerates the ugliness of human nature; it finds a sort of morose satisfaction in building for itself not castles but dungeons in Spain. What I am saying applies especially to the French realists who are more logical in their disillusion than the men of other nations. They often establish the material environment of their heroes with photographic literalness, but in their dealings with what should be the specifically human side of these characters they often resemble Rousseau at his worst: they put pure logic into the service of pure emotion, and this is a way of achieving, not the real, but a maximum of unreality. The so-called realistic writers abound in extreme examples of the romantic imagination. The peasants of Zola are not real, they are an hallucination. If a man is thus to let his imagination run riot, he might, as Lemaître complains, have imagined something more agreeable.

The same kinship between realism and romanticism might be brought out in a writer whom Zola claimed as his master—

Balzac. I do not refer to the side of Balzac that is related to what the French call *le bas romantisme*—his lapses into the weird and the melodramatic, his occasional suggestions of the claptrap of Anne Radcliffe and the Gothic romance—but to his general thesis and his handling of it. Balzac's attitude towards the society of his time is, like the attitude of Rousseau towards the society of his time, satirical, but on entirely different grounds: he would show the havoc wrought in this society by its revolutionary emancipation from central control of the kind that had been provided traditionally by the monarchy and the Catholic Church, and the consequent disruption of the family by the violent and egoistic expansion of the individual along the lines of his ruling passion. But Balzac's imagination is not on the side of his thesis; not, that is, on the side of the principle of control; on the contrary, it revels in its vision of a world in which men are overstepping all ethical bounds in their quest of power and pleasure, of a purely naturalistic world that is governed solely by the law of cunning and the law of force. His imagination is so fascinated by this vision that, like the imagination of Rousseau, though in an entirely different way, he simply parts company with reality. Judged by the ultimate quality of his imagination, and this, let me repeat, is always the chief thing to consider in a creative artist, Balzac is a sort of inverted idealist. Compared with the black fictions he conjures up in his painting of Paris, the actual Paris seems pale and insipid. His Paris is not real in short, but an hallucination—a lurid land of heart's desire. As Leslie Stephen puts it, for Balzac Paris is hell, but then hell is the only place worth living in. The empire of chimeras over which he holds sway is about as far on one side of reality as George Sand's kingdom of dreams is on the other. George Sand, more perhaps than any other writer of her time, continues Rousseau in his purely idyllic manner. Her idealized peasants are not any further from the truth and are certainly more agreeable than the peasants of Balzac, who foreshadow the peasants of Zola.

The writer, however, who shows the conflict between the romantic imagination and the real better than either Balzac or Zola, better than any other writer perhaps of the modern French movement, is Flaubert. The fondness of this founder of realism for reality may be inferred from a passage in one of his letters to George Sand: "I had in my very youth a complete presentiment of life. It was like a sickly kitchen smell escaping from a basement window." In his attitude towards the society of his time, he is, in the same sense, but in a far greater degree than Rousseau, satirical. The stupidity and mediocrity of the bourgeois are his target, just as Rousseau's target is the artificiality of the drawing-room. At the same time that he shrinks back with nausea from this reality, Flaubert is like Gautier "full of nostalgias," even the nostalgia of the Middle Ages. "I am a Catholic," he exclaims, "I have in my heart something of the green ooze of the Norman Cathedrals." Yet he cannot acquiesce in a mediæval or any other dream. Even Rousseau says that he was "tormented at times by the nothingness of his chimeras." Flaubert was tormented far more by the nothingness of his. Perhaps indeed the predominant flavor in Flaubert's writing as a whole is that of an acrid disillusion. He portrays satirically the real and at the same time mocks at the ideal that he craves emotionally and imaginatively (this is only one of the innumerable forms assumed by the Rousseauistic warfare between the head and the heart). He oscillates rapidly between the pole of realism as he conceives it, and the pole of romance, and so far as any serious philosophy is concerned, is left suspended in the void. Madame Bovary is the very type of the Rousseauistic idealist, misunderstood in virtue of her exquisite faculty of feeling. She aspires to a "love beyond all loves," an infinite satisfaction that her commonplace husband and environment quite deny her. At bottom Flaubert's heart is with Madame Bovary. "I am Madame Bovary," he exclaims. Yet he exposes pitilessly the "nothingness of her chimeras," and pursues her to the very dregs of her disillusion. I have already mentioned Flaubert's cult for "Don Quixote." His intellectual origins were all there, he says; he had known it by heart even when a boy. It has been said that "Madame Bovary" bears the same relationship to æsthetic romanticism that "Don Quixote" does to the romanticism of actual adventure of the Middle Ages. Yet "Don Quixote" is the most genial, "Madame Bovary" the least genial of masterpieces. This difference comes out no less clearly in a comparison of M. Homais with Sancho Panza than in a comparison of Madame Bovary with the Knight, and is so fundamental as to throw doubt on the soundness of the whole analogy.

In M. Homais and like figures Flaubert simply means to symbolize contemporary life and the immeasurable abyss of platitude in which it is losing itself through its lack of imagination and ideal. Yet this same platitude exercises on him a horrid fascination. For his execration of the philistine is the nearest approach in his idealism to a positive content, to an escape from sheer emptiness and unreality. This execration must therefore be cherished if he is to remain convinced of his own superiority. "If it were not for my indignation," he confesses in one place, "I should fall flat." Unfortunately we come to resemble what we habitually contemplate. "By dint of railing at idiots," says Flaubert, "one runs the risk of becoming idiotic one's self."

In his discourse on the "Immortality of the Soul" (1659) Henry More speaks of "that imagination which is most free, such as we use in romantic inventions." The price that the romantic imagination pays for its freedom should by this time be obvious: the freer it becomes the farther it gets away from reality. We have seen that the special form of unreality encouraged by the æsthetic romanticism of Rousseau is the dream of the simple life, the return to a nature that never existed, and that this dream made its special appeal to an age that was suffering from an excess of artificiality and conventionalism. Before entering upon the next stage of our subject it might be well to consider for a moment wherein the facts of primitive life, so far as we can ascertain them, differ from Rousseau's dream of primitive life; why we are justified in assuming that the noble savage of Rousseau, or the Greek of Schiller, or Hölderlin, or the man of the Middle Ages of Novalis never had any equivalent in reality. More or less primitive men have existed and still exist and have been carefully studied. Some of them actually recall by various traits, their gentleness, for example, Rousseau's aboriginal man, and the natural pity that is supposed to guide him. Why then will any one familiar with the facts of aboriginal life smile when Rousseau speaks of the savage "attached to no place, having no prescribed task, obeying no one, having no other law than his own will," [21] and therefore displaying independence and initiative? The answer is of course that genuine savages are, with the possible exception of children, the most conventional and imitative of beings. What one takes to be natural in them is often the result of a long and, in the Rousseauistic sense, artificial discipline. The tendency to take for pure and unspoiled nature what is in fact a highly modified nature is one that assumes many forms. "When you see," says Rousseau, "in the happiest people in the world bands of peasants regulate the affairs of state under an oak tree and always behave sensibly, can you keep from despising the refinements of other nations which make themselves illustrious and miserable with so much art and mystery?" Rousseau is viewing these peasants through the Arcadian glamour. In much the same way Emerson saw a proof of the consonance of democracy with human nature in the working of the New England town-meeting. But both Rousseau's Swiss and Emerson's New Englanders had been moulded by generations of austere religious discipline and so throw little light on the relation of democracy to human nature in itself.

A somewhat similar illusion is that of the man who journeys into a far country and enjoys in the highest degree the sense of romantic strangeness. He has escaped from the convention of his own society and is inclined to look on the men and women he meets in the foreign land as Arcadian apparitions. But these men and women have not escaped from *their* convention. On the contrary, what most delights him in them (for example, what most delighted Lafcadio Hearn in the Japanese) may be the result of an extraordinarily minute and tyrannical discipline imposed in the name of the general sense upon the impulses of the individual.

The relation of convention to primitive life is so well understood nowadays that the Rousseauist has reversed his argument. Since primitive folk (let us say the Bushmen of Australia) are more conventional than the Parisian and Londoner we may infer that at some time in the future when the ideal is at last achieved upon earth, conventions will have disappeared entirely. But this is simply to transfer the Golden Age from the past to the future, and also to miss the real problem: for there is a real problem—perhaps indeed the gravest of all problems—involved in the relation of the individual to convention. If we are to grasp the nature of this problem we should perceive first of all that the significant contrast is not that between conditions more or less primitive and civilization, but that between a civilization that does not question its conventions and a civilization that has on the contrary grown self-conscious and critical. Thus the Homeric Greeks, set up by Schiller as exemplars of the simple life, were plainly subject to the conventions of an advanced civilization. The Periclean Greeks were also highly civilized, but unlike the Homeric Greeks, were becoming self-conscious and critical. In the same way the European thirteenth century, in some respects the most civilized that the world has seen, was governed by a great convention that imposed very strict limits upon the liberty of the individual. The critical spirit was already awake and tugging at the leashes of the outer authority that confined it, but it did not actually break them. Dante and St. Thomas Aquinas did not, for example, inquire into the basis of the mediæval convention in the same way that Socrates and the sophists inquired into the traditional opinions of Greece. But in the eighteenth century, especially in France, and from that time down to the present day, the revolt against convention has assumed proportions quite comparable to anything that took place in ancient Greece. Perhaps no other age has witnessed so many individuals who were, like Berlioz, eager to make all traditional barriers crack in the interest of their "genius" and its full expression. The state of nature in the name of which Rousseau himself assailed convention, though in itself only a chimera, a mere Arcadian projection upon the void, did indeed tend in a rationalistic pseudo-classic age to new forms of imaginative activity. In the form that concerns us especially the imagination is free to give its magic and glamour and infinitude to the emancipated emotions. This type of romanticism did not result in any recovery of the supposed primitive virtues, but it did bring about a revaluation of the received notions of morality that can scarcely be studied too carefully.

CHAPTER FOUR

ROMANTIC MORALITY: THE IDEAL

The period that began in the late eighteenth century and in the midst of which we are still living has witnessed an almost unparalleled triumph, as I have just said, of the sense of the individual (*sens propre*) over the general sense of mankind (*sens commun*). Even the collectivistic schemes that have been opposed to individualism during this period are themselves, judged by traditional standards, violently individualistic. Now the word individualism needs as much as any other general terms to be treated Socratically: we need in the interests of our present subject to discriminate between different varieties of individualism. Perhaps as good a working classification as any is to distinguish three main varieties: a man may wish to act, or think, or feel, differently from other men, and those who are individualistic in any one of these three main ways may have very little in common with one another. To illustrate concretely, Milton's plea in his "Areopagitica" for freedom of conscience makes above all for individualism of action. (*La foi qui n'agit pas est-ce une foi sincère?*) Pierre Bayle, on the other hand, pleads in his Dictionary and elsewhere for tolerance, not so much because he wishes to act or feel in his own way as because he wishes to think his own thoughts. Rousseau is no less obviously ready to subordinate both thought and action to sen-

sibility. His message is summed up once for all in the exclamation of Faust, "Feeling is all." He urges war on the general
sense only because of the restrictions it imposes on the free expansion of his emotions and the enhancing of these emotions
by his imagination.

Now the warfare that Rousseau and the individualists of
feeling have waged on the general sense has meant in practice
a warfare on two great traditions, the classical and the Christian. I have already pointed out that these two traditions,
though both holding the idea of imitation, were not entirely in
accord with one another, that the imitation of Horace differs
widely from the imitation of Christ. Yet their diverging from
one another is as nothing compared with their divergence from
the individualism of the primitivist. For the man who imitates
Christ in any traditional sense this world is not an Arcadian
dream but a place of trial and probation. "Take up your cross
and follow me." The following of this great exemplar required
that the instinctive self, which Rousseau would indulge, should
be either sternly rebuked or else mortified utterly. So far from
Nature and God being one, the natural man is so corrupt, according to the more austere Christian, that the gap between
him and the divine can be traversed only by a miracle of grace.
He should therefore live in fear and trembling as befits a being
upon whom rests the weight of the divine displeasure. "It is an
humble thing to be a man." Humility indeed is, in the phrase
of Jeremy Taylor, the special ornament and jewel of the Chris-
tain religion, and one is tempted to add, of all religion in so far
as it is genuine. Genuine religion must always have in some
form the sense of a deep inner cleft between man's ordinary
self and the divine. But some Christians were more inclined
from the start, as we can see in the extreme forms of the
doctrine of grace, to push their humility to an utter despair
of human nature. The historical explanation of this despair is
obvious: it is a sharp rebound from the pagan riot; an excessive
immersion in this world led to an excess of otherworldliness.
At the same time the conviction as to man's helplessness was
instilled into those, who, like St. Augustine, had witnessed in
some of its phases the slow disintegration of the Roman Empire. Human nature had gone bankrupt; and for centuries it

needed to be administered, if I may continue the metaphor, in receivership. The doctrine of grace was admirably adapted to this end.

The pagan riot from which the church reacted so sharply, was not, however, the whole of the ancient civilization. I have already said that there was at the heart of this civilization at its best a great idea—the idea of proportionateness. The ancients were in short not merely naturalistic but humanistic, and the idea of proportion is just as fundamental in humanism as is humility in religion. Christianity, one scarcely need add, incorporated within itself, however disdainfully, many humanistic elements from Greek and Roman culture. Yet it is none the less true that in his horror at the pagan worldliness the Christian tended to fly into the opposite extreme of unworldliness, and in this clash between naturalism and supernaturalism the purely human virtues of mediation were thrust more or less into the background. Yet by its very defect on the humanistic side the doctrine of grace was perhaps all the better fitted for the administration of human nature in receivership. For thus to make man entirely distrustful of himself and entirely dependent on God, meant in practice to make him entirely dependent on the Church. Man became ignorant and fanatical in the early Christian centuries, but he also became humble, and in the situation then existing that was after all the main thing. The Church as receiver for human nature was thus enabled to rescue civilization from the wreck of pagan antiquity and the welter of the barbarian invasions. But by the very fact that the bases of life in this world gradually grew more secure man became less otherworldly. He gradually recovered some degree of confidence in himself. He gave increasing attention to that side of himself that the ascetic Christian had repressed. The achievements of the thirteenth century which mark perhaps the culmination of Christian civilization were very splendid not only from a religious but also from a humanistic point of view. But although the critical spirit was already beginning to awake, it did not at that time, as I have already said, actually break away from the tutelage of the Church.

This emancipation of human nature from theological restraint took place in far greater measure at the Renaissance.

Human nature showed itself tired of being treated as a bankrupt, of being governed from without and from above. It aspired to become autonomous. There was in so far a strong trend in many quarters towards individualism. This rupture with external authority meant very diverse things in practice. For some who, in Lionardo's phrase, had caught a glimpse of the antique symmetry it meant a revival of genuine humanism; for others it meant rather a revival of the pagan and naturalistic side of antiquity. Thus Rabelais, in his extreme opposition to the monkish ideal, already proclaims, like Rousseau, the intrinsic excellence of man, while Calvin and others attempted to revive the primitive austerity of Christianity that had been corrupted by the formalism of Rome. In short, naturalistic, humanistic, and religious elements are mingled in almost every conceivable proportion in the vast and complex movement known as the Renaissance; all these elements indeed are often mingled in the same individual. The later Renaissance finally arrived at what one is tempted to call the Jesuitical compromise. There was a general revamping of dogma and outer authority, helped forward by a society that had taken alarm at the excesses of the emancipated individual. If the individual consented to surrender his moral autonomy, the Church for its part consented to make religion comparatively easy and pleasant for him, to adapt it by casuistry and other devices to a human nature that was determined once for all to take a less severe and ascetic view of life. One might thus live inwardly to a great extent on the naturalistic level while outwardly going through the motions of a profound piety. There is an unmistakable analogy between the hollowness of a religion of this type and the hollowness that one feels in so much neo-classical decorum. There is also a formalistic taint in the educational system worked out by the Jesuits—a system in all respects so ingenious and in some respects so admirable. The Greek and especially the Latin classics are taught in such a way as to become literary playthings rather than the basis of a philosophy of life; a humanism is thus encouraged that is external and rhetorical rather than vital, and this humanism is combined with a religion that tends to stress submission to outer authority at the expense of inwardness and individuality. The re-

proach has been brought against this system that it is equally
unfitted to form a pagan hero or a Christian saint. The reply
to it was Rousseau's educational naturalism—his exaltation of
the spontaneity and genius of the child.

Voltaire says that every Protestant is a Pope when he has his
Bible in his hand. But in practice Protestantism has been very
far from encouraging so complete a subordination of the general sense to the sense of the individual. In the period
that elapsed between the first forward push of individualism in
the Renaissance and the second forward push in the eighteenth
century, each important Protestant group worked out its creed
or convention and knew how to make it very uncomfortable
for any one of its members who rebelled against its authority.
Protestant education was also, like that of the Jesuits, an attempt to harmonize Christian and classical elements.

I have already spoken elsewhere of what was menacing all
these attempts, Protestant as well as Catholic, to revive the
principle of authority, to put the general sense once more on a
traditional and dogmatic basis and impose it on the sense of the
individual. The spirit of free scientific enquiry in the Renaissance had inspired great naturalists like Kepler and Galileo,
and had had its prophet in Bacon. So far from suffering any
setback in the seventeenth century, science had been adding
conquest to conquest. The inordinate self-confidence of the
modern man would seem to be in large measure an outcome
of this steady advance of scientific discovery, just as surely as
the opposite, the extreme humility that appears in the doctrine
of grace, reflects the despair of those who had witnessed the
disintegration of the Roman Empire. The word humility, if
used at all nowadays, means that one has a mean opinion of
one's self in comparison with other men, and not that one perceives the weakness and nothingness of human nature in itself
in comparison with what is above it. But it is not merely the
self-confidence inspired by science that has undermined the traditional disciplines, humanistic and religious, and the attempts
to mediate between them on a traditional basis; it is not merely
that science has fascinated man's imagination, stimulated his
wonder and curiosity beyond all bounds and drawn him away
from the study of his own nature and its special problems to

the study of the physical realm. What has been even more decisive in the overthrow of the traditional disciplines is that science has won its triumphs not by accepting dogma and tradition but by repudiating them, by dealing with the natural law, not on a traditional but on a positive and critical basis. The next step that might logically have been taken, one might suppose, would have been to put the human law likewise on a positive and critical basis. On the contrary the very notion that man is subject to two laws has been obscured. The truths of humanism and religion, being very much bound up with certain traditional forms, have been rejected along with these forms as obsolescent prejudice, and the attempt has been made to treat man as entirely the creature of the natural law. This means in practice that instead of dying to his ordinary self, as the austere Christian demands, or instead of imposing a law of decorum upon his ordinary self, as the humanist demands, man has only to develop his ordinary self freely.

At the beginning, then, of the slow process that I have been tracing down in briefest outline from mediæval Christianity, we find a pure supernaturalism; at the end, a pure naturalism. If we are to understand the relationship of this naturalism to the rise of a romantic morality, we need to go back, as we have done in our study of original genius, to the England of the early eighteenth century. Perhaps the most important intermediary stage in the passage from a pure supernaturalism to a pure naturalism is the great deistic movement which flourished especially in the England of this period. Deism indeed is no new thing. Deistic elements may be found even in the philosophy of the Middle Ages. But for practical purposes one does not need in one's study of deism to go behind English thinkers like Shaftesbury and his follower Hutcheson. Shaftesbury is a singularly significant figure. He is not only the authentic precursor of innumerable naturalistic moralists in England, France, and Germany, but one may also trace in his writings the connection between modern naturalistic morality and ancient naturalistic morality in its two main forms—Stoic and Epicurean. The strict Christian supernaturalist had maintained that the divine can be known to man only by the outer miracle of revelation, supplemented by the inner miracle of grace.

The deist maintains, on the contrary, that God reveals himself also through outer nature which he has fitted exquisitely to the needs of man, and that inwardly man may be guided aright by his unaided thoughts and feelings (according to the predominance of thought or feeling the deist is rationalistic or sentimental). Man, in short, is naturally good and nature herself is beneficent and beautiful. The deist finally pushes this harmony in God and man and nature so far that the three are practically merged. At a still more advanced stage God disappears, leaving only nature and man as a modification of nature, and the deist gives way to the pantheist who may also be either rationalistic or emotional. The pantheist differs above all from the deist in that he would dethrone man from his privileged place in creation, which means in practice that he denies final causes. He no longer believes, for example, like that sentimental deist and disciple of Rousseau, Bernardin de St. Pierre, that Providence has arranged everything in nature with an immediate eye to man's welfare; that the markings on the melon, for instance, "seem to show that it is destined for the family table." [1]

Rousseau himself, though eschewing this crude appeal to final causes, scarcely got, in theory at least, beyond the stage of emotional deism. The process I have been describing is illustrated better in some aspects by Diderot who began as a translator of Shaftesbury and who later got so far beyond mere deism that he anticipates the main ideas of the modern evolutionist and determinist. Diderot is at once an avowed disciple of Bacon, a scientific utilitarian in short, and also a believer in the emancipation of the emotions. Rousseau's attack on science is profoundly significant for other reasons, but it is unfortunate in that it obscures the connection that is so visible in Diderot between the two sides of the naturalistic movement. If men had not been so heartened by scientific progress they would have been less ready, we may be sure, to listen to Rousseau when he affirmed that they were naturally good. There was another reason why men were eager to be told that they were naturally good and that they could therefore trust the spontaneous overflow of their emotions. This reason is to be sought in the inevitable recoil from the opposite doctrine of total depravity and the mortal constraint that it had put on the instincts of the natural man. I have said that many churchmen, notably the Jesuits, sought to dissimulate the full austerity of Christian doctrine and thus retain their authority over a world that was moving away from austerity and so threatening to escape them. But other Catholics, notably the Jansenists, as well as Protestants like the Calvinists, were for insisting to the full on man's corruption and for seeking to maintain on this basis what one is tempted to call a theological reign of terror. One whole side of Rousseau's religion can be understood only as a protest against the type of Christianity that is found in a Pascal or a Jonathan Edwards. The legend of the abyss that Pascal saw always yawning at his side has at least a symbolical value. It is the wont of man to oscillate violently between extremes, and each extreme is not only bad in itself but even worse by the opposite extreme that it engenders. From a God who is altogether fearful, men are ready to flee to a God who is altogether loving, or it might be more correct to say altogether lovely. "Listen, my children," said Mother Angélique of Port-Royal to her nuns a few hours before her death, "listen well to what I say. Most people do not know what death is, and never give the matter a thought. But my worst forebodings were as nothing compared with the terrors now upon me." In deliberate opposition to such expressions of the theological terror, Rousseau imagined the elaborate complacency and self-satisfaction of the dying Julie, whose end was not only calm but æsthetic (*le dernier jour de sa vie en fut aussi le plus charmant*).

A sensible member of Edwards's congregation at Northampton might conceivably have voted with the majority to dismiss him, not only because he objected to this spiritual terrorism in itself, but also because he saw the opposite extreme that it would help to precipitate—the boundless sycophancy of human nature from which we are now suffering.

The effusiveness, then, that began to appear in the eighteenth century is one sign of the progress of naturalism, which is itself due to the new confidence inspired in man by scientific discovery coupled with a revulsion from the austerity of Christian dogma. This new effusiveness is also no less palpably a revulsion from the excess of artificial decorum and this revulsion was in turn greatly promoted by the rapid increase in power and influence at this time of the middle class. Reserve is traditionally aristocratic. The plebeian is no less traditionally expansive. It cannot be said that the decorous reserve of the French aristocracy that had been more or less imitated by other European aristocracies was in all respects commendable. According to this decorum a man should not love his wife, or if he did, should be careful not to betray the fact in public. It was also good "form" to live apart from one's children and bad form to display one's affection for them. The protest against a decorum that repressed even the domestic emotions may perhaps best be followed in the rise of the middle class drama. According to strict neo-classic decorum only the aristocracy had the right to appear in tragedy, whereas the man of the middle class was relegated to comedy and the man of the people to farce. The intermediate types of play that multiply in the eighteenth century (*drame bourgeois, comédie larmoyante,* etc.) are the reply of the plebeian to this classification. He is beginning to insist that his emotions too shall be taken seriously. But at the same time he is, under the influence of the new naturalistic philosophy, so bent on affirming his own goodness that in getting rid of artificial decorum he gets rid of true decorum likewise and so strikes at the very root of the drama. For true drama in contradistinction to mere melodrama requires in the background a scale of ethical values, or what amounts to the same thing, a sense of what is normal and representative and decorous, and the quality of the characters is revealed by their responsible choices good or bad with reference to some ethical scale, choices that the characters reveal by their actions and not by any explicit moralizing. But in the middle class drama there is little action in this sense: no one *wills* either his goodness or badness, but appears more or less as the creature of accident or fate (in a very un-Greek sense), or of a defective social order; and so instead of true dramatic conflict and proper motivation one tends to get domestic tableaux in which the characters weep in unison. For it is understood not only that man (especially the bourgeois) is good but that the orthodox way for this goodness to manifest itself is to overflow through the eyes. Perhaps never before or since have tears been shed with such a strange facility. At no other time have there been so many persons who, with streaming eyes, called upon heaven and earth to bear witness to their innate excellence. A man would be ashamed, says La Bruyère, speaking from the point of view of *l'honnête homme* and his decorum, to display his emotions at the theatre. By the time of Diderot he would have been ashamed not to display them. It had become almost a requirement of good manners to weep and sob in public. At the performance of the "Père de Famille" in 1769 we are told that every handkerchief was in use. The Revolution seems to have raised doubts as to the necessary connection between tearfulness and goodness. The "Père de Famille" was hissed from the stage in 1811. Geoffroy commented in his feuilleton: "We have learned by a fatal experience that forty years of declamation and fustian about sensibility, humanity and benevolence have served only to prepare men's hearts for the last excesses of barbarism."

The romanticist indulged in the luxury of grief and was not incapable of striking an attitude. But as a rule he disdained the facile lachrymosity of the man of feeling as still too imitative and conventional. For his part, he has that within which passes show. To estimate a play solely by its power to draw tears is, as Coleridge observes, to measure it by a virtue that it possesses in common with the onion; and Chateaubriand makes a similar observation. Yet one should not forget that the romantic emotionalist derives directly from the man of feeling. One may indeed study the transition from the one to the other in Chateaubriand himself. For example, in his early work, the "Natchez," he introduces a tribe of Sioux Indians who are still governed by the natural pity of Rousseau, as they prove by weeping on the slightest occasion. Lamartine again is close to Rousseau when he expatiates on the "genius" that is to be found in a tear; and Musset is not far from Diderot when he exclaims, "Long live the melodrama at which Margot wept" (*Vive le mélodrame où Margot a pleuré*).

Though it is usual to associate this effusiveness with Rousseau it should be clear from my brief sketch of the rise of the forces that were destined to overthrow the two great traditions —the Christian tradition with its prime emphasis on humility and the classical with its prime emphasis on decorum—that Rousseau had many forerunners. It would be easy enough, for example, to cite from English literature of the early eighteenth-century domestic tableaux[2] that look forward equally to the middle class drama and to Rousseau's picture of the virtues of Julie as wife and mother. Yet Rousseau, after all, deserves his preëminent position as the arch-sentimentalist by the very audacity of his revolt in the name of feeling from both humility and decorum. Never before and probably never since has a man of such undoubted genius shown himself so lacking in humility and decency (to use the old-fashioned synonym for decorum) as Rousseau in the "Confessions." Rousseau feels himself so good that he is ready as he declares to appear before the Almighty at the sound of the trump of the last judgment, with the book of his "Confessions" in his hand, and there to issue a challenge to the whole human race: "Let a single one assert to Thee if he dare: I am better than that man." As Horace Walpole complains he meditates a gasconade for the end of the world. It is possible to maintain with M. Lemaître that Rousseau's character underwent a certain purification as he grew older, but never at any time, either at the beginning or at the end, is it possible, as M. Lemaître admits, to detect an atom of humility—an essential lack that had already been noted by Burke.

The affront then that Rousseau puts upon humility at the very opening of his "Confessions" has like so much else in his life and writings a symbolical value. He also declares war in the same passage in the name of what he conceives to be his true self—that is his emotional self—against decorum or decency. I have already spoken of one of the main objections to decorum: it keeps one tame and conventional and interferes with the explosion of original genius. Another and closely allied grievance against decorum is implied in Rousseau's opening assertion in the "Confessions" that his aim is to show a man in all the truth of his nature, and human nature can be known in its truth only, it should seem, when stripped of its last shred of reticence. Rousseau therefore already goes on the principle recently proclaimed by the Irish Bohemian George Moore, that the only thing a man should be ashamed of is of being ashamed. If the first objection to decorum—that it represses original genius—was urged especially by the romanticists, the second objection—that decorum interferes with truth to nature —was urged especially by the so-called realists of the later nineteenth century (and realism of this type is, as has been said, only romanticism going on all fours). Between the Rousseauistic conception of nature and that of the humanist the gap is especially wide. The humanist maintains that man attains to the truth of his nature only by imposing decorum upon his ordinary self. The Rousseauist maintains that man attains to this truth only by the free expansion of his ordinary self. The humanist fears to let his ordinary self unfold freely at the expense of decorum lest he merit some such comment as that made on the "Confessions" by Madame de Boufflers who had been infatuated with Rousseau during his lifetime: that it was the work not of a man but of an unclean animal.[3]

The passages of the "Confessions" that deserve this verdict do not, it is hardly necessary to add, reflect directly Rousseau's moral ideal. In his dealings with morality as elsewhere he is, to come back to Schiller's distinction, partly idyllic and partly satirical. He is satiric in his attitude towards the existing forms—forms based upon the Christian tradition that man is naturally sinful and that he needs therefore the discipline of fear and humility, or else forms based upon the classical tradition that man is naturally one-sided and that he needs therefore to be disciplined into decorum and proportionateness. He is idyllic in the substitutes that he would offer for these traditional forms. The substitutes are particularly striking in their refusal to allow any place for fear. Fear, according to Ovid, created the first Gods, and religion has been defined by an old English poet as the "mother of form and fear." Rousseau would put in the place of form a fluid emotionalism, and as for fear, he would simply cast it out entirely, a revulsion, as I have pointed out, from the excessive emphasis on fear in the more austere forms of Christianity. Be "natural," Rousseau says, and eschew priests and doctors, and you will be emancipated from fear.

Rousseau's expedient for getting rid of man's sense of his own sinfulness on which fear and humility ultimately rest is well known. Evil, says Rousseau, foreign to man's constitution, is introduced into it from without. The burden of guilt is thus conveniently shifted upon society. Instead of the old dualism between good and evil in the breast of the individual, a new dualism is thus set up between an artificial and corrupt society and "nature." For man, let me repeat, has, according to Rousseau, fallen from nature in somewhat the same way as in the old theology he fell from God, and it is here that the idyllic element comes in, for, let us remind ourselves once more, Rousseau's nature from which man has fallen is only an Arcadian dream.

The assertion of man's natural goodness is plainly something very fundamental in Rousseau, but there is something still more fundamental, and that is the shifting of dualism itself, the virtual denial of a struggle between good and evil in the breast of the individual. That deep inner cleft in man's being on which religion has always put so much emphasis is not genuine. Only get away from an artificial society and back to nature and the inner conflict which is but a part of the artificiality will give way to beauty and harmony. In a passage in his "Supplément au voyage de Bougainville," Diderot puts the underlying thesis of the new morality almost more clearly than Rousseau: "Do you wish to know in brief the tale of almost all our woe? There once existed a natural man; there has been introduced within this man an artificial man and there has arisen in the cave a civil war which lasts throughout life."

The denial of the reality of the "civil war in the cave" involves an entire transformation of the conscience. The conscience ceases to be a power that sits in judgment on the ordinary self and inhibits its impulses. It tends, so far as it is recognized at all, to become itself an instinct and an emotion. Students of the history of ethics scarcely need to be told that this transformation of the conscience was led up to by the English deists, especially by Shaftesbury and his disciple Hutcheson.[4] Shaftesbury and Hutcheson are already æsthetic in all senses of the word; æsthetic in that they tend to base conduct upon feeling, and æsthetic in that they incline to identify the good and the beautiful. Conscience is ceasing for both of them to be an inner check on the impulses of the individual and becoming a moral *sense,* a sort of expansive instinct for doing good to others. Altruism, as thus conceived, is opposed by them to the egoism of Hobbes and his followers.

But for the full implications of this transformation of conscience and for æsthetic morality in general one needs to turn to Rousseau. Most men according to Rousseau are perverted by society, but there are a few in whom the voice of "nature" is still strong and who, to be good and at the same time beautiful, have only to let themselves go. These, to use a term that came to have in the eighteenth century an almost technical meaning, are the "beautiful souls." The *belle âme* is practically indistinguishable from the *âme sensible* and has many points in common with the original genius. Those whose souls are beautiful are a small transfigured band in the midst of a philistine multitude. They are not to be judged by the same rules as those of less exquisite sensibility. "There are unfortunates too privileged to follow the common pathway." [5] The beautiful soul is unintelligible to those of coarser feelings. His very superiority, his preternatural fineness of sensation, thus predestines him to suffering. We are here at the root of romantic melancholy as will appear more fully later.

The most important aspect of the whole conception is, however, the strictly ethical—the notion that the beautiful soul has only to be instinctive and temperamental to merit the praise that has in the past been awarded only to the purest spirituality. "As for Julie," says Rousseau, "who never had any other guide but her heart and could have no surer guide, she gives herself up to it without scruple, and to do right, has only to do all that it asks of her." [6] Virtue indeed, according to Rousseau, is not merely an instinct but a passion and even a voluptuous passion, moving in the same direction as other passions, only superior to them in vehemence. "Cold reason has never done anything illustrious; and you can triumph over the passions only by opposing them to one another. When the passion of virtue arises, it dominates everything and holds everything in equipoise." [7]

This notion of the soul that is spontaneously beautiful and therefore good made an especial appeal to the Germans and indeed is often associated with Germany more than with any

other land.⁸ But examples of moral æstheticism are scarcely
less frequent elsewhere from Rousseau to the present. No
one, for example, was ever more convinced of the beauty of
his own soul than Renan. "Morality," says Renan, "has been
conceived up to the present in a very narrow spirit, as obedience to a law, as an inner struggle between opposite laws. As
for me, I declare that when I do good I obey no one, I fight
no battle and win no victory. The cultivated man has only to
follow the delicious incline of his inner impulses." ⁹ Therefore,
as he says elsewhere, "Be beautiful and then do at each moment whatever your heart may inspire you to do. This is the
whole of morality." ¹⁰

The doctrine of the beautiful soul is at once a denial and a
parody of the doctrine of grace; a denial because it rejects original sin; a parody because it holds that the beautiful soul acts
aright, not through any effort of its own but because nature
acts in it and through it even as a man in a state of grace
acts aright not through any merit of his own but because God
acts in him and through him. The man who saw everything
from the angle of grace was, like the beautiful soul or the original genius, inclined to look upon himself as exceptional and
superlative. Bunyan entitles the story of his own inner life
"Grace abounding to the chief of sinners." But Bunyan flatters
himself. It is not easy to be chief in such a lively competition.
Humility and pride were evidently in a sort of grapple with
one another in the breast of the Jansenist who declared that
God had killed three men in order to compass his salvation.
In the case of the beautiful soul the humility disappears, but
the pride remains. He still looks upon himself as superlative
but superlative in goodness. If all men were like himself,
Renan declares, it would be appropriate to say to them: Ye are
Gods and sons of the most high.¹¹ The partisan of grace holds
that works are of no avail compared with the gratuitous and
unmerited illumination from above. The beautiful soul clings
to his belief in his own innate excellence, no matter how flagrant the contradiction may be between this belief and his deeds.
One should not fail to note some approximation to the point of
view of the beautiful soul in those forms of Christianity in
which the sense of sin is somewhat relaxed and the inner light

very much emphasized—for example among the German pie-
tists and the quietists of Catholic countries.[12] We even hear
of persons claiming to be Christians who as the result of de-
bauchery have experienced a spiritual awakening (*Dans la brute
assoupie, un ange se réveille*). But such doctrines are mere
excrescences and eccentricities in the total history of Christianity. Even in its extreme insistence on grace, Christianity has always tended to supplement rather than contradict the supreme
maxim of humanistic morality as enunciated by Cicero: "The
whole praise of virtue is in action." The usual result of the
doctrine of grace when sincerely held is to make a man feel
desperately sinful at the same time that he is less open to re-
proach than other men in his actual behavior. The beautiful
soul on the other hand can always take refuge in his feelings
from his real delinquencies. According to Joubert, Chateaubriand was not disturbed by actual lapses in his conduct because of his persuasion of his own innate rectitude.[13] "Her
conduct was reprehensible," says Rousseau of Madame de Warens, "but her heart was pure." It does not matter what you do
if only through it all you preserve the sense of your own loveliness. Indeed the more dubious the act the more copious would
seem to be the overflow of fine sentiments to which it stimulates the beautiful soul. Rousseau dilates on his "warmth of
heart," his "keenness of sensibility," his "innate benevolence
for his fellow creatures," his "ardent love for the great, the
true, the beautiful, the just," on the "melting feeling, the lively
and sweet emotion that he experiences at the sight of everything that is virtuous, generous and lovely," and concludes:
"And so my third child was put into the foundling hospital."

If we wish to see the psychology of Rousseau writ large
we should turn to the French Revolution. That period abounds
in persons whose goodness is in theory so superlative that it
overflows in a love for all men, but who in practice are filled
like Rousseau in his later years with universal suspicion. There
was indeed a moment in the Revolution when the madness of
Rousseau became epidemic, when suspicion was pushed to such
a point that men became "suspect of being suspect." One of
the last persons to see Rousseau alive at Ermenonville was
Maximilien Robespierre. He was probably a more thoroughgo-

ing Rousseauist than any other of the Revolutionary leaders.
Perhaps no passage that could be cited illustrates with more
terrible clearness the tendency of the new morality to convert
righteousness into self-righteousness than the following from
his last speech before the Convention at the very height of the
Reign of Terror. Himself devoured by suspicion, he is repelling
the suspicion that he wishes to erect his own power on the
ruins of the monarchy. The idea, he says, that "he can descend
to the infamy of the throne will appear probable only to those
perverse beings who have not even the right to believe in virtue. But why speak of virtue? Doubtless virtue is a natural
passion. But how could they be familiar with it, these venal
spirits who never yielded access to aught save cowardly and
ferocious passions? . . . Yet virtue exists as you can testify,
feeling and pure souls; it exists, that tender, irresistible, imperious passion, torment and delight of magnanimous hearts,
that profound horror of tyranny, that compassionate zeal for
the oppressed, that sacred love for one's country, that still more
sublime and sacred love for humanity, without which a great
revolution is only a glittering crime that destroys another
crime; it exists, that generous ambition to found on earth the
first Republic of the world; that egoism of undegenerate men
who find a celestial voluptuousness in the calm of a pure conscience and the ravishing spectacle of public happiness (!). You
feel it at this moment burning in your souls. I feel it in mine.
But how could our vile calumniators have any notion of it?"
etc.

In Robespierre and other revolutionary leaders one may
study the implications of the new morality—the attempt to
transform virtue into a natural passion—not merely for the individual but for society. M. Rod entitled his play on Rousseau
"The Reformer." Both Rousseau and his disciple Robespierre
were reformers in the modern sense,—that is they are concerned not with reforming themselves, but other men. Inasmuch as there is no conflict between good and evil in the
breast of the beautiful soul he is free to devote all his efforts
to the improvement of mankind, and he proposes to achieve
this great end by diffusing the spirit of brotherhood. All the
traditional forms that stand in the way of this free emotional

expansion he denounces as mere "prejudices," and inclines to look on those who administer these forms as a gang of conspirators who are imposing an arbitrary and artificial restraint on the natural goodness of man and so keeping it from manifesting itself. With the final disappearance of the prejudices of the past and those who base their usurped authority upon them, the Golden Age will be ushered in at last; everybody will be boundlessly self-assertive and at the same time temper this self-assertion by an equally boundless sympathy for others, whose sympathy and self-assertion likewise know no bounds. The world of Walt Whitman will be realized, a world in which there is neither inferior nor superior but only comrades. This vision (such for example as appears at the end of Shelley's "Prometheus") of a humanity released from all evil artificially imposed from without, a humanity "where all things flow to all, as rivers to the sea" and "whose nature is its own divine control," is the true religion of the Rousseauist. It is this image of a humanity glorified through love that he sets up for worship in the sanctuary left vacant by "the great absence of God."

This transformation of the Arcadian dreamer into the Utopist is due in part, as I have already suggested, to the intoxication produced in the human spirit by the conquests of science. One can discern the coöperation of Baconian and Rousseauist from a very early stage of the great humanitarian movement in the midst of which we are still living. Both Baconian and Rousseauist are interested not in the struggle between good and evil in the breast of the individual, but in the progress of mankind as a whole. If the Rousseauist hopes to promote the progress of society by diffusing the spirit of brotherhood, the Baconian or utilitarian hopes to achieve the same end by perfecting its machinery. It is scarcely necessary to add that these two main types of humanitarianism may be contained in almost any proportion in any particular person. By his worship of man in his future material advance, the Baconian betrays no less surely than the Rousseauist his faith in man's natural goodness. This lack of humility is especially conspicuous in those who have sought to develop the positive observations of science into a closed system with the aid of logic and pure mathematics. Pascal already remarked sarcastically of Descartes that he had no need of God except to give an initial fillip to his mechanism. Later the mechanist no longer grants the need of the initial fillip. According to the familiar anecdote, La Place when asked by Napoleon in the course of an explanation of his "Celestial Mechanics" where God came in, replied that he had no need of a God in his system. As illustrating the extreme of humanitarian arrogance one may take the following from the physicist and mathematician, W. K. Clifford: "The dim and shadowy outlines of the superhuman deity fade slowly from before us; and as the mist of his presence floats aside, we perceive with greater and greater clearness the shape of a yet grander and nobler figure—of Him who made all gods and shall unmake them. From the dim dawn of history and from the inmost depths of every soul the face of our father Man looks out upon us with the fire of eternal youth in his eyes and says, 'Before Jehovah was, I am.' " The fire, one is tempted to say, of eternal lust! Clifford is reported to have once hung by his toes from the cross-bar of a weathercock on a church-tower. As a bit of intellectual acrobatics the passage I have just quoted has some analogy with this posture. Further than this, man's intoxication with himself is not likely to go. The attitude of Clifford is even more extreme in its way than that of Jonathan Edwards in his. However, there are already signs that the man of science is becoming, if not humble, at least a trifle less arrogant.

One can imagine the Rousseauist interrupting at this point to remark that one of his chief protests has always been against the mechanical and utilitarian and in general the scientific attitude towards life. This is true. Something has already been said about this protest and it will be necessary to say more about it later. Yet Rousseauist and Baconian agree, as I have said, in turning away from the "civil war in the cave" to humanity in the lump. They agree in being more or less rebellious towards the traditional forms that put prime emphasis on the "civil war in the cave"—whether the Christian tradition with its humility or the classical with its decorum. No wonder Prometheus was the great romantic hero. Prometheus was at once a rebel, a lover of man and a promoter of man's material progress. We have been living for over a century in what may be termed an age of Promethean individualism.

The Rousseauist especially feels an inner kinship with Prometheus and other Titans. He is fascinated by every form of insurgency. Cain and Satan are both romantic heroes. To meet the full romantic requirement, however, the insurgent must also be tender-hearted. He must show an elemental energy in his explosion against the established order and at the same time a boundless sympathy for the victims of it. One of Hugo's poems tells of a Mexican volcano that in sheer disgust at the cruelty of the members of the Inquisition spits lava upon them. This compassionate volcano symbolizes in both of its main aspects the romantic ideal. Hence the enormous international popularity of Schiller's "Robbers." One may find innumerable variants of the brigand Karl Moor who uses his plunder "to support meritorious young men at college." The world into which we enter from the very dawn of romanticism is one of "glorious rascals," and "beloved vagabonds."

Sublime convicts, [says M. Lasserre] idlers of genius, angelic female poisoners, monsters inspired by God, sincere comedians, virtuous courtesans, metaphysical mountebanks, faithful adulterers, form only one half—the sympathetic half of humanity according to romanticism. The other half, the wicked half, is manufactured by the same intellectual process under the suggestion of the same revolutionary instinct. It comprises all those who hold or stand for a portion of any discipline whatsoever, political, religious, moral or intellectual—kings, ministers, priests, judges, soldiers, policemen, husbands and critics.[14]

The Rousseauist is ever ready to discover beauty of soul in any one who is under the reprobation of society. The figure of the courtesan rehabilitated through love that has enjoyed such popularity during the past hundred years goes back to Rousseau himself.[15] The underlying assumption of romantic morality is that the personal virtues, the virtues that imply self-control, count as naught compared with the fraternal spirit and the readiness to sacrifice one's self for others. This is the ordinary theme of the Russian novel in which one finds, as Lemaître remarks, "the Kalmuck exaggerations of our French romantic ideas." For example Sonia in "Crime and Punishment" is glorified because she prostitutes herself to procure a livelihood for her family. One does not however need to go to Russia for what is scarcely less the assumption of contemporary America. If it can only be shown that a person is sympathetic we are inclined to pardon him his sins of unrestraint, his lack, for example, of common honesty. As an offset to the damaging facts brought out at the investigation of the sugar trust, the defense sought to establish that the late H. O. Havemeyer was a beautiful soul. It was testified that he could never hear little children sing without tears coming into his eyes. His favorite song, some one was unkind enough to suggest, was "little drops of water, little grains of sand." The newspapers again reported not long ago that a notorious Pittsburgh grafter had petitioned for his release from the penitentiary on the grounds that he wished to continue his philanthropic activities among the poor. Another paragraph that appeared recently in the daily press related that a burglar while engaged professionally in a house at Los Angeles discovered that the lady of the house had a child suffering from croup, and at once came to her aid, explaining that he had six children of his own. No one could really think amiss of this authentic descendant of Schiller's Karl Moor. For love, according to the Rousseauist, is not the fulfillment of the law but a substitute for it. In "Les Misérables" Hugo contrasts Javert who stands for the old order based on obedience to the law with the convict Jean Valjean who stands for the new regeneration of man through love and self-sacrifice. When Javert awakens to the full ignominy of his rôle he does the only decent thing—he commits suicide. Hugo indeed has perhaps carried the new evangel of sympathy as a substitute for all the other virtues further than any one else and with fewer weak concessions to common sense. Sultan Murad, Hugo narrates, was "sublime." He had his eight brothers strangled, caused his uncle to be sawn in two between two planks, opened one after the other twelve children to find a stolen apple, shed an ocean of blood and "sabred the world." One day while passing in front of a butcher-shop he saw a pig bleeding to death, tormented by flies and with the sun beating upon its wound. Touched by pity, the Sultan pushes the pig into the shade with his foot and with an "enormous and super-human gesture" drives away the flies. When Murad dies the pig appears before the Almighty and, pleading for him against the accusing host of his victims, wins his pardon. Moral: "A succored pig outweighs a world oppressed" [16] (*Un pourceau secouru vaut un monde égorgé*).

This subordination of all the other values of life to sympathy is achieved only at the expense of the great humanistic virtue —decorum or a sense of proportion. Now not to possess a sense of proportion is, however this lack may be manifested, to be a pedant; and, if there is ever a humanistic reaction, Hugo, one of the chief products of the age of original genius, will scarcely escape the charge of pedantry. But true religion also insists on a hierarchy of the virtues. Burke speaks at least as much from a religious as from a humanistic point of view when he writes:

> *The greatest crimes do not arise so much from a want of feeling for others as from an over-sensibility for ourselves and an over-indulgence to our own desires. . . . They [the 'philosophes'] explode or render odious or contemptible that class of virtues which restrain the appetite. These are at least nine out of ten of the virtues. In the place of all this they substitute a virtue which they call humanity or benevolence. By these means their morality has no idea in it of restraint or indeed of a distinct and settled principle of any kind. When their disciples are thus left free and guided only by present feeling, they are no longer to be depended on for good and evil. The men who today snatch the worst criminals from justice will murder the most innocent persons to-morrow.* [17]

The person who seeks to get rid of ninety per cent of the virtues in favor of an indiscriminate sympathy does not simply lose his scale of values. He arrives at an inverted scale of values. For the higher the object for which one feels sympathy the more the idea of obligation is likely to intrude—the very thing the Rousseauist is seeking to escape. One is more irresponsible and therefore more spontaneous in the Rousseauistic sense in lavishing one's pity on a dying pig. Medical men have given a learned name to the malady of those who neglect the members of their own family and gush over animals (zoöphilpsychosis). But Rousseau already exhibits this "psychosis." He abandoned his five children one after the other, but had we are told an unspeakable affection for his dog.[18]

Rousseau's contemporary, Sterne, is supposed to have lavished a somewhat disproportionate emotion upon an ass. But the ass does not really come into his own until a later stage of the movement. Nietzsche has depicted the leaders of the nineteenth century as engaged in a veritable onolatry or ass-worship. The opposition between neo-classicist and Rousseauist is indeed symbolized in a fashion by their respective attitude towards the ass. Neo-classical decorum was, it should be remembered, an all-pervading principle. It imposed a severe hierarchy, not only upon objects, but upon the words that express these objects. The first concern of the decorous person was to avoid lowness, and the ass he looked upon as hopelessly low— so low as to be incapable of ennoblement even by a resort to periphrasis. Homer therefore was deemed by Vida to have been guilty of outrageous indecorum in comparing Ajax to an ass. The partisans of Homer sought indeed to prove that the ass was in the time of Homer a "noble" animal or at least that the word ass was "noble." But the stigma put upon Homer by Vida—reinforced as it was by the similar attacks of Scaliger and others—remained.

The rehabilitation of the ass by the Rousseauist is at once a protest against an unduly squeamish decorum, and a way of proclaiming the new principle of unbounded expansive sympathy. In dealing with both words and what they express, one should show a democratic inclusiveness. Something has already been said of the war the romanticist waged in the name of local color against the impoverishment of vocabulary by the neo-classicists. But the romantic warfare against the aristocratic squeamishness of the neo-classic vocabulary goes perhaps even deeper. Take, for instance, Wordsworth's view as to the proper language of poetry. Poetical decorum had become by the end of the eighteenth century a mere varnish of conventional elegance. Why should mere polite prejudice, so Wordsworth reasoned, and the "gaudiness and inane phraseology" in which it resulted be allowed to interfere with the "spontaneous overflow of powerful emotion"? And so he proceeds to set up a view of poetry that is only the neo-classical view turned upside down.

For the proper subjects and speech of poetry he would turn from the highest class of society to the lowest, from the aristocrat to the peasant. The peasant is more poetical than the aristocrat because he is closer to nature, for Wordsworth as he himself avows, is less interested in the peasant for his own sake than because he sees in him a sort of emanation of the landscape.[19]

One needs to keep all this background in mind if one wishes to understand the full significance of a poem like "Peter Bell." Scaliger blames Homer because he stoops to mention in his description of Zeus something so trivial as the eyebrows. Wordsworth seeks to bestow poetical dignity and seriousness on the "long left ear" of an ass.[20] The ass is thus exalted, one scarcely need add, because of his compassionateness. The hard heart of Peter Bell is at last melted by the sight of so much goodness. He aspires to be like the ass and finally achieves his wish.

The French romanticists, Hugo, for instance, make an attack on decorum somewhat similar to that of Wordsworth. Words formerly lived, says Hugo, divided up into castes. Some had the privilege of mounting into the king's coaches at Versailles, whereas others were relegated to the rabble. I came along and clapped a red liberty cap on the old dictionary. I brought about a literary '93,[21] etc. Hugo's attack on decorum is also combined with an even more violent assertion than Wordsworth's of the ideal of romantic morality—the supremacy of pity. He declares in the "Legend of the Ages" that an ass that takes a step aside to avoid crushing a toad is "holier than Socrates and greater than Plato." [22] For this and similar utterances Hugo deserves to be placed very nearly if not quite at the head of romantic onolaters.

We have said that the tremendous burden put upon sympathy in romantic morality is a result of the assumption that the "civil war in the cave" is artificial and that therefore the restraining virtues (according to Burke ninety per cent of the virtues) which imply this warfare are likewise artificial. If the "civil war in the cave" should turn out to be not artificial but a fact of the gravest import, the whole spiritual landscape would change immediately. Romantic morality would in that case be not a reality but a mirage. We need at all events to grasp the central issue firmly. Humanism and religion have always asserted in some form or other the dualism of the human spirit. A man's spirituality is in inverse ratio to his immersion in temperament. The whole movement from Rousseau to Bergson is, on the other hand, filled with the glorification of instinct. To become spiritual the beautiful soul needs only to expand along the lines of temperament and with this process the cult of pity or sympathy does not interfere. The romantic moralist tends to favor expansion on the ground that it is vital, creative, infinite, and to dismiss whatever seems to set bounds to expansion as something inert, mechanical, finite. In its onslaughts on the veto power whether within or without the breast of the individual it is plain that no age has ever approached the age of original genius in the midst of which we are still living. Goethe defines the devil as the spirit that always says no, and Carlyle celebrates his passage from darkness to light as an escape from the Everlasting Nay to the Everlasting Yea. We rarely pause to consider what a reversal of traditional wisdom is implied in such conceptions. In the past, the spirit that says no has been associated rather with the divine. Socrates tells us that the counsels of his "voice" were always negative, never positive.[23] According to the ancient Hindu again the divine is the "inner check." God, according to Aristotle, is pure Form. In opposition to all this emphasis on the restricting and limiting power, the naturalist, whether scientific or emotional, sets up a program of formless, fearless expansion; which means in practice that he recognizes no bounds either to intellectual or emotional curiosity.

I have said that it is a part of the psychology of the original genius to offer the element of wonder and surprise awakened by the perpetual novelty, the infinite otherwiseness of things, as a substitute for the awe that is associated with their infinite oneness; or rather to refuse to discriminate between these two infinitudes and so to confound the two main directions of the human spirit, its religious East, as one may say, with its West of wonder and romance. This confusion may be illustrated by the romantic attitude towards what is perhaps the most Eastern of all Eastern lands—India. The materials for the study of India in the Occident were accumulated by Englishmen towards the end of the eighteenth century, but the actual interpretation of this material is due largely to German romanticists, notably to Friedrich Schlegel.[24] Alongside the romantic Hellenist and the romantic mediævalist we find the romantic Indianist. It is to India even more than to Spain that one needs to turn, says Friedrich Schlegel, for the supremely romantic[25]—that is, the wildest and most unrestrained luxuriance of imagination. Now in a country so vast and so ancient as India you can find in some place or at some period or other almost anything you like. If, for example, W. B. Yeats waxes enthusiastic over Tagore we may be sure that there is in the work of Tagore something akin to æsthetic romanticism. But if we take India at the top of her achievement in the early Buddhistic movement, let us say, we shall find something very different. The early Buddhistic movement in its essential aspects is at the extreme opposite pole from romanticism. The point is worth making because certain misinterpretations that still persist both of Buddhism and other movements in India can be traced ultimately to the bad twist that was given to the whole subject by romanticists like the Schlegels. The educated Frenchman, for instance, gets his ideas of India largely from certain poems of Leconte de Lisle who reflects the German influence. But the sense of universal and meaningless flux that pervades these poems without any countervailing sense of a reality behind the shows of nature is a product of romanticism, working in coöperation with science, and is therefore antipodal to the absorption of the true Hindu in the oneness of things. We are told, again, that Schopenhauer was a Buddhist. Did he not have an image of Buddha in his bedroom? But no doctrine perhaps is more remote from the genuine doctrine of Buddha than that of this soured and disillusioned romanticist. The nature of true Buddhism and its opposition to all forms of romanticism is worth dwelling on for a moment. Buddha not only asserted the human law with unusual power but he also did what, in the estimation of some, needs doing in our own day—he put this law, not on a traditional, but on a positive and critical basis. This spiritual positivism of Buddha is, reduced to its simplest terms, a psychology of desire. Not only is the world outside of man in a constant state of flux and change, but there is an element within man that is in constant flux and change also makes itself felt practically as an element of expansive desire. What is unstable in him longs for what is unstable in the outer world. But he may escape from the element of flux and change, nay he must aspire to do so, if he wishes to be released from sorrow. This is to substitute the noble for the ignoble craving. The permanent or ethical element in himself towards which he should strive to move is known to him practically as a power of inhibition or inner check upon expansive desire. Vital impulse (*élan vital*) may be subjected to vital control (*frein vital*). Here is the Buddhist equivalent of the "civil war in the cave" that the romanticist denies. Buddha does not admit a soul in man in the sense that is often given to the word, but on this opposition between vital impulse and vital control as a psychological fact he puts his supreme emphasis. The man who drifts supinely with the current of desire is guilty according to Buddha of the gravest of all vices—spiritual or moral indolence (*pamāda*). He on the contrary who curbs or reins in his expansive desires is displaying the chief of all the virtues, spiritual vigilance or strenuousness (*appamāda*). The man who is spiritually strenuous has entered upon the "path." The end of this path and the goal of being cannot be formulated in terms of the finite intellect, any more than the ocean can be put into a cup. But progress on the path may be known by its fruits— negatively by the extinction of the expansive desires (the literal meaning of Nirvâna), positively by an increase in peace, poise, centrality.

A man's rank in the scale of being is, then, according to the Buddhist determined by the quality of his desires; and it is within his power to determine whether he shall let them run wild or else control them to some worthy end. We hear of the fatalistic East, but no doctrine was ever less fatalistic than that of Buddha. No one ever put so squarely upon the individual what the individual is ever seeking to evade—the burden of moral responsibility. "Self is the lord of self. Who else can be the lord? . . . You yourself must make the effort. The Buddhas are only teachers." [26] But does not all this emphasis on self, one may ask, tend to hardness and indifference towards others, towards the undermining of that compassion to which the romantic moralist is ready to sacrifice all the other virtues? Buddha may be allowed to speak for himself; "Even as a mother cherishes her child, her only child, so let a man cultivate a boundless love towards all beings." [27] Buddha thus seems to fulfil Pascal's requirement for a great man: he unites in himself opposite virtues and occupies all the space between them.

Enough has been said to make plain that the infinite indeterminate desire of the romanticist and the Buddhist repression of desire are the most different things conceivable. Chateaubriand it has been said was an "invincibly restless soul," a soul of desire (*une âme de désir*), but these phrases are scarcely more applicable to him than to many other great romanticists. They are fitly symbolized by the figures that pace to and fro in the Hall of Eblis and whose hearts are seen through their transparent bosoms to be lapped in the flames of unquenchable longing. The romanticist indeed bases, as I have said, on the very intensity of his longing his claims to be an idealist and even a mystic. William Blake, for example, has been proclaimed a true mystic. The same term has also been applied to Buddha. Without pretending to have fathomed completely so unfathomable a being as Buddha or even the far less unfathomable William Blake, one may nevertheless assert with confidence that Buddha and Blake stand for utterly incompatible views of life. If Blake is a mystic then Buddha must be something else. To be assured on this point one needs only to compare the "Marriage of Heaven and Hell" with the "Dhammapada," an anthology of some of the most authentic and authoritative material in early Buddhism. "He who desires but acts not, breeds pestilence. . . . The road of excess leads to the palace of wisdom," says Blake. "Even in heavenly pleasures he finds no satisfaction; the disciple who is fully awakened delights only in the destruction of all desires. . . . Good is restraint in all things," says Buddha. Buddha would evidently have dismissed Blake as a madman, whereas Blake would have looked on Buddhism as the ultimate abomination. My own conviction is that Buddha was a genuine sage well worthy of the homage rendered him by multitudes of men for more than twenty-four centuries, whereas Blake was only a romantic æsthete who was moving in his imaginative activity towards madness and seems at the end actually to have reached the goal.

I have been going thus far afield to ancient India and to Buddha, not that I might, like a recent student of Buddhism, enjoy "the strangeness of the intellectual landscape," but on the contrary that I might suggest that there is a centre of normal human experience and that Buddhism, at least in its ethical aspects, is nearer to this centre than æsthetic romanticism. Buddha might perhaps marvel with more reason at our strangeness than we at his. Buddha's assertion of man's innate moral laziness in particular accords more closely with what most of us have experienced than Rousseau's assertion of man's natural goodness. This conception of the innate laziness of man seems to me indeed so central that I am going to put it at the basis of the point of view I am myself seeking to develop, though this point of view is not primarily Buddhistic. This conception has the advantage of being positive rather than dogmatic. It works out in practice very much like the original sin of the Christian theologian. The advantage of starting with indolence rather than sin is that many men will admit that they are morally indolent who will not admit that they are sinful. For theological implications still cluster thickly about the word sin, and these persons are still engaged more or less consciously in the great naturalistic revolt against theology.

The spiritual positivist then will start from a fact of immediate perception—from the presence namely in the breast of the individual of a principle of vital control (*frein vital*), and he will measure his spiritual strenuousness or spiritual sloth by the degree to which he exercises or fails to exercise this power. In accordance with the keenness of a man's perception of a specially human order that is known practically as a curb upon his ordinary self, he may be said to possess insight. The important thing is that the insight should not be sophisticated, that a man should not fall away from it into some phantasmagoria of the intellect or emotions. A man sometimes builds up a whole system of metaphysics as a sort of screen between himself and his obligations either to himself or others. Mrs. Barbauld suspected that Coleridge's philosophy was only a mask for indolence.

Carlyle's phrase for Coleridge was even harsher: "putrescent indolence," a phrase that might be applied with more justice perhaps to Rousseau. One may learn from Rousseau the art of sinking to the region of instinct that is below the rational level instead of struggling forward to the region of insight that is above it, and at the same time passing for a sublime enthusiast; the art of looking backwards and downwards, and at the same time enjoying the honor that belongs only to those who look forwards and up. We need not wonder at the warm welcome that this new art received. I have said that that man has always been accounted a benefactor who has substituted for the reality of spiritual discipline some ingenious art of going through the motions and that the decorum of the neo-classical period had largely sunk to this level. Even in the most decorous of modern ages, that of Louis XIV, it was very common, as every student of the period knows, for men to set up as personages in the grand manner and at the same time behind the façade of conventional dignity to let their appetites run riot. It would have been perfectly legitimate at the end of the eighteenth century to attack in the name of true decorum a decorum that had become the "varnish of vice" and "mask of hypocrisy." What Rousseau actually opposed to pseudo-decorum was perhaps the most alluring form of sham spirituality that the world has ever seen—a method not merely of masking but of glorifying one's spiritual indolence. "You wish to have the pleasures of vice and the honor of virtue," wrote Julie to Saint-Preux in a moment of unusual candor. The Rousseauist may indulge in the extreme of psychic unrestraint and at the same time pose as a perfect idealist or even, if one is a Chateaubriand, as a champion of religion. Chateaubriand's life according to Lemaître was a "magnificent series of attitudes."

I do not mean to assert that the Rousseauist is always guilty of the pose and theatricality of which there is more than a suggestion in Chateaubriand. There is, however, much in the Rousseauistic view of life that militates against a complete moral honesty. "Of all the men I have known," says Rousseau, "he whose character derives most completely from his temperament alone is Jean-Jacques." [28] The ugly things that have a way of happening when impulse is thus left uncontrolled do not, as we have seen, disturb the beautiful soul in his complacency. He can always point an accusing finger at something or somebody else. The faith in one's natural goodness is a constant encouragement to evade moral responsibility. To accept responsibility is to follow the line of maximum effort, whereas man's secret desire is to follow, if not the line of least, at all events the line of lesser resistance. The endless twisting and dodging and proneness to look for scapegoats that results is surely the least reputable aspect of human nature. Rousseau writes to Madame de Francueil (20 April, 1751) that it was her class, the class of the rich, that was responsible for his having had to abandon his children. With responsibility thus shifted from one's self to the rich, the next step is inevitable, namely to start a crusade against the members of a class which, without any warrant from "Nature," oppresses its brothers, the members of other classes, and forces them into transgression. A man may thus dodge his duties as a father, and at the same time pose as a paladin of humanity. Rousseau is very close here to our most recent agitators. If a working girl falls from chastity, for example, do not blame her, blame her employer. She would have remained a model of purity if he had only added a dollar or two a week to her wage. With the progress of the new morality every one has become familiar with the type of the perfect idealist who is ready to pass laws for the regulation of everybody and everything except himself, and who knows how to envelop in a mist of radiant words schemes the true driving power of which is the desire to confiscate property.

The tendency to make of society the universal scapegoat is not, one scarcely needs add, to be ascribed entirely to the romantic moralist. It is only one aspect of the denial of the human law, of the assumption that because man is partly subject to the natural law he is entirely subject to it; and in this dehumanizing of man the rationalist has been at least as guilty as the emotionalist. If the Rousseauist hopes to find a substitute for all the restraining virtues in sympathy, the rationalistic naturalist, who is as a rule utilitarian with a greater or smaller dash of pseudo-science, hopes to find a substitute for these same virtues in some form of machinery. The legislative mill to which our "uplifters" are so ready to resort is a familiar example. If our modern society continues to listen to those who are seeking to persuade it that it is possible to find mechanical or emotional equivalents for self-control, it is likely, as Rousseau said of himself, to show a "great tendency to degenerate."

The fact on which the moral positivist would rest his effort to rehabilitate self-control is, as I have said, the presence in man of a restraining, informing and centralizing power that is anterior to both intellect and emotion. Such a power, it must be freely granted, is not present equally in all persons; in some it seems scarcely to exist at all. When released from outer control, they are simply unchained temperaments; whereas in others this super-rational perception seems to be singularly vivid and distinct. This is the psychological fact that underlies what the theologian would term the mystery of grace.

Rousseau himself was not quite so temperamental as might be inferred from what has been said about his evasion of ethical effort. There were moments when the dualism of the spirit came home to him, moments when he perceived that the conscience is not itself an expansive emotion but rather a judgment and a check upon expansive emotion. Yet his general readiness to subordinate his ethical self to his sensibility is indubitable. Hence the absence in his personality and writing of the note of masculinity. There is indeed much in his make-up that reminds one less of a man than of a high-strung impressionable woman. Woman, most observers would agree, is more natural in Rousseau's sense, that is, more temperamental, than man. One should indeed always temper these perilous comparisons of the sexes with the remark of La Fontaine that in this matter he knew a great many men who were women. Now to be temperamental is to be extreme, and it is in this sense perhaps that the female of the species may be said to be "fiercer than the male." Rousseau's failure to find "any intermediary term between everything and nothing" would seem to be a feminine rather than a masculine trait. Decorum in the case of women, even more perhaps than in the case of men, tends to be a mere conformity to what is established rather than the immediate perception of a law of measure and proportion that sets bounds to the expansive desires. "Women believe innocent everything that they dare," says Joubert, whom no one will accuse of being a misogynist. Those who are thus temperamental have more need than others of outer guidance. "His feminine nature," says C. E. Norton of Ruskin, "needed support such as it never got." [29]

If women are more temperamental than men it is only fair to add that they have a greater fineness of temperament. Women, says Joubert again, are richer in native virtues, men in acquired virtues. At times when men are slack in acquiring virtues in the truly ethical sense—and some might maintain that the present is such a time—the women may be not only men's equals but their superiors. Rousseau had this feminine fineness of temperament. He speaks rightly of his "exquisite faculties." He also had no inconsiderable amount of feminine charm. The numerous members of the French aristocracy whom he fascinated may be accepted as competent witnesses on this point. The mingling of sense and spirit that pervades Rousseau, his pseudo-Platonism as I have called it elsewhere, is also a feminine rather than a masculine trait.

There is likewise something feminine in Rousseau's preference for illusion. Illusion is the element in which woman even more than man would seem to live and move and have her being. It is feminine and also romantic to prefer to a world of sharp definition a world of magic and suggestiveness. W. Bagehot (it will be observed that in discussing this delicate topic I am prone to take refuge behind authorities) attributes the triumph of an art of shifting illusion over an art of clear and firm outlines to the growing influence of women.[30] Woman's being is to that of man, we are told, as is moonlight unto sunlight—and the moon is the romantic orb. The whole of German romance in particular is bathed in moonshine.[31]

The objection of the classicist to the so-called enlightenment of the eighteenth century is that it did not have in it sufficient light. The primitivists on the contrary felt that it had too much light—that the light needed to be tempered by darkness. Even the moon is too effulgent for the author of "Hymns to the Night." No movement has ever avowed more openly its partiality for the dim and the crepuscular. The German romanticists have been termed "twilight men." What many of them

admire in woman, as in children and plants, is her unconscious-
ness and freedom from analysis—an admiration that is also a
tribute in its way to the "night side" of nature.[32]

Discussions of the kind in which I have been indulging regarding the unlikeness of woman and man are very dreary unless one puts at least equal emphasis on their fundamental likeness. Woman, before being woman, is a human being and so
subject to the same law as man. So far as men and women
both take on the yoke of this law, they move towards a common centre. So far as they throw it off and live temperamentally, there tends to arise the most odious of all forms of warfare—that between the sexes. The dictates of the human law
are only too likely to yield in the case of both men and women
to the rush of outer impressions and the tumult of the desires
within. This is what La Rochefoucauld means when he says
that "the head is always the dupe of the heart." Nevertheless
feeling is even more likely to prevail over judgment in woman
than it is in man. To be judicial indeed to the point of hardness and sternness has always been held to be unfeminine. It is
almost woman's prerogative to err on the side of sympathy.
But even woman cannot be allowed to substitute sympathy for
true conscience—that is for the principle of control. In basing
conduct on feeling Rousseau may be said to have founded a
new sophistry. The ancient sophist at least made man the measure of all things. By subordinating judgment to sensibility
Rousseau may be said to have made woman the measure of all
things.

The affirmation of a human law must ultimately rest on the
perception of a something that is set above the flux upon which
the flux itself depends—on what Aristotle terms an unmoved
mover. Otherwise conscience becomes a part of the very flux
and element of change it is supposed to control. In proportion
as he escapes from outer control man must be conscious of
some such unmoved mover if he is to oppose a definite aim or
purpose to the indefinite expansion of his desires. Having some
such firm centre he may hope to carry through to a fortunate
conclusion the "civil war in the cave." He may, as the wise are
wont to express it, build himself an island in the midst of the
flood. The romantic moralist, on the other hand, instead of

building himself an island is simply drifting with the stream. For feeling not only shifts from man to man, it is continually shifting in the same man; so that morality becomes a matter of mood, and romanticism here as elsewhere might be defined as the despotism of mood. At the time of doing anything, says Mrs. Shelley, Shelley deemed himself right; and Rousseau says that in the act of abandoning his own children he felt "like a member of Plato's republic."

The man who makes self-expression and not self-control his primary endeavor becomes subject to every influence, "the very slave of circumstance and impulse borne by every breath." [33] This is what it means in practice no longer to keep a firm hand on the rudder of one's personality, but to turn one's self over to "nature." The partisan of expression becomes the thrall of his impressions so that the whole Rousseauistic conception may be termed indifferently impressionistic or expressionistic. For the beautiful soul in order to express himself has to indulge his emotions instead of hardening and bracing them against the shock of circumstance. The very refinement of sensibility which constitutes in his own eyes his superiority to the philistine makes him quiver responsively to every outer influence; he finally becomes subject to changes in the weather, or in Rousseau's own phrase, the "vile plaything of the atmosphere and seasons."

This rapid shifting of mood in the romanticist, in response to inner impulse or outer impression, is almost too familiar to need illustration. Here is an example that may serve for a thousand from that life-long devotee of the great god Whim—Hector Berlioz. When at Florence, Berlioz relates in his Memoirs, he received a letter from the mother of Camille, the woman he loved, informing him of Camille's marriage to another. "In two minutes my plans were laid. I must hurry to Paris to kill two guilty women and one innocent man; for, this act of justice done, I too must die." Accordingly he loads his pistols, supplies himself with a disguise as a lady's maid, so as to be able to penetrate into the guilty household, and puts into his pockets "two little bottles, one of strychnine, the other of laudanum." While awaiting the departure of the diligence he "rages up and down the streets of Florence like a mad dog." Later, as the diligence is traversing a wild mountain road, he suddenly lets out a " 'Ha'! so hoarse, so savage, so diabolic that the startled driver bounded aside as if he had indeed a demon for his fellow-traveller." But on reaching Nice he is so enchanted by the climate and environment that he not only forgets his errand, but spends there "the twenty happiest days" of his life! There are times, one must admit, when it is an advantage to be temperamental.

In this exaltation of environmental influences one should note again the coöperation of Rousseauist and Baconian, of emotional and scientific naturalist. Both are prone to look upon man as being made by natural forces and not as making himself. To deal with the substitutes that Rousseauist and Baconian have proposed for traditional morality is in fact to make a study of the varieties—and they are numerous—of naturalistic fatalism. The upshot of the whole movement is to discredit moral effort on the part of the individual. Why should a man believe in the efficacy of this effort, why should he struggle to acquire character if he is convinced that he is being moulded like putty by influences beyond his control—the influence of climate, for example? Both science and romanticism have vied with one another in making of man a mere stop on which Nature may play what tune she will. The Æolian harp enjoyed an extraordinary popularity as a romantic symbol. The man of science for his part is ready to draw up statistical tables showing what season of the year is most productive of suicide and what type of weather impels bank-cashiers most irresistibly to embezzlement. A man on a mountain top, according to Rousseau, enjoys not only physical but spiritual elevation, and when he descends to the plain the altitude of his mind declines with that of his body. Ruskin's soul, says C. E. Norton, "was like an Æolian harp, its strings quivering musically in serene days under the touch of the soft air, but as the clouds gathered and the winds arose, vibrating in the blast with a tension that might break the sounding board itself." It is not surprising Ruskin makes other men as subject to "skyey influences" as himself. "The mountains of the earth are," he says, "its natural cathedrals. True religion can scarcely be achieved away from them. The curate or hermit of the field and fen, however simple his life or painful his lodging, does not often attain the spirit of the hill pastor or recluse: we may find in him a decent virtue or a contented ignorance, rarely the *prophetic vision or the martyr's passion*." The corruptions of Romanism "are traceable for the most part to lowland prelacy." [34]

Is then the Rousseauist totally unable to regulate his impressions? It is plain that he cannot control them from within because the whole idea of a vital control of this kind is, as we have seen, foreign to the psychology of the beautiful soul. Yet it is, according to Rousseau, possible to base morality on the senses—on outer perception that is—and at the same time get the equivalent of a free will based on inner perception. He was so much interested in this subject that he had planned to devote to it a whole treatise to be entitled "Sensitive morality or the materialism of the sage." A man cannot resist an outer impression but he may at least get out of its way and put himself in the way of another impression that will impel him to the desired course of conduct. "The soul may then be put or maintained in the state most favorable to virtue." "Climates, seasons, sounds, colors, darkness, light, the elements, food, noise, silence, movement, rest, everything, acts on our physical frame." By a proper adjustment of all these outer elements we may govern in their origins the feelings by which we allow ourselves to be dominated.[35]

Rousseau's ideas about sensitive morality are at once highly chimerical and highly significant. Here as elsewhere one may say with Amiel that nothing of Rousseau has been lost. His point of view has an inner kinship with that of the man of science who asserts that man is necessarily the product of natural forces, but that one may at least modify the natural forces. For example, moral effort on the part of the individual cannot overcome heredity. It is possible, however, by schemes of eugenics to regulate heredity. The uneasy burden of moral responsibility is thus lifted from the individual, and the moralist in the old-fashioned sense is invited to abdicate in favor of the biologist. It would be easy enough to trace similar assumptions in the various forms of socialism and other "isms" almost innumerable of the present hour.

Perhaps the problem to which I have already alluded may as

well be faced here. How does it happen that Rousseau who attacked both science and literature as the chief sources of human degeneracy should be an arch-æsthete, the authentic ancestor of the school of art for art's sake and at the same time by his sensitive (or æsthetic) morality play into the hands of the scientific determinist? If one is to enter deeply into the modern movement one needs to consider both wherein scientific and emotional naturalists clash and wherein they agree. The two types of naturalists agree in their virtual denial of a superrational realm. They clash above all in their attitude towards what is on the rational level. The scientific naturalist is assiduously analytical. Rousseau, on the other hand, or rather one whole side of Rousseau, is hostile to analysis. The arts and sciences are attacked because they are the product of reflection. "The man who reflects is a depraved animal," because he has fallen away from the primitive spontaneous unity of his being. Rousseau is the first of the great anti-intellectualists. By assailing both rationalism and pseudo-classic decorum in the name of instinct and emotion he appealed to men's longing to get away from the secondary and the derivative to the immediate. True decorum satisfies the craving for immediacy because it contains within itself an element of superrational perception. The "reason" of a Plato or an Aristotle also satisfies the craving for immediacy because it likewise contains within itself an element of superrational perception. A reason or a decorum of this kind ministers to another deep need of human nature—the need to lose itself in a larger whole. Once eliminate the superrational perception and reason sinks to the level of rationalism, consciousness becomes mere self-consciousness. It is difficult, as St. Evremond said, for man to remain in the long run in this doubtful middle state. Having lost the unity of insight, he will long for the unity of instinct. Hence the paradox that this most self-conscious of all movements is filled with the praise of the unconscious. It abounds in persons who, like Walt Whitman, would turn and live with the animals, or who, like Novalis, would fain strike root into the earth with the plant. Animals[36] and plants are not engaged in any moral struggle, they are not inwardly divided against themselves.

Here is the source of the opposition between the abstract and analytical head, deadly to the sense of unity, and the warm immediate heart that unifies life with the aid of the imagination—an opposition that assumes so many forms from Rousseau to Bergson. The Rousseauist always betrays himself by arraigning in some form or other, "the false secondary power by which we multiply distinctions." One should indeed remember that there were obscurantists before Rousseau. Pascal also arrays the heart against the head; but his heart is at the farthest remove from that of Rousseau; it stands for a superrational perception. Christians like Pascal may indulge with comparative impunity in a certain amount of obscurantism. For they have submitted to a tradition that supplies them with distinctions between good and evil and at the same time controls their imagination. But for the individualist who has broken with tradition to deny his head in the name of his heart is a deadly peril. He above all persons should insist that the power by which we multiply distinctions, though secondary, is not false—that the intellect, of however little avail in itself, is invaluable when working in coöperation with the imagination in the service of either inner or outer perception. It is only through the analytical head and its keen discriminations that the individualist can determine whether the unity and infinitude towards which his imagination is reaching (and it is only through the imagination that one can have the sense of unity and infinitude) is real or merely chimerical. Need I add that in making these distinctions between imagination, intellect, feeling, etc., I am not attempting to divide man up into more or less watertight compartments, into hard and fast "faculties," but merely to express, however imperfectly, certain obscure and profound facts of experience?

The varieties of what one may term the rationalistic error, of the endeavor of the intellect to emancipate itself from perception and set up as an independent power, are numerous. The variety that was perhaps formerly most familiar was that of the theologian who sought to formulate intellectually what must ever transcend formulation. The forms of the rationalistic error that concern our present subject can be traced back for the most part to Descartes, the father of modern philosophy, and are indeed implicit in his famous identification of though and being (*Je pense, donc je suis*). The dogmatic and arrogant rationalism that denies both what is above and what is below itself, both the realm of awe and the realm of wonder, which prevailed among the Cartesians of the Enlightenment, combined, as I have said, with pseudo-classic decorum to produce that sense of confinement and smugness against which the original genius protested. Man will always crave a view of life to which perception lends immediacy and the imagination infinitude. A view of life like that of the eighteenth century that reduces unduly the rôle of both imagination and perception will always seem to him unvital and mechanical. "The Bounded," says Blake, "is loathed by its possessor. The same dull round even of a Universe would soon become a Mill with complicated wheels."

The mechanizing of life against which the romanticist protested may, as I said, be largely associated with the influence of Descartes. It is not, however, the whole truth about Descartes to say that he forgot the purely instrumental rôle of the intellect and encouraged it to set up as an independent power. As a matter of fact he also used the intellect as an instrument in the service of outer perception. Taking as his point of departure the precise observations that science was accumulating, he sought to formulate mathematically the natural law. Now the more one reduces nature to a problem of space and movement, the more one is enabled to measure nature; and the method of exact measurement may be justified, if not on metaphysical, at least on practical grounds. It helps one, if not to understand natural forces, at least to control them. It thereby increases man's power and ministers to utility. In a word, the intellect when thus pressed into the service of outer perception makes for material efficiency. In a sense science becomes scientific only in proportion as it neglects the qualitative differences between phenomena, e.g. between light and sound, and treats them solely from the point of view of quantity. But the penalty that science pays for this quantitative method is a heavy one. The farther it gets away from the warm immediacy of perception the less real it becomes; for that only is real to a man that he immediately perceives. Perfectly pure science tends to become a series of abstract mathematical formulæ without any real content. By his resort to such a method the man of science is in constant danger of becoming a mere rationalist. At the bottom he is ignorant of the reality that lies behind natural phenomena; he must ever be ignorant of it, for it lays hold upon the infinite, and so must elude a finite being like man. But the desire to conceal his own ignorance from himself and others, the secret push for power and prestige that lies deep down in the breast of the man of science as in that of every other man, impels him to attach an independent value to the operations of the intellect that have only an instrumental value in the service of outer perception and to conceive that he has locked up physical nature in his formulæ. The man of science thus falls victim to a special form of metaphysical illusion. The gravity of the error of the scientific intellectualist is multiplied tenfold when he conceives that his formulæ cover not merely the natural law but the human law as well, when he strives, like Taine, to convert man himself into a "walking theorem," a "living geometry." This denial of every form of spontaneity was rightly felt by the romanticists to be intolerable.

Goethe contrasts the smug satisfaction of Wagner in his dead formulæ that give only what is external and secondary, with Faust's fierce craving for immediacy and therefore his impatience with an analysis that gives only the dry bones from which the vital breath has departed. Wagner is a philistine because he is not tormented by the thirst for the infinite. Faust, on the other hand, reaches out beyond the mere intellect towards the spirit that is behind the shows of nature, but this spirit appears to him and reduces him to despair by declaring that he is trying to grasp something that is not only infinite but alien to him. Instead of turning from this alien spirit to the spirit that is relevant to man, a spirit that sets bounds to every inordinate craving, including the inordinate craving for knowledge (*libido sciendi*), Faust gives himself to the devil in what was, in the time of the youthful Goethe, the newest fashion: he becomes a Rousseauist. Instead of striking into the ascending path of insight, he descends to the level of impulse. Seen from this level the power by which we multiply distinctions seems to him, as it was to seem later to Wordsworth, not merely secondary but false, and so definition yields to indiscriminate feeling (*Gefühl ist alles*). In general the Rousseau-istic reply to the Cartesian attempt to identify thought and being is the identification of being with emotion (*je sens, donc je suis*).

The Mephistopheles of Goethe has often been taken as a symbol of the iconoclastic and Voltairian side of the eighteenth century. The rationalists assailed the traditional forms that imply a superrational realm as mere "prejudice," and, failing to find in insight a substitute for these discarded forms, they succumbed in turn to the emotionalists. A "reason" that is not grounded in insight will always seem to men intolerably cold and negative and will prove unable to withstand the assault of the primary passions. The reason of a Plato or an Aristotle is on a different footing altogether because, as I have said, it includes an element of inner perception. One may note here that the difficulties of the present subject arise in no small degree from the ambiguities that cluster about the word reason. It may not only mean the imaginative insight[37] of a Plato and the abstract reasoning of a Descartes, but is often employed by the classicist himself as a synonym of good sense. Good sense may be defined as a correct perception of the ordinary facts of life and of their relation to one another. It may be of very many grades, corresponding to the infinite diversity of the facts to be perceived. A man may evidently have good sense in dealing with one order of facts, and quite lack it in dealing with some different order of facts. As the result of long observation and experience of a multitude of minute relationships, of the facts that ordinarily follow one another or coexist in some particular field, a man's knowledge of this field becomes at last, as it were, automatic and unconscious. A sea captain for example acquires at last an intuitive knowledge of the weather, the broker, an intuitive knowledge of stocks. The good sense or practical judgment of the sea captain in his particular calling and of the broker in his is likely to be greater than that of less experienced persons. One cannot, however, assert that a man's good sense is always in strict ratio to his experience. Some persons seem to have an innate gift for seeing things as they are, others a gift equally innate for seeing things as they are not.

Again the field in which one displays one's good sense or practical judgment may fall primarily under either the human law or the natural law, may belong in Aristotelian phrase to the domain either of the probable or of the necessary. To take a homely illustration, a man is free to choose the temperature of his bath, but only within the limits of natural necessity—in this case the temperature at which water freezes and that at which water boils. He will show his practical judgment by choosing water that is neither too hot nor too cold and this so far as he is concerned will be the golden mean. Here as elsewhere the golden mean is nothing mechanical, but may vary not only from individual to individual but in the same individual according to his age, the state of his health, etc. In determining what conforms to the golden mean or law of measure there must always be a mediation between the particular instance and the general principle, and it is here that intuition is indispensable. But even so there is a centre of normal human experience, and the person who is too far removed from it ceases to be probable. Aged persons may exist who find bathing in ice-water beneficial, but they are not representative. Now creative art, in distinct ratio to its dignity, deals not with what may happen in isolated cases but with what happens according to probability or necessity. It is this preoccupation with the universal that, as Aristotle says, makes poetry a more serious and philosophical thing than history. There enters indeed into true art an element of vital novelty and surprise. But the more cultivated the audience to which the creator addresses himself the more will it insist that the surprise be not won at the expense of motivation. It will demand that characters and incidents be not freakish, not too remote from the facts that normally follow one another or coexist, whether in nature or human nature. One needs, in short, to deal with both art and life from some ethical centre. The centre with reference to which one has good sense may be only the ethos of one's time and country, but if one's good sense has, as in the case of the great poets, the support of the imagination, it may pass beyond to something more abiding. "Of Pope's intellectual character," says Dr. Johnson, "the constituent and fundamental principle was good sense, a prompt and intuitive perception of consonance and propriety. He saw immediately of his own conceptions what was to be chosen, and what to be rejected." One may grant all this and at the same time feel the difference between the "reason" of a Pope and the reason of a Sophocles.

Good sense of the kind Dr. Johnson describes and decorum are not strictly speaking synonymous. To be decorous not only must one have a correct perception of what to do, but one must actually be able to do it; and this often requires a long and difficult training. We have seen that Rousseau's spite against eighteenth-century Paris was largely due to the fact that he had not acquired young enough the habits that would have made it possible for him to conform to its convention. "I affected," says Rousseau with singular candor, "to despise the politeness I did not know how to practice." As a matter of fact he had never adjusted himself to the decorum and good sense of any community. His attitude towards life was fundamentally Bohemian. But a person who was sensible and decorous according to the standards of some other country might have emphasized the differences between his good sense and decorum and the good sense and decorum of eighteenth-century Paris. The opponents of the traditional order in the eighteenth century were fond of introducing some Persian or Chinese to whom this order seemed no true order at all but only "prejudice" or "abuse." The conclusion would seem to be that because the good sense and decorum of one time and country do not coincide exactly with those of another time and country, therefore good sense and decorum themselves have in them no universal element, and are entirely implicated in the shifting circumstances of time and place. But behind the ethos of any particular country, that of Greece, for instance, there are, as Antigone perceived, the "unwritten laws of heaven," and something of this permanent order is sure to shine through even the most imperfect convention. Though no convention is final, though man and all he establishes are subject to the law of change, it is therefore an infinitely delicate and perilous task to break with convention. One can make this break only in favor of insight; which is much as if one should say that the only thing that may safely be opposed to common sense is a commoner sense, or if one prefers, a common sense that is becoming more and more imaginative. Even so, the wiser the man, one may surmise, the less likely he will be to indulge in a violent and theatrical rupture with his age, after the fashion of Rousseau. He will, like Socrates, remember the counsel of the Delphian oracle to follow the "usage of the city," [38] and while striving to gain a firmer hold upon the human law and to impose a more strenuous discipline upon his ordinary self, he will so far as possible conform to what he finds established. A student of the past cannot help being struck by the fact that men are found scattered through different times and countries and living under very different conventions who are nevertheless in virtue of their insight plainly moving towards a common centre. So much so that the best books of the world seem to have been written, as Emerson puts it, by one all-wise, all-seeing gentleman. A curious circumstance is that the writers who are most universal in virtue of their imaginative reason or inspired good sense are likewise as a rule the writers who realized most intensely the life of their own age. No other Spanish writer, for example, has so much human appeal as Cervantes, and at the same time no other brings us so close to the heart of sixteenth-century Spain. In the writings attributed to Confucius one encounters, mixed up with much that is almost inconceivably remote from us, maxims that have not lost their validity to-day; maxims that are sure to be reaffirmed wherever and whenever men attain to the level of humanistic insight. In the oldest Buddhist documents again one finds along with a great deal that is very expressive of ancient India, and thus quite foreign to our idiosyncrasy, a good sense which is even more imaginative and inspired, and therefore more universal, than that of Confucius, and which is manifested, moreover, on the religious rather than on the humanistic level. We are dealing here with indubitable facts, and should plant ourselves firmly upon them as against those who would exaggerate either the constant or the variable elements in human nature.

Enough has been said to show the ambiguities involved in the word reason. Reason may mean the abstract and geometrical reason of a Descartes, it may mean simply good sense, which may itself exist in very many grades ranging from an intuitive mastery of some particular field to the intuitive mastery of the ethos of a whole age, like the reason of a Pope. Finally reason may be imaginative and be thereby enabled to go beyond the convention of a particular time and country, and lay hold in varying degrees on "the unwritten laws of heaven." I have already traced in some measure the process by which reason in the eighteenth century had come to mean abstract and geometrical (or, as one may say, Cartesian) reason or else unimaginative good sense. Cartesian reason was on the one hand being pressed into the service of science and its special order of perceptions; on the other hand it was being used frequently in coöperation with an unimaginative good sense to attack the traditional forms that imply a realm of insight which is above both abstract reason and ordinary good sense. Men were emboldened to use reason in this way because they were flushed not only by the increasing mastery of man over nature through science, but by the positive and anti-traditional method through which this mastery had been won. Both those who proclaimed and those who denied a superrational realm were at least agreed in holding that the faith in any such realm was inseparable from certain traditional forms. Pascal, for example, held not only that insight in religion is annexed to the acceptance of certain dogmas—and this offended the new critical spirit—but furthermore that insight could exist even in the orthodox only by a special divine gift or grace, and this offended man's reviving confidence in himself. People were ready to applaud when a Voltaire declared it was time to "take the side of human nature against this sublime misanthropist." The insight into the law of decorum on which classicism must ultimately rest was in much the same way held to be inseparable from the Græco-Roman tradition; and so the nature of classical insight as a thing apart from any tradition tended to be obscured in the endless bickerings of ancients and moderns. The classical traditionalists, however, were less prone than the Christian traditionalists (Jansenists, Jesuits and Protestants) to weaken their cause still further by wrangling among themselves.

Inasmuch as both Christians and humanists failed to plant themselves on the fact of insight, the insight came more and more to be rejected along with the special forms from which it was deemed to be inseparable. As a result of this rejection "reason" was left to cope unaided with man's impulses and expansive desires. Now Pascal saw rightly that the balance of power in such a conflict between reason and impulse was held by the imagination, and that if reason lacked the support of insight the imagination would side with the expansive desires and reason would succumb. Moreover the superrational insight, or "heart" as Pascal calls it, that can alone keep man from being thus overwhelmed, comes, as he holds, not through reason but through grace and is at times actually opposed to reason. ("The heart," he says, "has reasons of which the reason knows nothing.") Instead of protesting against the asceticism of this view as the true positivist would do, instead of insisting that reason and imagination may pull together harmoniously in the service of insight, the romantic moralist opposed to the superrational "heart" of the austere Christian a subrational "heart," and this involved an attempt to base morality on the very element in human nature it is designed to restrain. The positivist will plant himself first of all on the fact of insight and will define it as the immediate perception of a something anterior to both thought and feeling, that is known practically as a power of control over both. The beautiful soul, as we have seen, has no place for any such power in his scheme of things, but hopes to satisfy all ethical elements simply by letting himself go. Rousseau (following Shaftesbury and Hutcheson) transforms conscience itself from an inner check into an expansive emotion. While thus corrupting conscience in its very essence he does not deny conscience. On the contrary he grows positively rhapsodic over conscience and other similar words. "Rousseau took wisdom from men's souls," says Joubert, "by talking to them of virtue." In short, Rousseau displays the usual dexterity of the sophist in juggling with ill-defined general terms. If one calls for sharp definition one is at once dismissed as a mere rationalist who is retreating into a false secondary power from a warm immediacy. The traditional distinctions regarding good and bad were thus discarded at the same time that discredit was cast on the keen analysis with which it would have been possible to build up new distinctions

—all in favor of an indiscriminate emotionalism. This discomfiture of both tradition and analysis in the field of the human law would not have been so easy if at the same time man's active attention and effort had not been concentrated more and more on the field of the natural law. In that field imagination and the analytical intellect were actually pulling together in the service of perception with the result that man was constantly gaining in power and utility. Emotional romanticists and scientific utilitarians have thus, in spite of their surface clashes, coöperated during the past century in the dehumanizing of man.

It is not enough to say of the representatives of both sides of this great naturalistic movement that they eliminate the veto power from human nature while continuing to use the old words, like virtue and conscience, that imply a veto power. We have seen that they actually attack the veto power as synonymous with evil. The devil is conceived as the spirit that always says no. A purely affirmative morality is almost necessarily an emotional morality. If there is no region of insight above the reason which is felt by the natural man as an element of vital control, and if cold reason, reason unsupported by insight, never has done anything illustrious, as Rousseau truly says, it follows that the only way to put driving power behind reason is to turn virtue into a passion—a passion that differs from other passions merely in its greater imperiousness. For the beautiful soul virtue, as we have seen in the case of Robespierre, is not only a tender, imperious and voluptuous passion but even an intoxication. "I was, if not virtuous," says Rousseau, "at least intoxicated with virtue." In its extreme manifestations romantic morality is indeed only one aspect, and surely the most singular aspect, of the romantic cult of intoxication. No student of romanticism can fail to be struck by its pursuit of delirium, vertigo and intoxication for their own sake. It is important to see how all these things are closely related to one another and how they all derive from the attempt to put life on an emotional basis. To rest conscience, for example, on emotion is to rest it on what is always changing, not only from man to man but from moment to moment in the same man. "If," as Shelley says, "nought is, but that it feels itself to be," it will feel itself to be very different things at different times. No part of man is exempt from the region of flux and change. There is, as James himself points out, a kinship between such a philosophy of pure motion and vertigo. Faust after all is only consistent when having identified the spirit that says no, which is the true voice of conscience, with the devil, he proceeds to dedicate himself to vertigo (*dem Taumel weih' ich mich*). Rousseau also, as readers of the "Confessions" will remember, deliberately courted giddiness by gazing down on a waterfall from the brink of a precipice (making sure first that the railing on which he leaned was good and strong). This naturalistic dizziness became epidemic among the Greeks at the critical moment of their break with traditional standards. "Whirl is King," cried Aristophanes, "having driven out Zeus." The modern sophist is even more a votary of the god Whirl than the Greek, for he has added to the mobility of an intellect that has no support in either tradition or insight the mobility of feeling. Many Rousseauists were, like Hazlitt, attracted to the French Revolution by its "grand whirling movements."

Even more significant than the cult of vertigo is the closely allied cult of intoxication. "Man being reasonable," says Byron, with true Rousseauistic logic, "must therefore get drunk. The best of life is but intoxication." The subrational and impulsive self of the man who has got drunk is not only released from the surveillance of reason in any sense of the word, but his imagination is at the same time set free from the limitations of the real. If many Rousseauists have been rightly accused of being "lovers of delirium," that is because in delirium the fancy is especially free to wander wild in its own empire of chimeras. To compose a poem, as Coleridge is supposed to have composed "Kubla Khan," in an opium dream without any participation of his rational self is a triumph of romantic art. "I should have taken more opium when I wrote it," said Friedrich Schlegel in explanation of the failure of his play "Alarcos." What more specially concerns our present topic is the carrying over of this subrational "enthusiasm" into the field of ethical values, and this calls for certain careful distinctions. Genuine religion— whether genuine Christianity or genuine Buddhism—is plainly unfriendly in the highest degree to every form of intoxication.

Buddhism, for example, not only prohibits the actual use of intoxicants but it pursues implacably all the subtler intoxications of the spirit. The attitude of the humanist towards intoxication is somewhat more complex. He recognizes how deep in man's nature is the craving for some blunting of the sharp edge of his consciousness and at least a partial escape from reason and reality; and so he often makes a place on the recreative side of life for such moments of escape even if attained with the aid of wine. *Dulce est desipere in loco.* Pindar, who displays so often in his verse the high seriousness of the ethical imagination, is simply observing the decorum of the occasion when he celebrates in a song for the end of a feast "the time when the wearisome cares of men have vanished from their reasons and on a wide sea of golden wealth we are all alike voyaging to some visionary shore. He that is penniless is then rich, and even they that are wealthy find their hearts expanding, when they are smitten by the arrows of the vine." The true Greek, one scarcely needs add, put his final emphasis, as befitted a child of Apollo, not on intoxication but on the law of measure and sobriety—on preserving the integrity of his mind, to render literally the Greek word for the virtue that he perhaps prized the most.[39] One must indeed remember that alongside the Apollonian element in Greek life is the orgiastic or Dyonisiac element. But when Euripides sides imaginatively with the frenzy of Dionysus, as he does in his "Bacchae," though ostensibly preaching moderation, we may affirm that he is falling away from what is best in the spirit of Hellas and revealing a kinship with the votaries of the god Whirl. The cult of intoxication has as a matter of fact appeared in all times and places where men have sought to get the equivalent of religious vision and the sense of oneness that it brings without rising above the naturalistic level. True religious vision is a process of concentration, the result of the imposition of the veto power upon the expansive desires of the ordinary self. The various naturalistic simulations of this vision are, on the contrary, expansive, the result of a more or less complete escape from the veto power, whether won with the aid of intoxicants or not. The emotional romanticists from Rousseau down have left no doubt as to the type of vision they represented. Rousseau dilates with a sort of fellow feeling on the deep potations that went on in the taverns of patriarchal Geneva.[40] Renan looks with disfavor on those who are trying to diminish drunkenness among the common people. He merely asks that this drunkenness "be gentle, amiable, accompanied by moral sentiments." Perhaps this side of the movement is best summed up in the following passage of William James: "The sway of alcohol over mankind is unquestionably due to its power to stimulate the mystical faculties of human nature, usually crushed to earth by the cold facts and dry criticisms of the sober hour. Sobriety diminishes, discriminates and says no; drunkenness expands, unites, and says yes. It is, in fact, the great exciter of the *Yes* function in man. It brings its votary from the chill periphery of things to the radiant core. It makes him for the moment one with truth." [41]

The American distiller who named one of his brands "Golden Dream Whiskey" was evidently too modest. If an adept in the new psychology he might have set up as a pure idealist, as the opener up of an especially radiant pathway to the "truth."

The primitivist then attacks sober discrimination as an obstacle both to warm immediacy of feeling and to unity. He tends to associate the emotional unity that he gains through intoxication with the unity of instinct which he so admires in the world of the subrational. "The romantic character," says Ricarda Huch, "is more exposed to waste itself in debaucheries than any other; for only in intoxication, whether of love or wine, when the one half of its being, consciousness, is lulled to sleep, can it enjoy the bliss for which it envies every beast—the bliss of feeling itself one." [42] The desires of the animal, however, work within certain definite limits. They are not, like those of the primitivist, inordinate, the explanation being that they are less stimulated than the desires of the primitivist by the imagination. Even if he gets rid of intellect and moral effort, the primitivist cannot attain the unity of instinct because he remains too imaginative; at the same time he proclaims and proclaims rightly that the imagination is the great unifying power—the power that can alone save us from viewing things in "disconnection dead and spiritless." We should attend carefully at this point for we are coming to the heart of the great romantic sophism. The Rousseauist does not attain to the unity of the man whose impulses and desires are controlled and disciplined to some ethical centre. He does not, in spite of all his praise of the unconscious and of the "sublime animals," attain to the unity of instinct. In what sense then may he be said to attain unity? The obvious reply is that he attains unity only in dreamland. For the nature to which he would return, one cannot repeat too often, is nothing real, but a mere nostalgic straining of the imagination away from the real. It is only in dreamland that one can rest unity on the expansive forces of personality that actually divide not only one individual from another but the same individual from himself. It is only in dreamland that, in the absence of both inner and outer control, "all things" will "flow to all, as rivers to the sea." Such a unity will be no more than a dream unity, even though one term it the ideal and sophisticate in its favor all the traditional terms of religion and morality. A question that forces itself at every stage upon the student of this movement is *What is the value of unity without reality?* For two things are equally indubitable: first, that romanticism on the philosophical side, is a protest in the name of unity against the disintegrating analysis of the eighteenth-century rationalist; second, that what the primitivist wants in exchange for analysis is not reality but illusion. Rousseau who inclines like other æsthetes to identify the true with the beautiful was, we are told, wont to exclaim: "There is nothing beautiful save that which is not"; a saying to be matched with that of "La Nouvelle Héloïse": "The land of chimeras is alone worthy of habitation." Similar utterances might be multiplied from French, English, and German romanticists.[43] To be sure, the word "reality" is perhaps the most slippery of all general terms. Certain recent votaries of the god Whirl, notably Bergson, have promised us that if we surrender to the flux we shall have a "vision" not only of unity but also of reality; and so they have transferred to the cult of their divinity all the traditional language of religion.

We do not, however, need for the present to enter into a discussion as to the nature of reality, but simply to stick to strict psychological observation. From this point of view it is not hard to see that the primitivist makes his primary appeal not to man's need for unity and reality but to a very different need. Byron has told us what this need is in his tale ("The Island") of a ship's crew that overpowered its officers and then set sail for Otaheite; what impelled these Arcadian mutineers was not the desire for a genuine return to aboriginal life with its rigid conventions, but

> *The wish—which ages have not yet subdued*
> *in man—to have no master save his mood.*

Now to have no master save one's mood is to be wholly temperamental. In Arcadia—the ideal of romantic morality—those who are wholly temperamental unite in sympathy and brotherly love. It remains to consider more fully what this triumph of temperament means in the real world.

CHAPTER FIVE

ROMANTIC MORALITY: THE REAL

The fundamental thing in Rousseauistic morality is not, as we have seen, the assertion that man is naturally good, but the denial of the "civil war in the cave." Though this denial is not complete in Rousseau himself, nothing is more certain than that his whole tendency is away from this form of dualism. The beautiful soul does the right thing not as a result of effort, but spontaneously, unconsciously and almost inevitably. In fact the beautiful soul can scarcely be said to be a voluntary agent at all. "Nature" acts in him and for him. This minimizing of moral struggle and deliberation and choice, this drift towards a naturalistic fatalism, as it may be termed, is a far more significant thing in Rousseau than his optimism. One may as a matter of fact eliminate dualism in favor of nature and at the same time look on nature as evil. This is precisely what one is likely to do if one sees no alternative to temperamental living, while judging those who live temperamentally not by their "ideal," that is by their feeling of their own loveliness, but by what they actually do. One will become a realist in the sense that came to be attached to this word during the latter part of the nineteenth century. Rousseau himself is often realistic in this sense when he interrupts his Arcadian visions to tell us what actually occurred. In the "Confessions," as I have said,

passages that recall Lamartine alternate with passages that recall Zola, and the transition from one type of passage to the
other is often disconcertingly sudden. In reading these realistic
passages of Rousseau we are led to reflect that his "nature" is
not, in practice, so remote from Taine's nature as might at first
appear. "What we call *nature,*" says Taine, "is this brood of
secret passions, often maleficent, generally vulgar, always blind,
which tremble and fret within us, ill-covered by the cloak of
decency and reason under which we try to disguise them; we
think we lead them and they lead us; we think our actions our
own, they are theirs." [1]

The transition from an optimistic to a pessimistic naturalism
can be followed with special clearness in the stages by which
the sentimental drama of the eighteenth century passes over
into the realistic drama of a later period. Petit de Julleville contrasts the beginning and the end of this development as
follows: "[In the eighteenth century] to please the public you
had to say to it: 'You are all at least at bottom good, virtuous,
full of feeling. Let yourselves go, follow your instincts; listen to
nature and you will do the right thing spontaneously.' How
changed times are! Nowadays[2] any one who wishes to please, to
be read and petted and admired, to pass for great and become
very rich, should address men as follows: 'You are a vile pack
of rogues, and profligates, you have neither faith nor law; you
are impelled by your instincts alone and these instincts are ignoble. Do not try though to mend matters, that would be of no
use at all.' " [3]

The connecting link between these different forms of the
drama is naturalistic fatalism, the suppression of moral responsibility for either man's goodness or badness. Strictly speaking,
the intrusion of the naturalistic element into the realm of ethical values and the subversion by it of deliberation and choice
and of the normal sequence of moral cause and effect is felt
from the human point of view not as fate at all, but as chance.
Emotional romanticism joins at this point with other forms of
romanticism, which all show a proclivity to prefer to strict motivation, to probability in the Aristotelian sense, what is fortui-
tous and therefore wonderful. This is only another way of
saying that the romanticist is moving away from the genuinely

dramatic towards melodrama. Nothing is easier than to establish the connection between emotional romanticism and the prodigious efflorescence of melodrama, the irresponsible quest for thrills, that has marked the past century. What perhaps distinguishes this movement from any previous one is the attempt to invest what is at bottom a melodramatic view of life with philosophic and even religious significance. By suppressing the "civil war in the cave" one strikes at the very root of true drama. It does not then much matter from the dramatic point of view whether the burden of responsibility for good or evil of which you have relieved the individual is shifted upon "nature" or society. Shelley, for example, puts the blame for evil on society. "Prometheus Unbound," in which he has developed his conception, is, judged as a play, only an ethereal melodrama. The unaccountable collapse of Zeus, a monster of unalloyed and unmotivated badness, is followed by the gushing forth in man of an equally unalloyed and unmotivated goodness. The whole genius of Hugo, again, as I have said in speaking of his use of antithesis, is melodramatic. His plays may be described as parvenu melodramas. They abound in every variety of startling contrast and strange happening, the whole pressed into the service of "problems" manifold and even of a philosophy of history. At the same time the poverty of ethical insight and true dramatic motivation is dissimulated under profuse lyrical outpourings and purple patches of local color. His Hernani actually glories in not being a responsible agent, but an "unchained and fatal force," [4] and so more capable of striking astonishment into himself and others. Yet the admirers of Hugo would not only promote him to the first rank of poets, but would have us share his own belief that he is a seer and a prophet.

It may be objected that the great dramatists of the past exalt this power of fate and thus diminish moral responsibility. But the very sharpest distinction must be drawn between the subrational fate of the emotional romanticist and the superrational fate of Greek tragedy. The fate of Æschylean tragedy, for instance, so far from undermining moral responsibility rather reinforces it. It is felt to be the revelation of a moral order of which man's experience at any particular moment is only an infinitesimal fragment. It does not seem, like the subrational fate of the emotional romanticist, the intrusion into the human realm of an alien power whether friendly or unfriendly. This point might be established by a study of the so-called fate drama in Germany (*Schicksaltragödie*), which, though blackly pessimistic, is closely related to the optimistic sentimental drama of the eighteenth century.[5] The German fate drama is in its essence ignoble because its characters are specimens of sensitive morality—incapable, that is, of opposing a firm human purpose to inner impulse or outer impression. The fate that thus wells up from the depths of nature and overwhelms their wills is not only malign and ironical, but as Grillparzer says, makes human deeds seem only "throws of the dice in the blind night of chance." [6] It would be easy to follow similar conceptions of fate down through later literature at least to the novels of Thomas Hardy.

Some of the earlier exponents of the sentimental drama, like Diderot, were not so certain as one might expect that the discarding of traditional decorum in favor of "nature" would result practically in a reign of pure loveliness. At one moment Diderot urges men to get rid of the "civil war in the cave" in order that they may be Arcadian, like the savages of the South Sea, but at other moments—as in "Rameau's Nephew"—he shows a somewhat closer grip on the problem of what will actually come to pass when a man throws off the conventions of a highly organized civilization and sets out to live temperamentally. Diderot sees clearly that he will be that least primitive of all beings, the Bohemian. Rameau's nephew, in his irresponsibility and emotional instability, in the kaleidoscopic shiftings of his mood, anticipates all the romantic Bohemians and persons of "artistic temperament" who were to afflict the nineteenth century. But he is more than a mere æsthete. At moments we can discern in him the first lineaments of the superman, who knows no law save the law of might. One should recollect that the actual influence of Diderot in France fell in the second rather than in the first half of the nineteenth century—was upon the realists rather than upon the romanticists. The same men that had a cult for Diderot admired the Vautrins and the Rastignacs of Balzac and the Julien Sorel of

Stendhal. These characters are little Napoleons. They live temperamentally in the midst of a highly organized society, but they set aside its conventions of right and wrong in favor, not of æsthetic enjoyment, but of power.

The ideal of romantic morality, as was seen in the last chapter, is altruism. The real, it should be clear from the examples I have been citing, is always egoism. But egoism may assume very different forms. As to the main forms of egoism in men who have repudiated outer control without acquiring self-control we may perhaps revive profitably the old Christian classification of the three lusts—the lust of knowledge, the lust of sensation, and the lust of power. Goethe indeed may be said to have treated these three main ways of being temperamental in three of his early characters—the lust of knowledge in "Faust," the lust of sensation in "Werther," and the lust of power in "Götz." If we view life solely from the naturalistic level and concern ourselves solely with the world of action, we are justified in neglecting, like Hobbes, the other lusts and putting supreme emphasis on the lust for power.[7] Professor F. J. Mather, Jr., has distinguished between "hard" and "soft" sentimentalists.[8] His distinction might perhaps be brought more closely into line with my own distinctions if I ventured to coin a word and to speak of hard and soft temperamentalists. The soft temperamentalist will prove unable to cope in the actual world with the hard temperamentalist, and is very likely to become his tool. Balzac has very appropriately made Lucien de Rubempré, the romantic poet and a perfect type of a soft temperamentalism, the tool of Vautrin, the superman.

Here indeed is the supreme opposition between the ideal and the real in romantic morality. The ideal to which Rousseau invites us is either the primitivistic anarchy of the "Second Discourse," in which egoism is tempered by "natural pity," or else a state such as is depicted in the "Social Contract," in which egoism is held in check by a disinterested "general will." The preliminary to achieving either of these ideals is that the traditional checks on human nature should be removed. But in exact proportion as this programme of emancipation is carried out what emerges in the real world is not the mythical will to brotherhood, but the ego and its fundamental will to power.

Give a bootblack half the universe, according to Carlyle, and he will soon be quarreling with the owner of the other half. He will if he is a very temperamental bootblack. Perhaps indeed all other evils in life may be reduced to the failure to check that something in man that is reaching out for more and ever for more. In a society in which the traditional inhibitions are constantly growing weaker, the conflict I have just sketched between the ideal and the real is becoming more and more acute. The soft temperamentalists are overflowing with beautiful professions of brotherly love, and at the same time the hard temperamentalists are reaching out for everything in sight; and inasmuch as the hard temperamentalists operate not in dreamland, but in the real world, they are only too plainly setting the tone. Very often, of course, the same temperamentalist has his hard and his soft side. The triumph of egoism over altruism in the relations between man and man is even more evident in the relations between nation and nation. The egoism that results from the inbreeding of temperament on a national scale runs in the case of the strong nations into imperialism.[9] We have not reflected sufficiently on the fact that the soft temperamentalist Rousseau is more than any other one person the father of *Kultur;*[10] and that the exponents of Kultur in our own day have been revealed as the hardest of hard temperamentalists.

To understand the particular craving that is met by Rousseauistic idealism one would need to go with some care into the psychology of the half-educated man. The half-educated man may be defined as the man who has acquired a degree of critical self-consciousness sufficient to detach him from the standards of his time and place, but not sufficient to acquire the new standards that come with a more thorough cultivation. It was pointed out long ago that the characteristic of the half-educated man is that he is incurably restless; that he is filled with every manner of desire. In contrast with him the uncultivated man, the peasant, let us say, and the man of high cultivation have few and simple desires. Thus Socrates had fewer and simpler desires than the average Athenian. But what is most noteworthy about the half-educated man is not simply that he harbors many desires and is therefore incurably restless, but that these desires are so often incompatible. He craves various good things, but is not willing to pay the price—not willing to make the necessary renunciations. He pushes to an extreme what is after all a universal human proclivity—the wish to have one's cake and eat it too. Thus, while remaining on the naturalistic level, he wishes to have blessings that accrue only to those who rise to the humanistic or religious levels. He wishes to live in "a universe with the lid off," to borrow a happy phrase from the pragmatist, and at the same time to enjoy the peace and brotherhood that are the fruits of restraint. The moral indolence of the Rousseauist is such that he is unwilling to adjust himself to the truth of the human law; and though living naturalistically, he is loath to recognize that what actually prevails on the naturalistic level is the law of cunning and the law of force. He thus misses the reality of both the human and the natural law and in the pursuit of a vague Arcadian longing falls into sheer unreality. I am indeed overstating the case so far as Rousseau is concerned. He makes plain in "Emile" that the true law of nature is not the law of love but the law of force. Emile is to be released from the discipline of the human law and given over to the discipline of nature; and this means in practice that he will have "to bow his neck beneath the hard yoke of physical necessity." In so far the "nature" of Emile is no Arcadian dream. Where the Arcadian dreaming begins is when Rousseau assumes that an Emile who has learned the lesson of force from Nature herself will not pass along this lesson to others, whether citizens of his own or some other country, but will rather display in his dealings with them an ideal fraternity. In the early stages of the naturalistic movement, in Hobbes and Shaftesbury, for example, egoism and altruism, the idea of power and the idea of sympathy, are more sharply contrasted than they are in Rousseau and the later romanticists. Shaftesbury assumes in human nature an altruistic impulse or will to brotherhood that will be able to cope successfully with the will to power that Hobbes declares to be fundamental. Many of the romanticists, as we have seen, combine the cult of power with the cult of brotherhood. Hercules, as in Shelley's poem, is to bow down before Prometheus, the lover of mankind. The extreme example, however, is probably William Blake. He proclaims himself of the devil's party, he glorifies a free expansion of energy, he looks upon everything that restricts this expansion as synonymous with evil. At the same time he pushes his exaltation of sympathy to the verge of the grotesque.[11]

Such indeed is the jumble of incompatibles in Blake that he would rest an illimitable compassion on the psychology of the superman. For nothing is more certain than that the "Marriage of Heaven and Hell" is among other things a fairly complete anticipation of Nietzsche. The reasons are worth considering why the idea of power and the idea of sympathy which Blake and so many other romanticists hoped to unite have once more come to seem antipodal, why in the late stages of the movement one finds a Nietzsche and a Tolstoy, just as in its early stages one finds a Hobbes and a Shaftesbury. It is plain, first of all, that what brought the two cults together for a time was their common hatred of the past. With the triumph over the past fairly complete, the incompatibility of power and sympathy became increasingly manifest. Nietzsche's attitude is that of a Prometheus whose sympathy for mankind has changed to disgust on seeing the use that they are actually making of their emancipation. Humanitarian sympathy seemed to him to be tending not merely to a subversion, but to an inversion of values, to a positive preference for the trivial and the ignoble. He looked with special loathing on that side of the movement that is symbolized in its homage to the ass. The inevitable flying apart of power and sympathy was further hastened in Nietzsche and others by the progress of evolution. Darwinism was dissipating the Arcadian mist through which nature had been viewed by Rousseau and his early followers. The gap is wide between Tennyson's nature red in tooth and claw" and the tender and pitiful nature of Wordsworth.[12] Nietzsche's preaching of ruthlessness is therefore a protest against the sheer unreality of those who wish to be natural and at the same time sympathetic. But how are we to get a real scale of values to oppose to an indiscriminate sympathy? It is here that Nietzsche shows that he is caught in the same fatal coil of naturalism as the humanitarian. He accepts the naturalistic corruption of conscience which underlies all other naturalistic corruptions. "The will to overcome an emotion," he says, "is ultimately only the will of another or of several other emotions." [13] All he can do with this conception of conscience is to set over against the humanitarian suppression of values a scale of values based on force and not a true scale of values based on the degree to which one imposes or fails to impose on one's temperamental self a human law of vital control. The opposition between a Nietzsche and a Tolstoy is therefore not specially significant; it is only that between the hard and the soft temperamentalist. To be sure Nietzsche can on occasion speak very shrewdly about the evils that have resulted from temperamentalism—especially from the passion for an untrammeled self-expression. But the superman himself is a most authentic descendant of the original genius in whom we first saw this passion dominant. The imagination of the superman, spurning every centre of control, traditional or otherwise, so coöperates with his impulses and desires as to give them "infinitude," that is so as to make them reach out for more and ever for more. The result is a frenzied romanticism.[14]

"Proportionateness is strange to us, let us confess it to ourselves," says Nietzsche. "Our itching is really the itching for the infinite, the immeasurable." How the humanitarian loses proportionateness is plain; it is by his readiness to sacrifice to sympathy the ninety per cent or so of the virtues that imply self-control. The superman would scarcely seem to redress the balance by getting rid of the same restraining virtues in favor of power. He simply oscillates wildly from the excess of which he is conscious in others or in himself into the opposite excess, at imminent peril in either case to the ethical basis of civilization. The patterns or models that the past had set up for imitation and with reference to which one might rein in his lusts and impose upon them proportionateness are rejected by every type of romantic expansionist, not only as Nietzsche says, because they do not satisfy the yearning for the infinite, but also, as we have seen, because they do not satisfy the yearning for unity and immediacy. Now so far as the forms of the eighteenth century were concerned the romantic expansionist had legitimate grounds for protest. But because the rationalism and artificial decorum of that period failed to satisfy, he goes on to attack the analytical intellect and decorum in general and this attack is entirely illegitimate. It may be affirmed on the contrary that the power by which we multiply distinctions is never so necessary as in an individualistic age, an age that has broken with tradition on the ground that it wishes to be more imaginative and immediate. There are various ways of being imaginative and immediate, and analysis is needed, not to build up some abstract system but to discriminate between the actual data of experience and so to determine which one of these ways it is expedient to follow if one wishes to become wise and happy. It is precisely at such moments of individualistic break with the past that the sophist stands ready to juggle with general terms, and the only protection against such juggling is to define these terms with the aid of the most unflinching analysis. Thus Bergson would have us believe that there are in France two main types of philosophy, a rationalistic type that goes back to Descartes and an intuitive type that goes back to Pascal,[15] and gives us to understand that, inasmuch as he is an intuitionist, he is in the line of descent from Pascal. Monstrous sophistries lurk in this simple assertion, sophistries which if they go uncorrected are enough to wreck civilization. The only remedy is to define the word intuition, to discriminate practically and by their fruits between subrational and superrational intuition. When analyzed and defined in this way subrational intuition will be found to be associated with vital impulse (*élan vital*) and superrational intuition with a power of vital control (*frein vital*) over this impulse; and furthermore it will be clear that this control must be exercised if men are to be drawn towards a common centre, not in dreamland, but in the real world. So far then from its being true that the man who analyzes must needs see things in disconnection dead and spiritless, it is only by analysis that he is, in an individualistic age, put on the pathway of true unity, and also of the rôle of the imagination in achieving this unity. For there is need to discriminate between the different types of imagination no less than between the different types of intuition. One will find through such analysis that the centre of normal human experience that is to serve as a check on impulse (so far at least as it is something distinct from the mere convention of one's age and time) can be apprehended only with the aid of the imagination. This is only another way of saying that the reality that is set above one's ordinary self is not a fixed absolute but can be glimpsed, if at all, only through a veil of illusion and is indeed inseparable from the illusion. This realm of insight cannot be finally formulated for the simple reason that it is anterior to formulæ. It must therefore from the point of view of an intellect it transcends seem infinite though in a very different sense from the outer infinite of expansive desire.

This inner or human infinite, so far from being incompatible with decorum, is the source of true decorum. True decorum is only the pulling back and disciplining of impulse to the proportionateness that has been perceived with the aid of what one may term the ethical or generalizing imagination. To dismiss like the romantic expansionist everything that limits or restricts the lust of knowledge or of power or of sensation as arbitrary and artificial is to miss true decorum and at the same time to sink, as a Greek would say, from ethos to pathos. If one is to avoid this error one must, as Hamlet counsels, "in the very torrent, tempest, and (as I may say) whirlwind of passion, acquire and beget a temperance that may give it smoothness." This is probably the best of all modern definitions of decorum simply because it is the most experimental. In general all that has been said about the ethical imagination is not to be taken as a fine-spun theory, but as an attempt however imperfect to give an account of actual experience.

One may report from observation another trait of truly ethical art, art which is at once imaginative and decorous. It is not merely intense, as art that is imaginative at the expense of decorum may very well be,[16] it has a restrained and humanized intensity—intensity on a background of calm. The presence of the ethical imagination whether in art or life[17] is always known as an element of calm.

In art that has the ethical quality, and I am again not setting up a metaphysical theory but reporting from observation, the calm that comes from imaginative insight into the universal is inextricably blended with an element of uniqueness—with a something that belongs to a particular time and place and individual. The truth to the universal, as Aristotle would say, gives the work verisimilitude and the truth to the particu-

lar satisfies man's deep-seated craving for novelty; so that the
best art unites the probable with the wonderful. But the probable, one cannot insist too often, is won no less than the wonderful with the aid of the imagination and so is of the very
soul of art. The romanticist who is ready to sacrifice the probable to the wonderful and to look on the whole demand for
verisimilitude as an academic superstition is prone to assume
that he has a monopoly of soul and imagination. But the word
soul is at least in as much need of Socratic definition as the
word intuition. It is possible, for example, with the aid of the
ethical imagination so to partake of the ultimate element of
calm as to rise to the religious level. The man who has risen to
this level has a soul, but it is a soul of peace. Both soul and
imagination are also needed to achieve the fine adjustment
and mediation of the humanist. It is not enough, however, to
have a religious or a humanistic soul if one is to be a creator
or even a fully equipped critic of art. For art rests primarily
not on ethical but æsthetic perception. This perception itself
varies widely according to the art involved. One may, for instance, be musically perceptive and at the same time lack poetic
perception. To be a creator in any art one must possess furthermore the technique of this art—something that is more or less
separable from its "soul" in any sense of the word. It is possible to put a wildly romantic soul into art, as has often been
done in the Far East, and at the same time to be highly conventional or traditional in one's technique. Writers like Mé-
rimée, Renan, and Maupassant again are faithful in the main
to the technique of French prose that was worked out during
the classical period, but combine with this technique an utterly
unclassical "soul."

Rules, especially perhaps rules as to what to avoid, may be
of aid in acquiring technique, but are out of place in dealing
with the soul of art. There one passes from rules to principles. The only rule, if we are to achieve art that has an ethical
soul, is to view life with some degree of imaginative wholeness.
Art that has technique without soul in either the classical or
romantic sense, and so fails either to inspire elevation or
awaken wonder, is likely to be felt as a barren virtuosity. The
pseudo-classicist was often unduly minute in the rules he laid

down for technique or outer form, as one may say, and then ignored the ethical imagination or inner form entirely, or else set up as a substitute mere didacticism. Since pseudo-classic work of this type plainly lacked soul and imagination, and since the romanticist felt and felt rightly that he himself had a soul and imagination, he concluded wrongly that soul and imagination are romantic monopolies. Like the pseudo-classicist, he inclines to identify high seriousness in art, something that can only come from the exercise of the ethical imagination at its best, with mere preaching, only he differs from the pseudo-classicist in insisting that preaching should be left to divines. One should insist, on the contrary, that the mark of genuinely ethical art, art that is highly serious, is that it is free from preaching. Sophocles is more ethical than Euripides for the simple reason that he views life with more imaginative wholeness. At the same time he is much less given to preaching than Euripides. He does not, as FitzGerald says, interrupt the action and the exhibition of character through action in order to "jaw philosophy."

It is not unusual for the modern artist to seek, like Euripides, to dissimulate the lack of true ethical purpose in his work by agitating various problems. But problems come and go, whereas human nature abides. One may agitate problems without number, and yet lack imaginative insight into the abiding element in human nature. Moreover, not being of the soul of art, the problem that one agitates is in danger of being a clogging intellectualism. Furthermore to seek in problems an equivalent for the definition and purpose that the ethical imagination alone can give is to renew, often in an aggravated form, the neo-classical error. The moralizing of the pseudo-classic dramatist, even though dull and misplaced, was usually sound enough in itself; whereas the moralizing of those who seek nowadays to use the stage as a pulpit, resting as it does on false humanitarian postulates, is in itself dubious. The problem play succeeds not infrequently in being at once dull and indecent.

The problem play is often very superior in technique or outer form to the earlier romantic drama, but it still suffers from the same lack of inner form, inasmuch as its social purpose cannot take the place of true human purpose based on imaginative insight into the universal. The lack of inner form in so much modern drama and art in general can be traced to the original unsoundness of the break with pseudo-classic formalism. To a pseudo-classic art that lacked every kind of perceptiveness the Rousseauist opposed æsthetic perceptiveness, and it is something, one must admit, thus to have discovered the senses. But to his æsthetic perceptiveness he failed, as I have already said, to add ethical perceptiveness because of his inability to distinguish between ethical perceptiveness and mere didacticism, and so when asked to put ethical purpose into art he replied that art should be pursued for its own sake (*l'art pour l'art*) and that "beauty is its own excuse for being." One should note here the transformation that this pure æstheticism brought about in the meaning of the word beauty itself. For the Greek beauty resided in proportion,[18] and proportion can be attained only with the aid of the ethical imagination. With the elimination of the ethical element from the soul of art the result is an imagination that is free to wander wild with the emancipated emotions. The result is likely to be art in which a lively æsthetic perceptiveness is not subordinated to any whole, art that is unstructural, however it may abound in vivid and picturesque details; and a one-sided art of this kind the romanticist does not hesitate to call beautiful. "If we let the reason sleep and are content to watch a succession of dissolving views," says Mr. Elton of Shelley's "Revolt of Islam," "the poem is seen at once to overflow with beauty." [19] Mere reason is not strictly speaking a sufficient remedy for this unstructural type of "beauty." Thus Chateaubriand's reason is on the side of proportion and all the classical virtues but his imagination is not (and we cannot repeat too often that it is what a man is imaginatively and not what he preaches that really counts). Instead of siding with his reason and aiding it to ethical perception Chateaubriand's imagination is the free playmate of his emotions. "What did I care for all these futilities" (i.e. his functions as cabinet minister), he exclaims, "I who never cared for anything except for my dreams, and even then on condition that they should last only for a night." When a man has once spoken in that vein sensible people will pay little heed to what he preaches; for they will be certain that the driving power of his work and personality is elsewhere. The imagination holds the balance of power between the reason and the perceptions of sense, and Chateaubriand's imagination is plainly on the side of sensuous adventure. This vagabondage of the imagination appears especially in his imagistic trend, in his pursuit of the descriptive detail for its own sake. To set out like Chateaubriand to restore the monarchy and the Christian religion and instead to become the founder of *"l'école des images à tout prix"* is an especially striking form of the contrast in romantic morality between the ideal and the real.

The attempt that we have been studying to divorce beauty from ethics led in the latter part of the eighteenth century to the rise of a nightmare subject—æsthetics. Shaftesbury indeed, as we have seen already, anticipates the favorite romantic doctrine that beauty is truth and truth beauty, which means in practice to rest both truth and beauty upon a fluid emotionalism. Thus to deal æsthetically with truth is an error of the first magnitude, but it is also an error, though a less serious one, to see only the æsthetic element in beauty. For beauty to be complete must have not only æsthetic perceptiveness but order and proportion; and this brings us back again to the problem of the ethical imagination and the permanent model or pattern with reference to which it seeks to impose measure and proportion upon sensuous perception and expansive desire. We should not hesitate to say that beauty loses most of its meaning when divorced from ethics even though every æsthete in the world should arise and denounce us as philistines. To rest beauty upon feeling as the very name æsthetics implies, is to rest it upon what is ever shifting. Nor can we escape from this endless mobility with the aid of physical science, for physical science does not itself rise above the naturalistic flux. After eliminating from beauty the permanent pattern and the ethical imagination with the aid of which it is perceived, a man will be ready to term beautiful anything that reflects his ordinary or temperamental self. Diderot is a sentimentalist and so he sees as much beauty in the sentimentalist Richardson as in Homer. If a man is psychically restless he will see beauty only in motion. The Italian futurist Marinetti says that for him a rushing motor car is more beautiful than the Victory of Samothrace. A complete sacrifice of the principle of repose in beauty (which itself arises from the presence of the ethical imagination) to the suggesting of motion such as has been seen in certain recent schools runs practically into a mixture of charlatanism and madness. "He that is giddy thinks the world goes round," says Shakespeare, and the exponents of certain ultra-modern movements in painting are simply trying to paint their inner giddiness. As a matter of fact the pretension of the æsthete to have a purely personal vision of beauty and then treat as a philistine every one who does not accept it is intolerable. Either beauty cannot be defined at all or we must say that only is beautiful which seems so to the right kind of man, and the right kind of man is plainly he whose total attitude towards life is correct, who views life with some degree of imaginative wholeness, which is only another way of saying that the problem of beauty is inseparable from the ethical problem. In an absolute sense nobody can see life steadily and see it whole; but we may at least move towards steadiness and wholeness. The æsthete is plainly moving in an opposite direction; he is becoming more and more openly a votary of the god Whirl. His lack of inner form is an error not of æsthetics but of general philosophy.

The romantic imagination, the imagination that is not drawn back to any ethical centre and so is free to wander wild in its own empire of chimeras, has indeed a place in life. To understand what this place is one needs to emphasize the distinction between art that has high seriousness and art that is merely recreative. The serious moments of life are moments of tension, of concentration on either the natural or the human law. But Apollo cannot always be bending the bow. Man needs at times to relax, and one way of relaxing is to take refuge for a time in some land of chimeras, to follow the Arcadian gleam. He may then come back to the real world, the world of active effort, solaced and refreshed. But it is only with reference to some ethical centre that we may determine what art is soundly recreative, in what forms of adventure the imagination may innocently indulge. The romanticist should recollect that among other forms of adventure is what Ben Jonson terms

"a bold adventure for hell"; and that a not uncommon nostalgia is what the French call *la nostalgie de la boue*—man's
nostalgia for his native mud. Because we are justified at
times, as Lamb urges, in wandering imaginatively beyond "the
diocese of strict conscience," it does not follow that we may,
like him, treat Restoration Comedy as a sort of fairyland; for
Restoration Comedy is a world not of pure but of impure imagination.

Lamb's paradox, however, is harmless compared with what
we have just been seeing in Chateaubriand. With a dalliant imagination that entitles him at best to play a recreative rôle, he
sets up as a religious teacher. Michelet again has been
described as an "entertainer who believes himself a prophet,"
and this description fits many other Rousseauists. The æsthete
who assumes an apocalyptic pose is an especially flagrant instance of the huddling together of incompatible desires. He
wishes to sport with Amaryllis in the shade and at the same
time enjoy the honors that belong only to the man who scorns
delights and lives laborious days. For the exercise of the ethical imagination, it is hardly necessary to say, involves effort.
Perhaps no one has ever surpassed Rousseau himself in the art
of which I have already spoken—that of giving to moral indolence a semblance of profound philosophy.

One cannot indeed always affirm that the Rousseauist is by
the quality of his imagination an entertainer pure and simple.
His breaking down of barriers and running together of the
planes of being results at times in ambiguous mixtures—gleams
of insight that actually seem to minister to fleshliness. One may
cite as an example the "voluptuous religiosity" that certain critics have discovered in Wagner.

The romanticist will at once protest against the application
of ethical standards to Wagner or any other musician. Music,
he holds, is the most soulful of the arts and so the least subject to ethics. For the same reason it is the chief of arts and
also—in view of the fact that romanticists have a monopoly of
soul—the most romantic. One should not allow to pass un-
challenged this notion that because music is filled with soul it
is therefore subject to no ethical centre, but should be treated
as a pure enchantment. The Greeks were as a matter of fact

much concerned with the ethical quality of music. Certain musical modes, the Doric for example, had as they believed a virile 'soul," other modes, like the Lydian, had the contrary ("Lap me in soft Lydian airs"). For the very reason that music is the most appealing of the arts (song, says Aristotle, is the sweetest of all things) they were especially anxious that this art should be guarded from perversion.[20] Without attempting a full discussion of a difficult subject for which I have no competency, it will be enough to point out that the plain song that prevailed in Christian churches for over a thousand years evidently had a very different "soul," a soul that inspired to prayer and peace, from much specifically romantic music that has a soul of restlessness, of infinite indeterminate desire. The result of the failure to recognize this distinction is very often a hybrid art. Berlioz showed a rather peculiar conception of religion when he took pride in the fact that his Requiem (!) Mass frightened one of the listeners into a fit.

The ethical confusion that arises from the romantic cult of "soul" and the closely allied tendency towards a hybrid art—art that lacks high seriousness without being frankly recreative—may also be illustrated from the field of poetry. Many volumes have been published and are still being published on Browning as a philosophic and religious teacher. But Browning can pass as a prophet only with the half-educated person, the person who has lost traditional standards and has at the same time failed to work out with the aid of the ethical imagination some fresh scale of values and in the meanwhile lives impulsively and glorifies impulse. Like the half-educated person, Browning is capable of almost any amount of intellectual and emotional subtlety, and like the half-educated person he is deficient in inner form: that is, he deals with experience impressionistically without reference to any central pattern or purpose.[21] It is enough that the separate moments of this experience should each stand forth like

> *The quick sharp scratch*
> *And blue spurt of a lighted match.*

One may take as an illustration of this drift towards the melodramatic the "Ring and the Book." The method of this poem is peripheral, that is, the action is viewed not from any centre but as refracted through the temperaments of the actors. The twelve monologues of which the poem is composed illustrate the tendency of romantic writing to run into some "song of myself" or "tale of my heart." The "Ring and the Book" is not only off the centre, but is designed to raise a positive prejudice against everything that is central. Guido, for example, had observed decorum, had done all the conventional things and is horrible. Pompilia, the beautiful soul, had the great advantage of having had an indecorous start. Being the daughter of a drab, she is not kept from heeding the voice of nature. Caponsacchi again shows the beauty of his soul by violating the decorum of the priesthood. This least representative of priests wins our sympathy not by his Christianity, but by his lyrical intensity:

> O lyric love, half angel and half bird,
> And all a wonder and a wild desire!

Browning here escapes for once from the clogging intellectualism that makes nearly all the "Ring and the Book" an indeterminate blend of verse and prose, and achieves true poetry though not of the highest type. The hybrid character of his art, due partly to a lack of outer form, to a defective poetical technique, arises even more from a lack of inner form—from an attempt to give a semblance of seriousness to what is at bottom unethical. The aged Pope may well meditate on the revolution that is implied in the substitution of the morality of the beautiful soul for that of St. Augustine.[22] In seeming to accept this revolution Browning's Pope comes near to breaking all records, even in the romantic movement, for paradox and indecorum.

At bottom the war between humanist and romanticist is so irreconcilable because the one is a mediator and the other an extremist. Browning would have us admire his Pompilia because her love knows no limit;[23] but a secular love like hers must know a limit, must be decorous in short, if it is to be distinguished from mere emotional intensity. It is evident that the romantic ideal of art for art's sake meant in the real world art for sensation's sake. The glorification of a love knowing no limit, that a Browning or a Hugo sets up as a substitute for philosophy and even for religion, is therefore closely affiliated in practice with the *libido sentiendi.* "It is hard," wrote Stendhal, in 1817, "not to see what the nineteenth century desires. A love of strong emotions is its true character." The romantic tendency to push every emotion to an extreme, regardless of decorum, is not much affected by what the romanticist preaches or by the problems he agitates. Doudan remarks of a mother who loses her child in Hugo's "Notre Dame de Paris," that "her rage after this loss has nothing to equal it in the roarings of a lioness or tigress who has been robbed of her young. She becomes vulgar by excess of despair. It is the saturnalia of maternal grief. You see that this woman belongs to a world in which neither the instincts nor the passions have that divine aroma which imposes on them some kind of measure— the dignity or decorum that contains a moral principle; . . . When the passions no longer have this check, they should be relegated to the menagerie along with leopards and rhinoceroses, and, strange circumstance, when the passions do recognize this check they produce more effect on the spectators than unregulated outbursts; they give evidence of more depth." This superlativeness, as one may say, that Hugo displays in his picture of maternal grief is not confined to the emotional romanticist. It appears, for example, among the intellectual romanticists of the seventeenth century and affected the very forms of language. Molière and others ridiculed the adjectives and adverbs with which the *précieuses* sought to express their special type of superlativeness and intensity (*extrêmement, furieusement, terriblement,* etc.). Alfred de Musset's assertion that the chief difference between classicist and romanticist is found in the latter's greater proneness to adjectives is not altogether a jest. It has been said that the pessimist uses few, the optimist many adjectives; but the use of adjectives and above all of superlatives would rather seem to grow with one's expansiveness, and no movement was ever more expansive than that we are studying. Dante, according to Rivarol, is very sparing of adjectives. His sentence tends to maintain itself by the verb and substantive alone. In this as in other respects Dante is at the opposite pole from the expansionist.

The romantic violence of expression is at once a proof of "soul" and a protest against the tameness and smugness of the pseudo-classicist. The human volcano must overflow at times in a lava of molten words. "Damnation!" cries Berlioz, "I could crush a red-hot iron between my teeth." [24] The disproportion between the outer incident and the emotion that the Rousseauist expends on it is often ludicrous.[25] The kind of force that the man attains who sees in emotional intensity a mark of spiritual distinction, and deems moderation identical with mediocrity, is likely to be the force of delirium or fever. What one sees in "Werther," says Goethe himself, is weakness seeking to give itself the prestige of strength; and this remark goes far. There is in some of the romanticists a suggestion not merely of spiritual but of physical anæmia.[26] Still the intensity is often that of a strong but unbridled spirit. Pleasure is pushed to the point where it runs over into pain, and pain to the point where it becomes an auxiliary of pleasure. The *âcre baiser* of the "Nouvelle Héloïse" that so scandalized Voltaire presaged even more than a literary revolution. The poems of A. de Musset in particular contain an extraordinary perversion of the Christian doctrine of purification through suffering. There is something repellent to the genuine Christian as well as to the worldling in what one is tempted to call Musset's Epicurean cult of pain.[27]

Moments of superlative intensity whether of pleasure or pain must in the nature of the case be brief—mere spasms or paroxysms; and one might apply to the whole school the term paroxyst and spasmodist assumed by certain minor groups during the past century. The Rousseauist is in general loath to rein in his emotional vehemence, to impair the zest with which he responds to the solicitations of sense, by any reference to the "future and sum of time," by any reference, that is, to an ethical purpose. He would enjoy his thrill pure and unalloyed, and this amounts in practice to the pursuit of the beautiful or sensation-crowded moment. Saint-Preux says of the days spent with Julie that a "sweet ecstasy" absorbed "their whole duration and gathered it together in a point like that of eternity. There was for me neither past nor future, and I enjoyed at one and the same time the delights of a thousand centuries." [28] The superlativist one might suppose could go no further. But in the deliberate sacrifice of all ethical values to the beautiful moment Browning has perhaps improved even on Rousseau:

> *Truth, that's brighter than gem,*
> *Trust, that's purer than pearl,—*
> *Brightest truth, purest trust in the universe—all were for me*
> *In the kiss of one girl.*

Browning entitles the poem from which I am quoting *Summum Bonum.* The supreme good it would appear is identical with the supreme thrill.

I have already said enough to make clear that the title of this chapter and the last is in a way a misnomer. There is no such thing as romantic morality. The innovations in ethics that are due to romanticism reduce themselves on close scrutiny to a vast system of naturalistic camouflage. To understand how this camouflage has been so successful one needs to connect Rousseauism with the Baconian movement. Scientific progress had inspired man with a new confidence in himself at the same time that the positive and critical method by which it had been achieved detached him from the past and its traditional standards of good and evil. To break with tradition on sound lines one needs to apply the utmost keenness of analysis not merely to the natural but to the human law. But man's analytical powers were very much taken up with the new task of mastering the natural law, so much so that he seemed incapable of further analytical effort, but longed rather for relaxation from his sustained concentration of intellect and imagination on the physical order. At the same time he was so elated by the progress he was making in this order that he was inclined to assume a similar advance on the moral plane and to believe that this advance could also be achieved collectively. A collective salvation of this kind without any need of a concentration of the intellect and imagination is precisely what was opened up to him by the Rousseauistic "ideal" of brotherhood. This "ideal," as I have tried to show, was only a projection of the Arcadian imagination on the void. But in the abdication of analysis and critical judgment, which would have reduced it to a purely recreative rôle, this Arcadian dreaming was enabled to set up as a serious philosophy, and to expand into innumerable Utopias. Many who might have taken alarm at the humanitarian revolution in ethics were reassured by the very fervor with which its promoters continued to utter the old words —conscience, virtue, etc. No one puts more stress than Rousseau himself on conscience, while in the very act of transforming conscience from an inner check into an expansive emotion.

We have seen that as a result of this transformation of conscience, temperament is emancipated from both inner and outer control and that this emancipation tends in the real world to the rise of two main types—the Bohemian and the superman, both unprimitive, inasmuch as primitive man is governed not by temperament but by convention; and that what actually tends to prevail in such a temperamental world in view of the superior "hardness" of the superman is the law of cunning and the law of force. So far as the Rousseauists set up the mere emancipation of temperament as a serious philosophy, they are to be held responsible for the results of this emancipation whether displayed in the lust of power or the lust of sensation. But the lust of power and the lust of sensation, such as they appear, for example, in the so-called realism of the later nineteenth century, are not in themselves identical with romanticism. Many of the realists, like Flaubert, as I have already pointed out, are simply bitter and disillusioned Rousseauists who are expressing their nausea at the society that has actually arisen from the emancipation of temperament in themselves and others. The essence of Rousseauistic as of other romance, I may repeat, is to be found not in any mere fact, not even in the fact of sensation, but in a certain quality of the imagination. Rousseauism is, it is true, an emancipation of impulse, especially of the impulse of sex. Practically all the examples I have chosen of the tense and beautiful moment are erotic. But what one has even here, as the imagination grows increasingly romantic, is less the reality than the dream of the beautiful moment, an intensity that is achieved only in the tower of ivory. This point can be made clear only by a fuller study of the romantic conception of love.

CHAPTER SIX

ROMANTIC LOVE

What first strikes one in Rousseau's attitude towards love is the separation, even wider here perhaps than elsewhere, between the ideal and the real. He dilates in the "Confessions" on the difference of the attachment that he felt when scarcely more than a boy for two young women of Geneva, Mademoiselle Vulson and Mademoiselle Goton. His attachment for the latter was real in a sense that Zola would have understood. His attachment for Mademoiselle Vulson reminds one rather of that of a mediæval knight for his lady. The same contrast runs through Rousseau's life. "Seamstresses, chambermaids, shopgirls," he says, "attracted me very little. I had to have fine ladies." [1] So much for the ideal; the real was Thérèse Levasseur.

We are not to suppose that Rousseau's love even when most ideal is really exalted above the fleshly level. Byron indeed says of Rousseau that "his was not the love of living dame but of ideal beauty," and if this were strictly true Rousseau might be accounted a Platonist. But any particular beautiful object is for Plato only a symbol or adumbration of a supersensuous beauty; so that an earthly love can be at best only a stepping-stone to the Uranian Aphrodite. The terrestrial and the heavenly loves are not in short run together, whereas the essence of Rousseauistic love is this very blending. "Rousseau," says Joubert, "had a voluptuous mind. In his writings the soul is always mingled with the body and never distinct from it. No one has ever rendered more vividly the impression of the flesh touching the spirit and the delights of their marriage." I need not, however, repeat here what I have said elsewhere[2] about this confusion of the planes of being, perhaps the most important aspect of romantic love.

Though Rousseau is not a true Platonist in his treatment of love, he does, as I have said, recall at times the cult of the mediæval knight for his lady. One may even find in mediæval love something that is remotely related to Rousseau's contrast between the ideal and the actual; for in its attitude towards woman as in other respects the Middle Ages tended to be extreme. Woman is either depressed below the human level as the favorite instrument of the devil in man's temptation (*mulier hominis confusio*), or else exalted above this level as the mother of God. The figure of Mary blends sense and spirit in a way that is foreign to Plato and the ancients. As Heine says very profanely, the Virgin was a sort of heavenly *dame du comptoir* whose celestial smile drew the northern barbarians into the Church. Sense was thus pressed into the service of spirit at the risk of a perilous confusion. The chivalric cult of the lady has obvious points of contact with the worship of the Madonna. The knight who is raised from one height of perfection to another by the light of his lady's eyes is also pressing sense into the service of spirit with the same risk that the process may be reversed. The reversal actually takes place in Rousseau and his followers: spirit is pressed into the service of sense in such wise as to give to sense a sort of infinitude. Baudelaire pays his homage to a Parisian grisette in the form of a Latin canticle to the Virgin.[3] The perversion of mediæval love is equally though not quite so obviously present in many other Rousseauists.

I have said that the Middle Ages inclined to the extreme; mediæval writers are, however, fond of insisting on "measure"; and this is almost inevitable in view of the large amount of classical, especially Aristotelian, survival throughout this period. But the two distinctively mediæval types, the saint and the knight, are neither of them mediators. They stand, however, on an entirely different footing as regards the law of measure. Not even Aristotle himself would maintain that the law of measure applies to saintliness, and in general to the religious realm. The saint in so far as he is saintly has undergone conversion, has in the literal sense of the word faced around and is looking in an entirely different direction from that to which the warnings "nothing too much" and "think as a mortal" apply. Very different psychic elements may indeed appear in any particular saint. A book has been published recently on the "Romanticism of St. Francis." The truth seems to be that though St. Francis had his romantic side, he was even more religious than romantic. One may affirm with some confidence of another mediæval figure, Peter the Hermit, that he was, on the other hand, much more romantic than religious. For all the information we have tends to show that he was a very restless person and a man's restlessness is ordinarily in inverse ratio to his religion.

If the saint transcends in a way the law of measure, the knight on the other hand should be subject to it. For courage and the love of woman—his main interests in life—belong not to the religious but to the secular realm. But in his conception of love and courage the knight was plainly not a mediator but an extremist: he was haunted by the idea of adventure, of a love and courage that transcend the bounds not merely of the probable but of the possible. His imagination is romantic in the sense I have tried to define—it is straining, that is, beyond the confines of the real. Ruskin's violent diatribe against Cervantes[4] for having killed "idealism" by his ridicule of these knightly exaggerations, is in itself absurd, but interesting as evidence of the quality of Ruskin's own imagination. Like other romanticists I have cited, he seems to have been not unaware of his own kinship to Don Quixote. The very truth about either the mediæval or modern forms of romantic love—love which is on the secular level and at the same time sets itself above the law of measure—was uttered by Dr. Johnson in his comment on the heroic plays of Dryden: "By admitting the romantic omnipotence of love he has recommended as laudable and worthy of imitation that conduct which through all ages the good have censured as vicious and the bad have despised as foolish."

The man of the Middle Ages, however extravagant in his imaginings, was often no doubt terrestrial enough in his practice. The troubadour who addressed his highflown fancies to some fair châtelaine (usually a married woman) often had relations in real life not unlike those of Rousseau with Thérèse Levasseur. Some such contrast indeed between the "ideal" and the "real" existed in the life of one of Rousseau's favorite poets, Petrarch. The lover may, however, run together the ideal and the real. He may glorify some comparatively commonplace person, crown as queen of his heart some Dulcinea del Toboso. Hazlitt employs appropriately in describing his own passion for the vulgar daughter of a London boarding-house keeper the very words of Cervantes: "He had courted a statute, hunted the wind, cried aloud to the desert." Hazlitt like other lovers of this type is in love not with a particular person but with his own dream. He is as one may say in love with love. No subject indeed illustrates like this of love the nostalgia, the infinite indeterminate desire of the romantic imagination. Something of this diffusive longing no doubt came into the world with Christianity. There is a wide gap between the sentence of St. Augustine that Shelley has taken as epigraph for his "Alastor" [5] and the spirit of the great Greek and Roman classics. Yet such is the abiding vitality of Greek mythology that one finds in Greece perhaps the best symbol of the romantic lover. Rousseau could not fail to be attracted by the story of Pygmalion and Galatea. His lyrical "monodrama" in poetical prose, "Pygmalion," is important not only for its literary but for its musical influence. The Germans in particular (including the youthful Goethe) were fascinated. To the mature Goethe Rousseau's account of the sculptor who became enamored of his own creation and breathed into it actual life by the sheer intensity of his desire seemed a delirious confusion of the planes of being, an attempt to drag ideal beauty down to the level of sensuous realization. But a passion thus conceived exactly satisfies the romantic requirement. For though the romanticist wishes to abandon himself to the rapture of love, he does not wish to transcend his own ego. The object with which Pygmalion is in love is after all only a projection of his own "genius." But such an object is not in any proper sense an object at all. There is in fact no object in the romantic universe—only subject. This subjective love amounts in practice to a use of the imagination to enhance emotional intoxication, or if one prefers, to the pursuit of illusion for its own sake.

This lack of definite object appears just as clearly in the German symbol of romantic love—the blue flower. The blue flower resolves itself at last, it will be remembered, into a fair feminine face[6]—a face that cannot, however, be overtaken. The color typifies the blue distance in which it always loses itself, "the never-ending quest after the ever-fleeting object of desire." The object is thus elusive because, as I have said, it is not, properly speaking, an object at all but only a dalliance of the imagination with its own dream. Cats, says Rivarol, do not caress us, they caress themselves upon us. But though cats may suffer from what the new realist calls the egocentric predicament, they can scarcely vie in the subtle involutions of their egoism with the romantic lover. Besides creating the symbol of the blue flower, Novalis treats romantic love in his unfinished tale "The Disciples at Saïs." He contemplated two endings to this tale—in the one, when the disciple lifts the veil of the inmost sanctuary of the temple at Saïs, Rosenblütchen (the equivalent of the blue flower) falls into his arms. In the second version what he sees when he lifts the mysterious veil is—"wonder of wonders—himself." The two endings are in substance the same.

The story of Novalis's attachment for a fourteen-year-old girl, Sophie von Kühn, and of his plans on her death for a truly romantic suicide—a swooning away into the night—and then of the suddenness with which he transferred his dream to another maiden, Julie von Charpentier, is familiar. If Sophie had lived and Novalis had lived and they had wedded, he might conceivably have made her a faithful husband, but she would no longer have been the blue flower, the ideal. For one's love is for something infinitely remote; it is as Shelley says in

what is perhaps the most perfect expression of romantic longing:

> *The desire of the moth for the star,*
> *Of the night for the morrow,*
> *The devotion to something afar*
> *From the sphere of our sorrow.*

The sphere of Shelley's sorrow at the time he wrote these
lines to Mrs. Williams was Mary Godwin. In the time of Har-
riet Westbrook, Mary had been the "star."

The romantic lover often feigns in explanation of his nostalgia that in some previous existence he had been enamored
of a nymph—an Egeria—or a woman transcending the ordinary mould—"some Lilith or Helen or Antigone." [7] Shelley in-
quires eagerly in one of his letters about the new poem by
Horace Smith, "The Nympholept." In the somewhat unclassical sense that the term came to have in the romantic movement, Shelley is himself the perfect example of the nympholept.
In this respect as in others, however, he merely continues Rousseau. "If it had not been for some memories of my youth and
Madame d'Houdetot," says Jean-Jacques, "the loves that I have
felt and described would have been only with sylphids." [8]

Chateaubriand speaks with aristocratic disdain of Rousseau's
Venetian amours, but on the "ideal" side he is not only his follower but perhaps the supreme French example of nympholepsy. He describes his lady of dreams sometimes like Rousseau
as the "sylphid," sometimes as his "phantom of love." He had
been haunted by this phantom almost from his childhood.
"Even then I glimpsed that to love and be loved in a way
that was unknown to me was destined to be my supreme felicity. . . . As a result of the ardor of my imagination, my tim-
idity and solitude, I did not turn to the outer world, but was
thrown back upon myself. In the absence of a real object, I
evoked by the power of my vague desires a phantom that was
never to leave me." To those who remember the closely parallel passages in Rousseau, Chateaubriand will seem to exaggerate the privilege of the original genius to look on himself as
unique when he adds: "I do not know whether the history of
the human heart offers another example of this nature." [9]

The pursuit of this phantom of love gives the secret key to Chateaubriand's life. He takes refuge in the American wilderness in order that he may have in this primitive Arcadia a more spacious setting for his dream.[10]

If one wishes to see how very similar these nympholeptic experiences are not only from individual to individual, but from country to country, one has only to compare the passages I have just been quoting from Chateaubriand with Shelley's "Epipsychidion." Shelley writes of his own youth:

> *There was a Being whom my spirit oft*
> *Met on its visioned wanderings, far aloft,*
> *In the clear golden prime of my youth's dawn,*
> *Upon the fairy isles of sunny lawn,*
> *Amid the enchanted mountains, and the caves*
> *Of divine sleep, and on the air-like waves*
> *Of wonder-level dream, whose tremulous floor*
> *Paved her light steps; on an imagined shore,*
> *Under the gray beak of some promontory*
> *She met me, robed in such exceeding glory,*
> *That I beheld her not, etc.*

At the time of writing "Epipsychidion" the magic vision happened to have coalesced for the moment with Emilia Viviani, though destined soon to flit elsewhere. Shelley invites his "soul's sister," the idyllic "she," who is at bottom only a projection of his own imagination, to set sail with him for Arcady. "Epipsychidion," indeed, might be used as a manual to illustrate the difference between mere Arcadian dreaming and a true Platonism.

Chateaubriand is ordinarily and rightly compared with Byron rather than with Shelley. He is plainly, however, far more of a nympholept than Byron. Mr. Hilary, indeed, in Peacock's "Nightmare Abbey" says to Mr. Cypress (Byron): "You talk like a Rosicrucian, who will love nothing but a sylph, who does not believe in the existence of a sylph, and who yet quarrels with the whole universe for not containing a sylph." [11] Certain distinctions would have to be made if one were attempting a complete study of love in Byron; yet after all the love of Don Juan and Haidée is one that Sapho or Catullus or Burns would have understood; and these poets were not nympholepts. They were capable of burning with love, but not, as Rousseau says of himself, "without any definite object." [12] Where Chateaubriand has some resemblance to Byron is in his actual libertinism. He is however nearer than Byron to the libertine of the eighteenth century—to the Lovelace who pushes the pursuit of pleasure to its final exasperation where it becomes associated with the infliction of pain. Few things are stranger than the blend in Chateaubriand of this Sadic fury[13] with the new romantic revery. Indeed almost every type of egotism that may manifest itself in the relations of the sexes and that pushed to the superlative pitch will be found in this theoretical classicist and champion of Christianity. Perhaps no more frenzied cry has ever issued from human lips than that uttered by Atala[14] in describing her emotions when torn between her religious vow and her love for Chactas: "What dream did not arise in this heart overwhelmed with sorrow. At times in fixing my eyes upon you, I went so far as to form desires as insensate as they were guilty; at one moment I seemed to wish that you and I were the only living creatures upon the earth; and then again, feeling a divinity that held me back in my horrible transports, I seemed to want this divinity to be annihilated provided that clasped in your arms I should roll from abyss to abyss with the ruins of God and the world." Longing is here pushed to a pitch where it passes over, as in Wagner's "Tristan and Isolde," into the desire for annihilation.

Actual libertinism is no necessary concomitant of nympholeptic longing. There is a striking difference in this respect between Poe, for example, and his translator and disciple, Baudelaire. Nothing could be less suggestive of voluptuousness than Poe's nostalgia. "His ecstasy," says Stedman, "is that of the nympholept seeking an evasive being of whom he has glimpses by moonlight, starlight, even fenlight, but never by noonday." The embodiments of his dream that flit through his tales and poems enhanced his popularity with the ultraromantic public in France. These strange apparitions nearly all of whom are epileptic, cataleptic, or consumptive made a natural appeal to a school that was known among its detractors as *l'école poitrinaire.* "Tender souls," says Gautier, "were specially touched by Poe's feminine figures, so vaporous, so transparent and of an almost spectral beauty." Perhaps the nympholepsy of Gérard de Nerval is almost equally vaporous and ethereal. He pursued through various earthly forms the queen of Sheba whom he had loved in a previous existence and hanged himself at last with what he believed to be her garter: an interesting example of the relation between the extreme forms of the romantic imagination and madness.[15]

The pursuit of a phantom of love through various earthly forms led in the course of the romantic movement to certain modifications in a famous legend—that of Don Juan. What is emphasized in the older Don Juan is not merely his libertinism but his impiety—the gratification of his appetite in deliberate defiance of God. He is animated by Satanic pride, by the lust of power as well as by the lust of sensation. In Molière's treatment of the legend we can also see the beginnings of the philanthropic pose.[16] With the progress of Rousseauism Don Juan tends to become an "idealist," to seek to satisfy in his amorous adventures not merely his senses but his "soul" and his thirst for the "infinite." [17] Along with this idealistic Don Juan we also see appearing at a very early stage in the movement the exotic Don Juan who wishes to have a great deal of strangeness added to his beauty. In his affair with the "Floridiennes," Chateaubriand shows the way to a long series of exotic lovers.

I said to my heart between sleeping and waking,
Thou wild thing that always art leaping or aching,
What black, brown or fair, in what clime, in what nation,
By turns has not taught thee a pit-a-pat-ation?

These lines are so plainly meant for Pierre Loti that one learns with surprise that they were written about 1724 by the Earl of Peterborough.[18]

Byron's Don Juan is at times exotic in his tastes, but, as I have said, he is not on the whole very nympholeptic—much less so than the Don Juan of Alfred de Musset, for example. Musset indeed suggests in many respects a less masculine Byron—Mademoiselle Byron as he has been called. In one whole side of his art as well as his treatment of love he simply continues like Byron the eighteenth century. But far more than Byron he aspires to ideal and absolute passion; so that the

Musset of the "Nuits" is rightly regarded as one of the supreme embodiments, and at the same time the chief martyr, of
the romantic religion of love. The outcome of his affair with
George Sand may symbolize fitly the wrecking of thousands of
more obscure lives by this mortal chimera. Musset and George
Sand sought to come together, yet what they each sought in
love is what the original genius seeks in all things—self-
expression. What Musset saw in George Sand was not the real
woman but only his own dream. But George Sand was not
content thus to reflect back passively to Musset his ideal. She
was rather a Galatea whose ambition it was to create her own
Pygmalion. "Your chimera is between us," Musset exclaims;
but his chimera was between them too. The more Titan and
Titaness try to meet, the more each is driven back into the
solitude of his own ego. They were in love with love rather
than with one another; and to be thus in love with love means
on the last analysis to be in love with one's own emotions. "To
love," says Musset, "is the great point. What matters the mis-
tress? What matters the flagon provided one have the intoxication?" [19] He then proceeds to carry a love of this quality up
into the presence of God and to present it to him as his justification for having lived. The art of speaking in tones of religious consecration of what is in its essence egoistic has never
been carried further than by the Rousseauistic romanticist. God
is always appearing at the most unexpected moments.[20] The
highest of which man is capable apparently is to put an un-
curbed imagination into the service of an emancipated temperament. The credo that Perdican recites at the end of the
second act of "On ne badine pas avec l'Amour" [21] throws light
on this point. Men and women according to this credo are
filled with every manner of vileness, yet there is something
"sacred and sublime," and that is the union of two of these
despicable beings.

The confusion of ethical values here is so palpable as scarcely
to call for comment. It is precisely when men and women set
out to love with this degree of imaginative and emotional unrestraint that they come to deserve all the opprobrious epithets
Musset heaps upon them. This radiant apotheosis of love and
the quagmire in which it actually lands one is, as I have said,

the whole subject of "Madame Bovary." I shall need to return to this particular disproportion between the ideal and the real when I take up the subject of romantic melancholy.

The romantic lover who identifies the ideal with the superlative thrill is turning the ideal into something very transitory. If the *summum bonum* is as Browning avers the "kiss of one girl," the *summum bonum* is lost almost as soon as found. The beautiful moment may however be prolonged in revery. The romanticist may brood over it in the tower of ivory, and when thus enriched by being steeped in his temperament it may become more truly his own than it was in reality. "Objects make less impression upon me than my memory of them," says Rousseau. He is indeed the great master of what has been termed the art of impassioned recollection. This art is far from being confined in its application to love, though it may perhaps be studied here to the best advantage. Rousseau, one should note, had very little intellectual memory, but an extraordinarily keen memory of images and sensations. He could not, as he tells us in the "Confessions," learn anything by heart, but he could recall with perfect distinctness what he had eaten for breakfast about thirty years before. In general he recalls his past feelings with a clearness and detail that are perhaps more feminine than masculine. "He seems," says Hazlitt, one of his chief disciples in the art of impassioned recollection, "to gather up the past moments of his being like drops of honey-dew to distil a precious liquor from them; his alternate pleasures and pains are the bead-roll that he tells over and piously worships; he makes a rosary of the flowers of hope and fancy that strewed his earliest years." [22] This highly developed emotional memory is closely associated with the special quality of the romantic imagination—its cult of Arcadian illusion and the wistful backward glance to the vanished paradise of childhood and youth when illusion was most spontaneous. "Let me still recall [these memories]," says Hazlitt, "that they may breathe fresh life into me, and that I may live that birthday of thought and romantic pleasure over again! Talk of the ideal! This is the only true ideal—the heavenly tints of Fancy reflected in the bubbles that float upon the spring-tide of human life." [23] Hazlitt converts criticism itself into an art of impassioned recollection. He loves to linger over the beautiful moments of his own literary life. The passing years have increased the richness of their temperamental refraction and bestowed upon them the "pathos of distance." A good example is his account of the two years of his youth he spent in reading the "Confessions" and the "Nouvelle Héloïse," and in shedding tears over them. "They were the happiest years of our life. We may well say of them, sweet is the dew of their memory and pleasant the balm of their recollection." [24]

Rousseau's own Arcadian memories are usually not of reading, like Hazlitt's, but of actual incidents, though he does not hesitate to alter these incidents freely, as in his account of his stay at Les Charmettes, and to accommodate them to his dream. He neglected the real Madame de Warens at the very time that he cherished his recollection of her because this recollection was the idealized image of his own youth. The yearning that he expresses at the beginning of his fragmentary "Tenth Promenade," written only a few weeks before his death, is for this idyllic period rather than for an actual woman.[25] A happy memory, says Musset, repeating Rousseau, is perhaps more genuine than happiness itself. Possibly the three best known love poems of Lamartine, Musset, and Hugo respectively—"Le Lac," "Souvenir," and "La Tristesse d'Olympio," all hinge upon impassioned recollection and derive very directly from Rousseau. Lamartine in particular has caught in the "Le Lac" the very cadence of Rousseau's reveries.[26]

Impassioned recollection may evidently be an abundant source of genuine poetry, though not, it must be insisted, of the highest poetry. The predominant rôle that it plays in Rousseau and many of his followers is simply a sign of an unduly dalliant imagination. Experience after all has other uses than to supply furnishings for the tower of ivory; it should control the judgment and guide the will; it is in short the necessary basis of conduct. The greater a man's moral seriousness, the more he will be concerned with doing rather than dreaming (and I include right meditation among the forms of doing). He will also demand an art and literature that reflect this, his main preoccupation. Between Wordsworth's definition of poetry as "emotion recollected in tranquillity," and Aristotle's definition of poetry as the imitation of human action according to probability or necessity, a wide gap plainly opens. One may prefer Aristotle's definition to that of Wordsworth and yet do justice to the merits of Wordsworth's actual poetical performance. Nevertheless the tendency to put prime emphasis on feeling instead of action shown in the definition is closely related to Wordsworth's failure not only in dramatic but in epic poetry, in all poetry in short that depends for its success on an element of plot and sustained narrative.

A curious extension of the art of impassioned recollection should receive at least passing mention. It has been so extended as to lead to what one may term an unethical use of literature and history. What men have done in the past and the consequences of this doing should surely serve to throw some light on what men should do under similar circumstances in the present. But the man who turns his own personal experience into mere dalliance may very well assume a like dalliant attitude towards the larger experience of the race. This experience may merely provide him with pretexts for revery. This narcotic use of literature and history, this art of creating for one's self an alibi as Taine calls it, is nearly as old as the romantic movement. The record of the past becomes a gorgeous pageant that lures one to endless imaginative exploration and lulls one to oblivion of everything except its variety and picturesqueness. It becomes everything in fact except a school of judgment. One may note in connection with this use of history the usual interplay between scientific and emotional naturalism. Both forms of naturalism tend to turn man into the mere product and plaything of physical forces—climate, heredity, and the like, over which his will has no control. Since literature and history have no meaning from the point of view of moral choice they may at least be made to yield the maximum of æsthetic satisfaction. Oscar Wilde argues in this wise for example in his dialogue "The Critic as Artist," and concludes that since man has no moral freedom or responsibility, and cannot therefore be guided in his conduct by the past experience of the race, he may at least turn this experience into an incomparable "bower of dreams." "The pain of Leopardi crying out against life becomes our pain. Theocritus blows on his pipe and we laugh with the lips of nymph and shepherd. In the wolfskin of Pierre Vidal we flee before the hounds, and in the armor of Lancelot we ride from the bower of the queen. We have whispered the secret of our love beneath the cowl of Abelard, and in the stained raiment of Villon have put our shame into song," etc.

The assumption that runs through this passage that the mere æsthetic contemplation of past experience gives the equivalent of actual experience is found in writers of far higher standing than Wilde—in Renan, for instance. The æsthete would look on his dream as a substitute for the actual, and at the same time convert the actual into a dream. (*Die Welt wird Traum, der Traum wird Welt.*) It is not easy to take such a programme of universal dreaming seriously. In the long run the dreamer himself does not find it easy to take it seriously. For his attempts to live his chimera result, as we have seen in the case of romantic love, in more or less disastrous defeat and disillusion. The disillusioned romanticist continues to cling to his dream, but intellectually, at least, he often comes at the same time to stand aloof from it. This subject of disillusion may be best be considered, along with certain other important aspects of the movement, in connection with the singular phenomenon known as romantic irony.

CHAPTER SEVEN

ROMANTIC IRONY

The first romanticist who worked out a theory of irony was Friedrich Schlegel.[1] The attempt to put this theory into practice, after the fashion of Tieck's plays, seemed, and seemed rightly, even to later representatives of the movement to be extravagant. Thus Hegel, who in his ideas on art continues in so many respects the Schlegels, repudiates irony. Formerly, says Heine, who is himself in any larger survey, the chief of German romantic ironists, when a man had said a stupid thing he had said it; now he can explain it away as "irony." Nevertheless one cannot afford to neglect this early German theory. It derives in an interesting way from the views that the partisans of original genius had put forth regarding the rôle of the creative imagination. The imagination as we have seen is to be free to wander wild in its own empire of chimeras. Rousseau showed the possibilities of an imagination that is at once extraordinarily rich and also perfectly free in this sense. I have said that Kant believed like the original genius that the nobility of art depends on the free "play" of the imagination; though he adds that art should at the same time submit to a purpose that is not a purpose—whatever that may mean. Schiller in his "Æsthetic Letters" relaxed the rationalistic rigor of Kant in favor of feeling and associated even more emphatically the ideality and creativeness of art with its free imaginative play, its emancipation from specific aim. The personal friction that arose between the Schlegels and Schiller has perhaps obscured somewhat their general indebtedness to him. The Schlegelian irony in particular merely pushes to an extreme the doctrine that nothing must interfere with the imagination in its creative play. "The caprice of the poet," as Friedrich Schlegel says, "suffers no law above itself." Why indeed should the poet allow any restriction to be placed upon his caprice in a universe that is after all only a projection of himself? The play theory of art is here supplemented by the philosophy of Fichte.[2] In justice to him it should be said that though his philosophy may not rise above the level of temperament, he at least had a severe and stoical temperament, and if only for this reason his "transcendental ego" is far less obviously ego than that which appears in the irony of his romantic followers. When a man has taken possession of his transcendental ego, according to the Schlegels and Novalis, he looks down on his ordinary ego and stands aloof from it. His ordinary ego may achieve poetry but his transcendental ego must achieve the poetry of poetry. But there is in him something that may stand aloof even from this aloofness and so on indefinitely. Romantic irony joins here with what is perhaps the chief preoccupation of the German romanticists, the idea of the infinite or, as they term it, the striving for endlessness (*Unendlichkeitstreben*). Now, according to the romanticist, a man can show that he lays hold imaginatively upon the infinite only by expanding beyond what his age holds to be normal and central—its conventions in short; nay more, he must expand away from any centre he has himself achieved. For to hold fast to a centre of any kind implies the acceptance of limitations and to accept limitations is to be finite, and to be finite is, as Blake says, to become mechanical; and the whole of romanticism is a protest against the mechanizing of life. No man therefore deserves to rank as a transcendental egotist unless he has learned to mock not merely at the convictions of others but at his own, unless he has become capable of self-parody. "Objection," says Nietzsche, "evasion, joyous distrust, and love of irony are signs of health; everything absolute belongs to pathology." [3]

One cannot repeat too often that what the romanticist always sees at the centre is either the mere rationalist or else the philistine; and he therefore inclines to measure his own distinction by his remoteness from any possible centre. Now thus to be always moving away from centrality is to be paradoxical, and romantic irony is, as Friedrich Schlegel says, identical with paradox. Irony, paradox and the idea of the infinite have as a matter of fact so many points of contact in romanticism that they may profitably be treated together.

Friedrich Schlegel sought illustrious sponsors in the past for his theory of irony. Among others he invoked the Greeks and put himself in particular under the patronage of Socrates. But Greek irony always had a centre. The ironical contrast is between this centre and something that is less central. Take for example the so-called irony of Greek tragedy. The tragic character speaks and acts in darkness as to his impending doom, regarding which the spectator is comparatively enlightened. To take another example, the German romanticists were especially absurd in their attempts to set up Tieck as a new Aristophanes. For Aristophanes, however wild and irresponsible he may seem in the play of his imagination, never quite loses sight of his centre, a centre from which the comic spirit proceeds and to which it returns. Above all, however far he may push his mockery, he never mocks at his own convictions; he never, like Tieck, indulges in self-parody. A glance at the parabasis of almost any one of his plays will suffice to show that he was willing to lay himself open to the charge of being unduly didactic rather than to the charge of being aimless. The universe of Tieck, on the other hand, is a truly romantic universe; it has no centre, or what amounts to the same thing, it has at its centre that symbol of spiritual stagnation, the philistine, and his inability to rise above a dull didacticism. The romanticist cherishes the illusion that to be a spiritual vagrant is to be exalted on a pinnacle above the plain citizen. According to Professor Stuart P. Sherman, the Irish dramatist Synge indulges in gypsy laughter from the bushes,[4] a good description of romantic irony in general.

The irony of Socrates, to take the most important example of Greek irony, is not of the centrifugal character. Socrates professes ignorance, and this profession seems very ironical, for it turns out that his ignorance is more enlightened, that is, more central than other men's swelling conceit of knowledge. It does not follow that Socrates is insincere in his profession of ignorance; for though his knowledge may be as light in comparison with that of the ordinary Athenian, he sees that in comparison with true and perfect knowledge it is only darkness. For Socrates was no mere rationalist; he was a man of insight, one would even be tempted to say a mystic were it not for the corruption of the term mystic by the romanticists. This being the case he saw that man is by his very nature precluded from true and perfect knowledge. A path, however, opens up before him towards this knowledge, and this path he should seek to follow even though it is in a sense endless, even though beyond any centre he can attain within the bounds of his finite experience there is destined always to be something still more central. Towards the mere dogmatist, the man who thinks he has achieved some fixed and final centre, the attitude of Socrates is that of scepticism. This attitude implies a certain degree of detachment from the received beliefs and conventions of his time, and it is all the more important to distinguish here between Socrates and the romanticists because of the superficial likeness; and also because there is between the Rousseauists and some of the Greeks who lived about the time of Socrates a real likeness. Promethean individualism was already rife at that time, and on the negative side it resulted then as since in a break with tradition, and on the positive side in an oscillation between the cult of force and the exaltation of sympathy, between admiration for the strong man and compassion for the weak. It is hardly possible to overlook these Promethean elements in the plays of Euripides. Antisthenes and the cynics, again, who professed to derive from Socrates, established an opposition between "nature" and convention even more radical in some respects than that established by Rousseau. Moreover Socrates himself was perhaps needlessly unconventional and also unduly inclined to paradox—as when he suggested to the jury who tried him that as an appropriate punishment he should be supported at the public expense in the prytaneum. Yet in his inner spirit and in spite of certain minor eccentricities, Socrates was neither a superman nor a Bohemian, but a humanist. Now that the critical spirit was abroad and the traditional basis for conduct was failing, he was chiefly concerned with putting conduct on a positive and critical basis. In establishing this basis his constant appeal is to actual experience and the more homely this experience the more it seems to please him. While working out the new basis for conduct he continues to observe the existing laws and customs; or if he gets away from the traditional discipline it is towards a stricter discipline; if he repudiates in aught the common sense of his day, it is in favor of a commoner sense. One may say indeed that Socrates and the Rousseauists (who are in this respect like some of the sophists) are both moving away from convention but in opposite directions. What the romanticist opposes to convention is his "genius," that is, his unique and private self. What Socrates opposes to convention is his universal and ethical self. According to Friedrich Schlegel, a man can never be a philosopher but only become one; if at any time he thinks that he is a philosopher he ceases to become one. The romanticist is right in thus thinking that to remain fixed at any particular point is to stagnate. Man is, as Nietzsche says, the being who must always surpass himself, but he has—and this is a point that Nietzsche did not sufficiently consider—a choice of direction in his everlasting pilgrimage. The man who is moving away from some particular centre will always seem paradoxical to the man who remains at it, but he may be moving away from it in either the romantic or the ethical direction. In the first case he is moving from a more normal to a less normal experience, in the second case he is moving towards an experience that is more profoundly representative. The New Testament abounds in examples of the ethical paradox—what one may term the paradox of humility. (A man must lose his life to find it, etc.) It is possible, however, to push even this type of paradox too far, to push it to a point where it affronts not merely some particular convention but the good sense of mankind itself, and this is a far graver matter. Pascal falls into this excess when he says that sickness is the natural state of the Christian. As a result of its supreme emphasis on humility Christianity from the start inclined unduly perhaps towards this type of paradox. It is hardly worth while, as Goethe said, to live seventy years in this world if all that one learn here below is only folly in the sight of God.

One of the most delicate of tasks is to determine whether a paradox occupies a position more or less central than the convention to which it is opposed. A somewhat similar problem is to determine which of two differing conventions has the greater degree of centrality. For one convention may as compared with another seem highly paradoxical. In 1870, it was announced at Peking that his Majesty the Emperor had had the good fortune to catch the small-pox. The auspiciousness of small-pox was part of the Chinese convention at this time, but to those of us who live under another convention it is a blessing we would willingly forego. But much in the Chinese convention, so far from being absurd, reflects the Confucian good sense, and if the Chinese decide to break with their convention, they should evidently consider long and carefully in which direction they are going to move—whether towards something more central, or something more eccentric.

As to the direction in which Rousseau is moving and therefore as to the quality of his paradoxes there can be little question. His paradoxes—and he is perhaps the most paradoxical of writers—reduce themselves on analysis to the notion that man has suffered a loss of goodness by being civilized, by having had imposed on his unconscious and instinctive self some humanistic or religious discipline—e.g., "The man who reflects is a depraved animal"; "True Christians are meant to be slaves"; decorum is only the "varnish of vice" or the "mask of hypoccrisy." Innumerable paradoxes of this kind will immediately occur to one as characteristic of Rousseau and his followers. These paradoxes may be termed in opposition to those of humility, the paradoxes of spontaneity. The man who holds them is plainly moving in an opposite direction not merely from the Christian but from the Socratic individualist. He is moving from the more representative to the less representative and not towards some deeper centre of experience, as would be the case if he were tending towards either humanism or religion. Wordsworth has been widely accepted not merely as a poet but as a religious teacher, and it is therefore important to note that his paradoxes are prevailingly of the Rousseauistic type. His verse is never more spontaneous or, as he would say, inevitable, than when it is celebrating the gospel of spontaneity. I have already pointed out some of the paradoxes that he opposes to pseudo-classic decorum: e.g., his attempt to bestow poetical dignity and importance upon the ass, and to make of it a model of moral excellence, also to find poetry in an idiot boy and to associate sublimity with a pedlar in defiance of the ordinary character of pedlars. In general Wordsworth indulges in Rousseauistic paradoxes when he urges us to look to peasants for the true language of poetry and would have us believe that man is taught by "woods and rills" and not by contact with his fellow men. He pushes this latter paradox to a point that would have made even Rousseau "stare and gasp" when he asserts that

> *One impulse from a vernal wood*
> *May teach you more of man*
> *Of moral evil and of good*
> *Than all the sages can.*

Another form of this same paradox that what comes from nature spontaneously is better than what can be acquired by conscious effort is found in his poem "Lucy Gray":

> *No mate, no comrade Lucy knew;*
> *She dwelt on a wide moor,*
> *The sweetest thing that ever grew*
> *Beside a human door!*

True maidenhood is made up of a thousand decorums; but this Rousseauistic maiden would have seemed too artificial if she had been reared in a house instead of "growing" out of doors; she might in that case have been a human being and not a "thing" and this would plainly have detracted from her spontaneity. Wordsworth's paradoxes about children have a similar origin. A child who at the age of six is a "mighty prophet, seer blest," is a highly improbable not to say impossible child. The "Nature" again of "Heart-Leap Well" which both feels and inspires pity is more remote from normal experience than the Nature "red in tooth and claw" of Tennyson. Wordsworth indeed would seem to have a penchant for paradox even when he is less obviously inspired by his naturalistic thesis.

A study of Wordsworth's life shows that he became progressively disillusioned regarding Rousseauistic spontaneity. He became less paradoxical as he grew older and in almost the same measure, one is tempted to say, less poetical. He returns gradually to the traditional forms until radicals come to look upon him as the "lost leader." He finds it hard, however, to wean his imagination from its primitivistic Arcadias; so that what one finds, in writing like the "Ecclesiastical Sonnets," is not imaginative fire but at best a sober intellectual conviction, an opposition between the head and the heart in short that suggests somewhat Chateaubriand and the "Genius of Christianity." [5] If Wordsworth had lost faith in his revolutionary and naturalistic ideal, and had at the same time refused to return to the traditional forms, one might then have seen in his work something of the homeless hovering of the romantic ironist. If, on the other hand, he had worked away from the centre that the traditional forms give to life towards a more positive and critical centre, if, in other words, he had broken with the past not on Rousseauistic, but on Socratic lines, he would have needed an imagination of different quality, an imagination less idyllic and pastoral and more ethical than that he usually displays.[6] For the ethical imagination alone can guide one not indeed to any fixed centre but to an ever increasing centrality. We are here confronted once more with the question of the infinite which comes very close to the ultimate ground of difference between classicist and romanticist. The centre that one perceives with the aid of the classical imagination and that sets bounds to impulse and desire may, as I have already said, be defined in opposition to the outer infinite of expansion as the inner or human infinite. If we moderns, to repeat Nietzsche, are unable to attain proportionateness it is because "our itching is really the itching for the infinite, the immeasurable." Thus to associate the infinite only with the immeasurable, to fail to perceive that the element of form and the curb it puts on the imagination are not external and artificial, but come from the very depths, is to betray the fact that one is a barbarian. Nietzsche and many other romanticists are capable on occasion of admiring the proportionateness that comes from allegiance to some centre. But after all the human spirit must be ever advancing, and its only motive powers, according to romantic logic, are wonder and curiosity; and so from the perfectly sound premise that man is the being who must always surpass himself, Nietzsche draws the perfectly unsound conclusion that the only way for man thus constantly to surpass himself and so show his infinitude is to spurn all limits and "live dangerously." The Greeks themselves, according to Renan, will some day seem the "apostles of ennui," for the very perfection of their form shows a lack of aspiration. To submit to form is to be static, whereas "romantic poetry," says Friedrich Schlegel magnificently, is "universal progressive poetry." Now the only effective counterpoise to the endless expansiveness that is implied in such a programme is the inner or human infinite of concentration. For it is perfectly true that there is something in man that is not satisfied with the finite and that, if he becomes stationary, he is at once haunted by the spectre of ennui. Man may indeed be defined as the insatiable animal; and the more imaginative he is the more insatiable he is likely to become, for it is the imagination that gives him access to the infinite in every sense of the word. In a way Baudelaire is right when he describes ennui as a "delicate monster" that selects as his prey the most highly gifted natures. Marguerite d'Angoulême already speaks of the "ennui proper to well-born spirits." Now religion seeks no less than romance an escape from ennui. Bossuet is at one with Baudelaire when he dilates on that "inexorable ennui which is the very substance of human life." But Bossuet and Baudelaire differ utterly in the remedies they propose for ennui. Baudelaire hopes to escape from ennui by dreaming of the superlative emotional adventure, by indulging in infinite, indeterminate desire, and becomes more and more restless in his quest for a something that at the end always eludes him. This infinite of nostalgia has nothing in common with the infinite of religion. No distinction is more important than that between the man who feels the divine discontent of religion, and the man who is suffering from mere romantic restlessness. According to religion man must seek the satisfaction that the finite fails to give by looking not without but within; and to look within he must in the literal sense of the word undergo conversion. A path will then be found to open up before him, a path of which he cannot see the end. He merely knows that to advance on this path is to increase in peace, poise, centrality; though beyond any calm he can attain is always a deeper centre of calm. The goal is at an infinite remove. This is the truth that St. Augustine puts theologically when he exclaims: "For thou hast made us for thyself and our heart is restless until it findeth peace in thee." [7] One should insist that this question of the two infinites is not abstract and metaphysical but bears on what is most concrete and immediate in experience. If the inner and human infinite cannot be formulated intellectually, it can be known practically in its effect on life and conduct. Goethe says of Werther that he "treated his heart like a sick child; its every wish was granted it." "My restless heart asked me for something else," says Rousseau. "René," says Chateaubriand, "was enchanted, tormented and, as it were, possessed by the demon of his heart." Mr. Galsworthy speaks in a similar vein of "the aching for the wild, the passionate, the new, that never quite dies in a man's heart." But is there not deep down in the human breast another heart that is felt as a power of control over this romantic heart and can keep within due bounds "its aching for the wild, the passionate, the new." This is the heart, it would seem, to which a man must hearken if he is not for a "little honey of romance" to abandon his "ancient wisdom and austere control."

The romantic corruption of the infinite here joins with the romantic corruption of conscience, the transformation of conscience from an inner check into an expansive emotion that I have already traced in Shaftesbury and Rousseau. But one should add that in some of its aspects this corruption of the idea of the infinite antedates the whole modern movement. At least the beginnings of it can be found in ancient Greece—especially in that "delirious and diseased Greece" of which Joubert speaks—the Greece of the neo-Platonists. There is already in the neo-Platonic notion of the infinite a strong element of expansiveness. Aristotle and the older Greeks conceived of the infinite in this sense as bad. That something in human nature which is always reaching out for more—whether the more of sensation or of power or of knowledge—was, they held, to be strictly reined in and disciplined to the law of measure. All the furies lie in wait for the man who overextends himself. He is ripening for Nemesis. "Nothing too much." "Think as a mortal." "The half is better than the whole." In his attitude towards man's expansive self the Greek as a rule stands for mediation, and not like the more austere Christian, for renunciation. Yet Plato frequently and Aristotle at times mount from the humanistic to the religious level. One of the most impressive passages in philosophy is that in which Aristotle, perhaps the chief exponent of the law of measure, affirms that one who has really faced about and is moving towards the inner infinite needs no warning against excess: "We should not give heed," he says, "to those who bid one think as a mortal, but so far as we can we should make ourselves immortal and do all with a view to a life in accord with the best Principle in us." [8] (This Principle, Aristotle goes on to say, is a man's true self.)

The earlier Greek distinction between an outer and evil infinite of expansive desire and an inner infinite that is raised above the flux and yet rules it, is, in the Aristotelian phrase, its "unmoved mover," became blurred, as I have said, during the Alexandrian period. The Alexandrian influence entered to some extent into Christianity itself and filtered through various channels down to modern times. Some of the romanticists went directly to the neo-Platonists, especially Plotinus. Still more were affected by Jacob Boehme, who himself had no direct knowledge of the Alexandrian theosophy. This theosophy appears nevertheless in combination with other elements in his writings. He appealed to the new school by his insistence on the element of appetency or desire, by his universal symbolizing, above all by his tendency to make of the divine an affirmative instead of a restrictive force—a something that pushes forward instead of holding back. The expansive elements are moderated in Boehme himself and in disciples like Law by genuinely religious elements—e.g., humility and the idea of conversion. What happens when the expansiveness is divorced from these elements, one may see in another English follower of Boehme—William Blake. To be both beautiful and wise one needs, according to Blake, only to be exuberant. The influence of Boehme blends in Blake with the new æstheticism. Jesus himself, he says, so far from being restrained "was all virtue, and acted from impulse not from rules." This purely æsthetic and impulsive Jesus has been cruelly maligned, as we learn from the poem entitled the "Everlasting Gospel," by being represented as humble and chaste. Religion itself thus becomes in Blake the mere sport of a powerful and uncontrolled imagination, and this we are told is mysticism. I have already contrasted with this type of mysticism something that goes under the same name and is yet utterly different—the mysticism of ancient India. Instead of conceiving of the divine in terms of expansion the Oriental sage defines it experimentally as the "inner check." No more fundamental distinction perhaps can be made than that between those who associate the good with the yes-principle and those who associate it rather with the no-principle. But I need not repeat what I have said elsewhere on the romantic attempt to discredit the veto power. Let no one think that this contrast is merely metaphysical. The whole problem of evil is involved in it and all the innumerable practical consequences that follow from one's attitude towards this problem. The passage in which Faust defines the devil as the "spirit that always says no" would seem to derive directly or indirectly from Boehme. According to Boehme good can be known only through evil. God therefore divides his will into two, the "yes" and the "no," and so founds an eternal contrast to himself in order to enter into a struggle with it, and finally to discipline and assimilate it. The object of all manifested nature is the transforming of the will which says "no" into the will which says "yes." [9] The opposition between good and evil tends to lose its reality when it thus becomes a sort of sham battle that God gets up with himself (without contraries is no progression, says Blake), or when, to take the form that the doctrine assumes in "Faust," the devil appears as the necessary though unwilling instrument of man's betterment. The recoil from the doctrine of total depravity was perhaps inevitable. What is sinister is that advantage has been taken of this recoil to tamper with the problem of evil itself. Partial evil we are told is universal good; or else evil is only good in the making.

For a Rousseau or a Shelley it is something mysteriously imposed from without on a spotless human nature; for a Wordsworth it is something one may escape by contemplating the speargrass on the wall. [10] For a Novalis sin is a mere illusion of which a man should rid his mind if he aspires to become a "magic idealist." [11] In spite of his quaint Tory prejudices Dr. Johnson is one of the few persons in recent times that one may term wise without serious qualification because he never dodges or equivocates in dealing with the problem of evil; he never fades away from the fact of evil into some theosophic or sentimental dream.

The rise of a purely expansive view of life in the eighteenth century was marked by a great revival of enthusiasm. The chief grievance of the expansionist indeed against the no-principle is that it kills enthusiasm. But concentration no less than expansion may have its own type of enthusiasm. It is therefore imperative in an age that has repudiated the traditional sanctions and set out to walk by the inner light that all general terms and in particular the term enthusiasm should be protected by a powerful dialectic. Nothing is more perilous than an uncritical enthusiasm, since it is only by criticism that one may determine whether the enthusiast is a man who is moving towards wisdom or is a candidate for Bedlam. The Rousseauist, however, exalts enthusiasm at the same time that he depreciates discrimination. "Enthusiasm," says Emerson, "is the height of man. It is the passage from the human to the divine." It is only too characteristic of Emerson and of the whole school to which he belongs, to put forth statements of this kind without any dialectical protection. The type of enthusiasm to which Emerson's praise might be properly applied, the type that has been defined as exalted peace, though extremely rare, actually exists. A commoner type of enthusiasm during the past century is that which has been defined as "the rapturous disintegration of civilized human nature." When we have got our fingers well burned as a result of our failure to make the necessary discriminations, we may fly to the opposite extreme like the men of the early eighteenth century among whom, as is well known, enthusiasm had become a term of vituperation. This dislike of enthusiasm was the natural recoil from the uncritical following of the inner light by the fanatics of the seventeenth century. Shaftesbury attacks this older type of enthusiasm and at the same time prepares the way for the new emotional enthusiasm. One cannot say, however, that any such sharp separation of types appears in the revival of enthusiasm that begins about the middle of the eighteenth century, though some of those who were working for this revival felt the need of discriminating:

> *That which concerns us therefore is to see*
> *What Species of Enthusiasts we be—*

says John Byrom in his poem on Enthusiasm. The different species, however—the enthusiasm of the Evangelicals and Wesleyans, the enthusiasm of those who like Law and his disciple Byrom hearken back to Boehme, the enthusiasm of Rousseau and the sentimentalists—tend to run together. To "let one's feelings run in soft luxurious flow," [12] is, as Newman says, at the opposite pole from spirituality. Yet much of this mere emotional facility appears alongside of genuinely religious elements in the enthusiasm of the Methodist. One may get a notion of the jumble to which I refer by reading a book like Henry Brooke's "Fool of Quality." Brooke is at one and the same time a disciple of Boehme and Rousseau while being more or less affiliated with the Methodistic movement. The book indeed was revised and abridged by John Wesley himself and in this form had a wide circulation among his followers.[13]

The enthusiasm that has marked the modern movement has plainly not been sufficiently critical. Perhaps the first discovery that any one will make who wishes to be at once critical and enthusiastic is that in a genuinely spiritual enthusiasm the inner light and the inner check are practically identical. He will find that if he is to rise above the naturalistic level he must curb constantly his expansive desires with reference to some centre that is set above the flux. Here let me repeat is the supreme rôle of the imagination. The man who has ceased to lean on outer standards can perceive his new standards or centre of control only through its aid. I have tried to show that to aim at such a centre is not to be stagnant and stationary but on the contrary to be at once purposeful and

progressive. To assert that the creativeness of the imagination is incompatible with centrality or, what amounts to
the same thing, with purpose, is to assert that the creativeness of the imagination is incompatible with reality or at
least such reality as man may attain. Life is at best a series
of illusions; the whole office of philosophy is to keep it from
degenerating into a series of delusions. If we are to keep it from
thus degenerating we need to grasp above all the difference
between the eccentric and the concentric imagination. To
look for serious guidance to an imagination that owes allegiance to nothing above itself is to run the risk of taking some cloud bank for terra firma. The eccentric imagination may give access to the "infinite," but it is an infinite
empty of content and therefore an infinite not of peace but of
restlessness. Can any one maintain seriously that there is aught
in common between the "striving for endlessness" of the German romanticists and the supreme and perfect Centre that
Dante glimpses at the end of the "Divine Comedy" and in the
presence of which he becomes dumb?

We are told to follow the gleam, but the counsel is somewhat ambiguous. The gleam that one follows may be that
which is associated with the concentric imagination and which
gives steadiness and informing purpose, or it may be the romantic will o' the wisp. One may, as I have said, in recreative
moments allow one's imagination to wander without control,
but to take these wanderings seriously is to engage in a sort of
endless pilgrimage in the void. The romanticist is constantly
yielding to the "spell" of this or the "lure" of that, or the
"call" of some other thing. But when the wonder and strangeness that he is chasing are overtaken, they at once cease to be
wondrous and strange, while the gleam is already dancing over
some other object on the distant horizon. For nothing is in itself romantic, it is only imagining that makes it so. Romanticism is the pursuit of the element of illusion in things for its
own sake; it is in short the cherishing of glamour. The word
glamour introduced into literary usage from popular Scotch
usage by Walter Scott itself illustrates this tendency. Traced
etymologically, it turns out to be the same word as grammar.
In an illiterate age to know how to write at all was a weird

and magical accomplishment,[14] but in an educated age, nothing is so drearily unromantic, so lacking in glamour as grammar.

The final question that arises in connection with this subject is whether one may quell the mere restlessness of one's spirit and impose upon it an ethical purpose. "The man who has no definite end is lost," says Montaigne. The upshot of the romantic supposition that purpose is incompatible with the freedom of the imagination is a philosophy like that of Nietzsche. He can conceive of nothing beyond whirling forever on the wheel of change ("the eternal recurrence") without any goal or firm refuge that is set above the flux. He could not help doubting at times whether happiness was to be found after all in mere endless, purposeless mutation.

> Have I still a goal? A haven towards which my sail is set? A good wind? Ah, he only who knoweth whither he saileth, knoweth what wind is good, and a fair wind for him.
> What still remaineth to me? A heart weary and flippant; an unstable will; fluttering wings; a broken backbone.
> . . . .
> Where is my home? For it do I ask and seek, and have sought, but have not found it. O eternal everywhere, O eternal nowhere, O eternal—in vain.[15]

To allow one's self to revolve passively on the wheel of change (samsāra) seemed to the Oriental sage the acme of evil. An old Hindu writer compares the man who does not impose a firm purpose upon the manifold solicitations of sense to a charioteer who fails to rein in his restless steeds[16]—a comparison suggested independently to Ricarda Huch by the lives of the German romanticists. In the absence of central control, the parts of the self tend to pull each in a different way. It is not surprising that in so centrifugal a movement, at least on the human and spiritual level, one should find so many instances of disintegrated and multiple personality. The fascination that the phenomenon of the double (Doppelgängerei) had for Hoffmann and other German romanticists is well known.[17] It may well be that some such disintegration of the self takes place under extreme emotional stress.[18] We should not fail to note here the usual coöperation between the emotional and the scientific naturalist. Like the romanticist, the scientific psychologist is more interested in the abnormal than in the normal. According to the Freudians, the personality that has become incapable of any conscious aim is not left entirely rudderless. The guidance that it is unable to give itself is supplied to it by some "wish," usually obscene, from the sub-conscious realm of dreams. The Freudian then proceeds to develop what may be true of the hysterical degenerate into a complete view of life.

Man is in danger of being deprived of every last scrap and vestige of his humanity by this working together of romanticism and science. For man becomes human only in so far as he exercises moral choice. He must also enter upon the pathway of ethical purpose if he is to achieve happiness. "Moods," says Novalis, "undefined emotions, not defined emotions and feelings, give happiness." The experience of life shows so plainly that this is not so that the romanticist is tempted to seek shelter once more from his mere vagrancy of spirit in the outer discipline he has abandoned. "To such unsettled ones as thou, seemeth at last even a prisoner blessed. Didst thou ever see how captured criminals sleep? They sleep quietly, they enjoy their new security. . . . Beware in the end lest a narrow faith capture thee, a hard rigorous delusion! For now everything that is narrow and fixed seduceth and tempteth thee." [19]

Various reasons have been given for romantic conversions to Catholicism—for example, the desire for confession (though the Catholic does not, like the Rousseauist, confess himself from the housetops), the æsthetic appeal of Catholic rites and ceremonies, etc. The sentence of Nietzsche puts us on the track of still another reason. The affinity of certain romantic converts for the Church is that of the jelly-fish for the rock. It is appropriate that Friedrich Schlegel, the great apostle of irony, should after a career as a heaven-storming Titan end by submitting to this most rigid of all forms of outer authority.

For it should now be possible to return after our digression on paradox and the idea of the infinite and the perils of aimlessness to romantic irony with a truer understanding of its significance. Like so much else in this movement it is an attempt to give to a grave psychic weakness the prestige of strength—unless indeed one conceives the superior personality to be the one that lacks a centre and principle of control. Man it has usually been held should think lightly of himself but should have some conviction for which he is ready to die. The romantic ironist, on the other hand, is often morbidly sensitive about himself, but is ready to mock at his own convictions. Rousseau was no romantic ironist, but the root of self-parody is found nevertheless in his saying that his heart and his head did not seem to belong to the same individual. Everything of course is a matter of degree. What poor mortal can say that he is perfectly at one with himself? Friedrich Schlegel is not entirely wrong when he discovers elements of irony based on an opposition between the head and the heart in writers like Ariosto and Cervantes, who love the very mediæval tales that they are treating in a spirit of mockery. Yet the laughter of Cervantes is not gypsy laughter. He is one of those who next to Shakespeare deserve the praise of having dwelt close to the centre of human nature and so can in only a minor degree be ranked with the romantic ironists.

In the extreme type of romantic ironist not only are intellect and emotion at loggerheads but action often belies both: he thinks one thing and feels another and does still a third. The most ironical contrast of all is that between the romantic "ideal" and the actual event. The whole of romantic morality is from this point of view, as I have tried to show, a monstrous series of ironies. The pacifist, for example, has been disillusioned so often that he should by this time be able to qualify as a romantic ironist, to look, that is, with a certain aloofness on his own dream. The crumbling of the ideal is often so complete indeed when put to the test that irony is at times, we may suppose, a merciful alternative to madness. When disillusion overtakes the uncritical enthusiast, when he finds that he has taken some cloud bank for terra firma, he continues to cling to his dream, but at the same time wishes to show that he is no longer the dupe of it; and so "hot baths of sentiment," as Jean Paul says of his novels, "are followed by cold douches of irony." The true German master of the genre is, however, Heine. Every one knows with what coldness his head came to survey the enthusiasms of his heart, whether in love or politics. One may again measure the havoc that life had wrought with Renan's ideals if one compares the tone of his youthful

"Future of Science" with the irony of his later writings. He compliments Jesus by ascribing to him an ironical detachment similar to his own. Jesus, he says, has that mark of the superior nature—the power to rise above his own dream and to smile down upon it. Anatole France, who is even more completely detached from his own dreams than his master Renan, sums up the romantic emancipation of imagination and sensibility from any definite centre when he says that life should have as its supreme witnesses irony and pity.

Irony is on the negative side, it should be remembered, a way of affirming one's escape from traditional and conventional control, of showing the supremacy of mood over decorum. "There are poems old and new which throughout breathe the divine breath of irony. . . . Within lives the poet's mood that surveys all, rising infinitely above everything finite, even above his own art, virtue or genius." [20] Decorum is for the classicist the grand masterpiece to observe because it is only thus he can show that he has a genuine centre set above his own ego; it is only by the allegiance of his imagination to this centre that he can give the illusion of a higher reality. The romantic ironist shatters the illusion wantonly. It is as though he would inflict upon the reader the disillusion from which he has himself suffered. By his swift passage from one mood to another (*Stimmungsbrechung*) he shows that he is subject to no centre. The effect is often that of a sudden breaking of the spell of poetry by an intrusion of the poet's ego. Some of the best examples are found in that masterpiece of romantic irony, "Don Juan." [21]

Closely allied to the irony of emotional disillusion is a certain type of misanthropy. You form an ideal of man that is only an Arcadian dream and then shrink back from man when you find that he does not correspond to your ideal. I have said that the romantic lover does not love a real person but only a projection of his mood. This substitution of illusion for reality often appears in the relations of the romanticist with other persons. Shelley, for example, begins by seeing in Elizabeth Hitchener an angel of light and then discovers that she is instead a "brown demon." He did not at any time see the real Elizabeth Hitchener. She merely reflects back to him two of his own moods. The tender misanthropy of the Rousseauist is at

the opposite pole from that of a Swift, which is the misanthropy of naked intellect. Instead of seeing human nature
through an Arcadian haze he saw it without any illusion at all.
His irony is like that of Socrates, the irony of intellect. Its bitterness and cruelty arise from the fact that his intellect does
not, like the intellect of Socrates, have the support of insight.
Pascal would have said that Swift saw man's misery without at
the same time seeing his grandeur. For man's grandeur is due
to his infinitude and this infinitude cannot be perceived directly,
but only through a veil of illusion; only, that is, through a
right use of the imagination. Literary distinctions of this kind
must of course be used cautiously. Byron's irony is prevailingly
sentimental, but along with this romantic element he has much
irony and satire that Swift would have understood perfectly.

The misanthropist of the Rousseauistic or Byronic type has
a resource that was denied to Swift. Having failed to find companionship among men he can flee to nature. Rousseau relates
how when he had taken refuge on St. Peter's Island he "exclaimed at times with deep emotion: Oh nature, oh my mother,
here I am under your protection alone. Here is no adroit and
rascally man to interpose between you and me." [22] Few aspects
of romanticism are more important than this attempt to find
companionship and consolation in nature.

CHAPTER EIGHT

ROMANTICISM AND NATURE

One of the most disquieting features of the modern movement is the vagueness and ambiguity of its use of the word
nature and the innumerable sophistries that have resulted. One
can sympathize at times with Sir Leslie Stephen's wish that the
word might be suppressed entirely. This looseness of definition
may be said to begin with the very rise of naturalism in the
Renaissance, and indeed to go back to the naturalists of Greek
and Roman antiquity.[1] Even writers like Rabelais and Molière
are not free from the suspicion of juggling dangerously on occasion with the different meanings of the word nature. But
the sixteenth and seventeenth centuries were not merely naturalistic, they were also humanistic, and what they usually
meant by nature, as I have pointed out, was the conception of
normal, representative human nature that they had worked out
with the aid of the ancients. There is undeniably an element of
narrowness and artificiality in this conception of nature, and a
resulting unfriendliness, as appears in Pope's definition of wit,
towards originality and invention. In his "Art of Poetry" Boileau says, "Let nature be your sole study." What he means by
nature appears a few lines later: "Study the court and become
familiar with the town." To this somewhat conventionalized
human nature the original genius opposed, as we have seen,

the cult of primitive nature. A whole revolution is implied in Byron's line:

I love not man the less, but nature more.

Any study of this topic must evidently turn on the question how far at different times and by different schools of thought the realm of man and the realm of nature (as Byron uses the word) have been separated and in what way, and also how far they have been run together and in what way. For there may be different ways of running together man and nature. Ruskin's phrase the "pathetic fallacy" is unsatisfactory because it fails to recognize this fact. The man who is guilty of the pathetic fallacy sees in nature emotions that are not really there but only in himself. Extreme examples of this confusion abound in Ruskin's own writings. Now the ancients also ran man and nature together, but in an entirely different way. The Greek we are told never saw the oak tree without at the same time seeing the dryad. There is in this and similar associations a sort of overflow of the human realm upon the forms of outer nature; whereas the Rousseauist instead of bestowing imaginatively upon the oak tree a conscious life and an image akin to his own and so lifting it up to his level, would, if he could, become an oak tree and so enjoy its unconscious and vegetative felicity. The Greek, one may say, humanized nature; the Rousseauist naturalizes man. Rousseau's great discovery was revery; and revery is just this imaginative melting of man into outer nature. If the ancients failed to develop in a marked degree this art of revery, it was not because they lacked naturalists. Both Stoics and Epicureans, the two main varieties of naturalists with which classical antiquity was familiar, inclined to affirm the ultimate identity of the human and the natural order. But both Stoics and Epicureans would have found it hard to understand the indifference to the intellect and its activities that Rousseauistic revery implies. The Stoics to be sure employed the intellect on an impossible and disheartening task—that of founding on the natural order virtues that the natural order does not give. The Epicureans remind one rather in much of their intellectual activity of the modern man of science. But the Epicurean was less prone than

the man of science to look on man as the mere passive creature of environment. The views of the man of science about
the springs of conduct often seem to coincide rather closely
with those of Rousseau about "sensitive morality." Geoffroy
Saint-Hilaire says that when reclining on the banks of the Nile
he felt awakening within himself the instincts of the crocodile.
The point of view is Rousseauistic perhaps rather than genuinely scientific. An Epicurus or a Lucretius would, we are
probably safe in assuming, have been disquieted by any such
surrender to the sub-rational, by any such encroachment of
the powers of the unconscious upon conscious control.

It is hard as a matter of fact to find in the ancients anything
resembling Rousseauistic revery, even when they yield to the
pastoral mood. Nature interests them as a rule less for its own
sake than as a background for human action; and when they
are concerned primarily with nature, it is a nature that has
been acted upon by man. They have a positive shrinking from
wild and uncultivated nature. "The green pastures and golden
slopes of England," says Lowell, "are sweeter both to the outward and to the inward eye that the hand of man has imme-
morially cared for and caressed them." This is an attitude
towards nature that an ancient would have understood perfectly. One may indeed call it the Virgilian attitude from the
ancient who has perhaps expressed it most happily. The man
who lives in the grand manner may indeed wish to impose on
nature some of the fine proportion and symmetry of which he
is conscious in himself and he may then from our modern
point of view carry the humanizing of nature too far. "Let us
sing of woods," says Virgil, "but let the woods be worthy of a
consul." This line has sometimes been taken to be a prophecy
of the Park of Versailles. We may sympathize up to a certain
point with the desire to introduce a human symmetry into nature (such as appears, for instance, in the Italian garden), but
the peril is even greater here than elsewhere of confounding
the requirements of a real with those of an artificial decorum.
I have already mentioned the neo-classicist who complained that
the stars in heaven were not arranged in sufficiently symmetrical patterns.

What has been said should make clear that though both

humanist and Rousseauist associate man with nature it is in very different ways, and that there is therefore an ambiguity in the expression "pathetic fallacy." It remains to show that men may not only associate themselves with nature in different ways but that they may likewise differ in their ways of asserting man's separateness from nature. The chief distinction to be made here is that between the humanist and the supernaturalist. Some sense of the gap between man and the "outworld" is almost inevitable and forces itself at times even upon those most naturalistically inclined:

> Nor will I praise a cloud however bright,
> Disparaging Man's gifts and proper food—
> Grove, isle, with every shape of sky-built dome,
> Though clad in colors beautiful and pure,
> Find in the heart of man no natural home.[2]

The Wordsworth who speaks here is scarcely the Wordsworth of Tintern Abbey or the Wordsworth whose "daily teachers had been woods and rills." He reminds us rather of Socrates who gave as his reason for going so rarely into the country, delightful as he found it when once there, that he did not learn from woods and rills but from the "men in the cities." This sense of the separateness of the human and the natural realm may be carried much further—to a point where an ascetic distrust of nature begins to appear. Something of this ascetic distrust is seen for example in the following lines from Cardinal Newman:

> There strayed awhile amid the woods of Dart
> One who could love them, but who durst not love;
> A vow had bound him ne'er to give his heart
> To streamlet bright or soft secluded grove.[3]

The origins of this latter attitude towards nature are to be sought in mediæval Christianity rather than in classical antiquity. No man who knows the facts would assert for a moment that the man of the Middle Ages was incapable of looking on nature with other feelings than those of ascetic distrust. It is none the less true that the man of the Middle Ages often saw in nature not merely something alien but a positive temptation and peril of the spirit. In his attitude towards nature as in other respects Petrarch is usually accounted the first modern. He did what no man of the mediæval period is supposed to have done before him, or indeed what scarcely any man of classical antiquity did: he ascended a mountain out of sheer curiosity and simply to enjoy the prospect. But those who tell of his ascent of Mt. Ventoux sometimes forget to add that the passage of Saint Augustine[4] that occurred to him at the top reflects the distrust of the more austere Christian towards the whole natural order. Petrarch is at once more ascetic and more romantic in his attitude towards nature than the Greek or Roman.

Traces of Petrarch's taste for solitary and even for wild nature are to be found throughout the Renaissance and the seventeenth century. But the recoil from supernaturalism that took place at this time led rather, as I have remarked, to a revival of the Græco-Roman humanism with something more of artifice and convention, and to an even more marked preference[5] of the town to the country. An age that aims first of all at urbanity must necessarily be more urban than rural in its predilections. It was a sort of condescension for the neo-classical humanist to turn from the central model he was imitating to mere unadorned nature, and even then he felt that he must be careful not to condescend too far. Even when writing pastorals he was warned by Scaliger to avoid details that are too redolent of the real country; he should indulge at most in an "urbane rusticity." Wild nature the neo-classicist finds simply repellent. Mountains he looks upon as "earth's dishonor and encumbering load." The Alps were regarded as the place where Nature swept up the rubbish of the earth to clear the plains of Lombardy. "At last," says a German traveller of the seventeenth century, "we left the horrible and wearisome mountains and the beautiful flat landscape was joyfully welcomed." The taste for mountain scenery is associated no doubt to some extent, as has been suggested, with the increasing ease and comfort of travel that has come with the progress of the utilitarian movement. It is scarcely necessary to point the contrast between the Switzerland of which Evelyn tells in his diary[6] and the Switzerland in which one may go by funicular to the top of the Jungfrau.

Those who in the eighteenth century began to feel the need of less trimness in both nature and human nature were not it is true entirely without neo-classic predecessors. They turned at times to painting—as the very word picturesque testifies— for the encouragement they failed to find in literature. A land-scape was picturesque when it seemed like a picture[7] and it might be not merely irregular but savage if it were to seem like some of the pictures of Salvator Rosa. This association of even wildness with art is very characteristic of eighteenth-century sentimentalism. It is a particular case of that curious blending in this period of the old principle of the imitation of models with the new principle of spontaneity. There was a moment when a man needed to show a certain taste for wildness if he was to be conventionally correct. "The fops," says Taine, de-scribing Rousseau's influence on the drawing-rooms, "dreamt between two madrigals of the happiness of sleeping naked in the virgin forest." The prince in Goethe's "Triumph of Sen-sibility" has carried with him on his travels canvas screens so painted that when placed in position they give him the illusion of being in the midst of a wild landscape. This taste for arti-ficial wildness can however best be studied in connection with the increasing vogue in the eighteenth century of the English garden as compared either with the Italian garden or the French garden in the style of Le Nôtre.[8] As a relief from the neo-classical symmetry, nature was broken up, often at great ex-pense, into irregular and unexpected aspects. Some of the Eng-lish gardens in France and Germany were imitated directly from Rousseau's famous description of this method of dealing with the landscape in the "Nouvelle Héloïse." [9] Artificial ruins were often placed in the English garden as a further aid to those who wished to wander imaginatively from the beaten path, and also as a provocative of the melancholy that was al-ready held to be distinguished. Towards the end of the century this cult of ruins was widespread. The veritable obsession with ruins that one finds in Chateaubriand is not unrelated to this sentimental fashion, though it arises even more perhaps from the real ruins that had been so plentifully supplied by the Rev-olution.

Rousseau himself, it should hardly be necessary to say,

stands for far more than an artificial wildness. Instead of imposing decorum on nature like the neo-classicist, he preached
constantly the elimination of decorum from man. Man should
flee from that "false taste for grandeur which is not made for
him" and which "poisons his pleasures" [10] to nature. Now "it
is on the summits of mountains, in the depths of forests, on
deserted islands that nature reveals her most potent charms." [11]
The man of feeling finds the savage and deserted nook filled
with beauties that seem horrible to the mere worldling.[12] Rousseau indeed did not crave the ultimate degree of wildness even
in the Alps. He did not get beyond what one may term the
middle zone of Alpine scenery—scenery that may be found
around the shores of Lake Leman. He was inclined to find
the most appropriate setting for the earthly paradise in the
neighborhood of Vevey. Moreover, others about the same time
and more or less independently of his influence were opposing
an even more primitive nature to the artificialities of civilization. The mountains of "Ossian" are, as has been said, mere
blurs, yet the new delight in mountains is due in no small
measure throughout Europe to the Ossianic influence.

The instinct for getting away from the beaten track, for exploration and discovery, has of course been highly developed at
other epochs, notably at the Renaissance. Much of the romantic interest in the wild and waste places of the earth did
not go much beyond what might have been felt in Elizabethan
England. Many of the Rousseauists, Wordsworth and Chateaubriand for example, not only read eagerly the older books of
travel but often the same books. The fascination of penetrating
to regions "where foot of man hath ne'er or rarely been," is
perennial. It was my privilege a few years ago to listen to Sir
Ernest Shackleton speak of his expedition across the Antarctic
continent and of the thrill that he and the members of his
party felt when they saw rising before them day after day
mountain peaks that no human eye had ever gazed upon. The
emotion was no doubt very similar to that of "stout Cortez"
when he first "stared at the Pacific." Chateaubriand must
have looked forward to similar emotions when he planned his
trip to North America in search of the North West Passage.
But the passion for actual exploration which is a form of the

romanticism of action is very subordinate in the case of Chateaubriand to emotional romanticism. He went into the wilderness first of all not to make actual discoveries but to affirm his freedom from conventional restraint, and at the same time to practice the new art of revery. His sentiments on getting into what was then the virgin forest to the west of Albany were very different we may assume from those of the early pioneers of America. "When," he says, "after passing the Mohawk I entered woods· which had never felt the axe, I was seized by a sort of intoxication of independence: I went from tree to tree, to right and left, saying to myself, 'Here are no more roads or cities or monarchy or republic or presidents or kings or men.' And in order to find out if I was restored to my original rights I did various wilful things that made my guide furious. In his heart he believed me mad." The disillusion that followed is also one that the early pioneers would have had some difficulty in understanding. For he goes on to relate that while he was thus rejoicing in his escape from conventional life to pure nature he suddenly bumped up against a shed, and under the shed he saw his first savages—a score of them both men and women. A little Frenchman named M. Violet, "bepowdered and befrizzled, with an apple-green coat, drugget waistcoat and muslin frill and cuffs, was scraping on a pocket fiddle" and teaching the Indians to dance to the tune of Madelon Friquet. M. Violet, it seemed, had remained behind on the departure from New York of Rochambeau's forces at the time of the American Revolution, and had set up as dancing-master among the savages. He was very proud of the nimbleness of his pupils and always referred to them as "ces messieurs sauvages et ces dames sauvagesses." "Was it not a crushing circumstance for a disciple of Rousseau," Chateaubriand concludes, "this introduction to savage life by a ball that the ex-scullion of General Rochambeau was giving to Iroquois? I felt very much like laughing, but I was at the same time cruelly humiliated."

In America, as elsewhere, Chateaubriand's chief concern is not with any outer fact or activity, but with his own emotions and the enhancement of these emotions by his imagination. In him as in many other romanticists the different elements of

Rousseauism—Arcadian longing, the pursuit of the dream woman, the aspiration towards the "infinite" (often identified with God)—appear at times more or less separately and then again almost inextricably blended with one another and with the cult of nature. It may be well to consider more in detail these various elements of Rousseauism and their relation to nature in about the order I have mentioned. The association of Arcadian longing with nature is in part an outcome of the conflict between the ideal and the real. The romantic idealist finds that men do not understand him: his "vision" is mocked and his "genius" is unrecognized. The result is the type of sentimental misanthropy of which I spoke at the end of the last chapter. He feels, as Lamartine says, that there is nothing in common between the world and him. Lamartine adds, however, "But nature is there who invites you and loves you. You will find in her the comprehension and companionship that you have failed to find in society." And nature will seem a perfect companion to the Rousseauist in direct proportion as she is uncontaminated by the presence of man. Wordsworth has described the misanthropy that supervened in many people on the collapse of the revolutionary idealism. He himself overcame it, though there is more than a suggestion in the manner of his own retirement into the hills of a man who retreats into an Arcadian dream from actual defeat. The suggestion of defeat is much stronger in Ruskin's similar retirement. Ruskin doubtless felt in later life, like Rousseau, that if he had failed to get on with men "it was less his fault than theirs." [13] Perhaps emotional misanthropy and the worship of wild nature are nowhere more fully combined than in Byron. He gives magnificent expression to the most untenable of paradoxes—that one escapes from solitude by eschewing human haunts in favor of some wilderness.[14] In these haunts, he says, he became like a "falcon with clipped wing," but found in nature the kindest of mothers.

Oh! she is fairest in her features wild,
Where nothing polished dare pollute her path:
To me by day or night she ever smiled
Though I have marked her when none other hath
And sought her more and more, and loved her best in wrath [15]

He not only finds companionship in nature but at the same time partakes of her infinitude—an infinitude, one should note, of feeling:

> *I live not in myself, but I become*
> *Portion of that around me; and to me*
> *High mountains are a feeling, but the hum*
> *Of human cities torture.*[16]

In his less misanthropic moods the Rousseauist sees in wild nature not only a refuge from society, but also a suitable setting for his companionship with the ideal mate, for what the French term *la solitude à deux*.

> *Oh! that the Desert were my dwelling-place*
> *With one fair Spirit for my minister,*
> *That I might all forget the human race*
> *And, hating no one, love but only her!* [17]

The almost innumerable passages in the romantic movement that celebrate this Arcadian companionship in the wilderness merely continue in a sense the pastoral mood that must be as old as human nature itself. But in the past the pastoral mood has been comparatively placid. It has not been associated in any such degree with misanthropy and wildness, with nympholeptic longing and the thirst for the infinite. The scene that Chateaubriand has imagined between Chactas and Atala in the primæval forest is surely the stormiest of Arcadias; so stormy indeed that it would have been unintelligible to Theocritus. It is not certain that it would have been intelligible to Shakespeare, who like the other Elizabethans felt at times that he too had been born in Arcadia. The Arcadian of the past was much less inclined to sink down to the subrational and to merge his personality in the landscape. Rousseau describes with a charm that has scarcely been surpassed by any of his disciples the reveries in which he thus descends below the level of his rational self. Time, no longer broken up by the importunate intellect and its analysis, is then felt by him in its unbroken flow; the result is a sort of "eternal present that leaves no sense of emptiness." Of such a moment of revery Rousseau says, anticipating Faust, that he "would like it to last forever." Bergson in his conception of the *summum bonum* as a state in which time is no longer cut up into artificial segments but is perceived in its continuous stream as a "present that endures" [18] has done little more than repeat Rousseau. The sight and sound of water seem to have been a special aid to revery in Rousseau's case. His accounts of the semi-dissolution of his conscious self that he enjoyed while drifting idly on the Lake of Bienne are justly celebrated. Lamartine's soul was, like that of Rousseau, lulled by "the murmur of waters." Nothing again is more Rousseauistic than the desire Arnold attributes to Maurice de Guérin—the desire "to be borne on forever down an enchanted stream." That too is why certain passages of Shelley are so near in spirit to Rousseau—for example, the boat revery in "Prometheus Unbound" in which an Arcadian nature and the dream companion mingle to the strains of music in a way that is supremely romantic.[19]

The association of nature with Arcadian longing and the pursuit of the dream woman is even less significant than its association with the idea of the infinite. For as a result of this latter association the nature cult often assumes the aspect of a religion. The various associations may indeed as I have said be very much blended or else may run into one another almost insensibly. No better illustration of this blending can be found perhaps than in Chateaubriand—especially in that compendium of Rousseauistic psychology, his "René." The soul of René, one learns, was too great to adjust itself to the society of men. He found that he would have to contract his life if he put himself on their level. Men, for their part, treated him as a dreamer, and so he is forced more and more by his increasing disgust for them into solitude. Now René rests the sense of his superiority over other men on two things: first, on his superlative capacity to feel grief;[20] secondly, on his thirst for the infinite. "What is finite," he says, "has no value for me." What is thus pushing him beyond all bounds is "an unknown good of which the instinct pursues me." "I began to ask myself what I desired. I did not know but I thought all of a sudden that the woods would be delicious to me!" What he found in this quest for the mystical something that was to fill the abyss of his existence was the dream woman. "I went down into the valley, I strode upon the mountain, summoning with all the force of my desire the ideal object of a future flame; I embraced this object in the winds; I thought that I heard it in the moanings of the river. All was this phantom of the imagination—both the stars in heaven and the very principle of life in the universe." I have already quoted a very similar passage and pointed out the equivalent in Shelley. No such close equivalent could be found in Byron, and Wordsworth, it is scarcely necessary to say, offers no equivalent at all. If one reads on, however, one finds passages that are Byronic and others that are Wordsworthian. Paganism, Chateaubriand complains, by seeing in nature only certain definite forms—fauns and satyrs and nymphs—had banished from it both God and the infinite. But Christianity expelled these thronging figures in turn and restored to the grottoes their silence and to the woods their revery. The true God thus became visible in his works and bestowed upon them his own immensity. What Chateaubriand understands by God and the infinite appears in the following description of the region near Niagara seen by moonlight. The passage is Byronic as a whole with a Wordsworthian touch at the end. "The grandeur, the amazing melancholy of this picture cannot be expressed in human language; the fairest night of Europe can give no conception of it. In vain in our cultivated fields does the imagination seek to extend itself. It encounters on every hand the habitations of men; but in these savage regions the soul takes delight in plunging into an ocean of forests, in hovering over the gulf of cataracts, in meditating on the shores of lakes and rivers and, so to speak, in finding itself alone in the presence of God." The relation between wild and solitary nature and the romantic idea of the infinite is here obvious. It is an aid to the spirit in throwing off its limitations and so in feeling itself "free." [21]

A greater spiritual elevation it is sometimes asserted is found in Wordsworth's communings with nature than in those of Rousseau and Chateaubriand. The difference perhaps is less one of spirit than of temperament. In its abdication of the intellectual and critical faculties, in its semi-dissolution of the conscious self, the revery of Wordsworth does not differ from that of Rousseau[22] and Chateaubriand, but the erotic element is absent. In the "Genius of Christianity" Chateaubriand gives a magnificent description of sunset at sea and turns the whole picture into a proof of God. Elsewhere he tells us that it was "not God alone that I contemplated on the waters in the splendor of his works. I saw an unknown woman and the miracle of her smile. . . . I should have sold eternity for one of her caresses. I imagined that she was palpitating behind that veil of the universe that hid her from my eyes," etc. Wordsworth was at least consistently religious in his attitude towards the landscape: he did not see in it at one moment God, and at another an unknown woman and the miracle of her smile. At the same time his idea of spirituality is very remote from the traditional conception. Formerly spirituality was held to be a process of recollection, of gathering one's self in, that is, towards the centre and not of diffusive emotion; so that when a man wished to pray he retired into his closet, and did not, like a Wordsworth or a Rousseau, fall into an inarticulate ecstasy before the wonders of nature. As for the poets of the past, they inclined as a rule to look on nature as an incentive not to religion but to love. Keble, following Wordsworth, protests on this ground against Aristophanes, and Catullus and Horace and Theocritus. He might have lengthened the list almost indefinitely. Chateaubriand bids us in our devotional moods to betake ourselves "to the religious forest." La Fontaine is at least as near to normal human experience and also at least as poetical when he warns "fair ones" to "fear the depths of the woods and their vast silence." [23]

No one would question that Wordsworth has passages of great ethical elevation. But in some of these passages he simply renews the error of the Stoics who also display at times great ethical elevation; he ascribes to the natural order virtues that the natural order does not give. This error persists to some extent even when he is turning away, as in the "Ode to Duty," from the moral spontaneity of the Rousseauist. It is not quite clear that the law of duty in the breast of man is the same law that preserves "the stars from wrong." His earlier assertion that the light of setting suns and the mind of man are identical in their essence is at best highly speculative, at least as speculative as the counter assertion of Sir Thomas Browne that "there is surely a piece of divinity in us; something that was before the elements, and owes no homage unto the sun." Furthermore this latter sense of the gap between man and nature seems to be more fully justified by its fruits in life and conduct, and this is after all the only test that counts in the long run.

One of the reasons why pantheistic revery has been so popular is that it seems to offer a painless substitute for genuine spiritual effort. In its extreme exponents, a Rousseau or a Walt Whitman, it amounts to a sort of ecstatic animality that sets up as a divine illumination. Even in its milder forms it encourages one to assume a tone of consecration in speaking of experiences that are æsthetic rather than truly religious. " 'T is only heaven that's given away," sings Lowell; " 'T is only God may be had for the asking." God and heaven are accorded by Lowell with such strange facility because he identifies them with the luxurious enjoyment of a "day in June." When pushed to a certain point the nature cult always tends towards sham spirituality.

> Oh World as God has made it
> —All is beauty,
> And knowing this is love, and
> Love is duty.

It seems to follow from these verses of Browning, perhaps the most flaccid spiritually in the English language, that to go out and mix one's self up with the landscape is the same as doing one's duty. As a method of salvation this is even easier and more æsthetic than that of the Ancient Mariner, who, it will be remembered, is relieved of the burden of his transgression by admiring the color of water-snakes!

The nature cult arose at a time when the traditional religious symbols were becoming incredible. Instead of working out new and firm distinctions between good and evil, the Rousseauist seeks to discredit all precise distinctions whether new or old, in favor of mere emotional intoxication. The passage to which I have already alluded, in which Faust breaks down the scruples of Marguerite by proclaiming the supremacy of feeling, surpasses even the lines I have cited from Browning as an example of sham spirituality:

Marguerite: *Dost thou believe in God?*
Faust: *My darling, who dares say,*
Yes, I in God believe?
Question or priest or sage, and they
Seem, in the answer you receive,
To mock the questioner.
Marguerite: *Then thou dost not believe?*
Faust: *Sweet one! my meaning do not misconceive!*
Him who dare name
And who proclaim,
Him I believe?
Who that can feel,
His heart can steel
To say: I believe him not?
The All-embracer,
All-sustainer,
Holds and sustains he not
Thee, me, himself?
Lifts not the Heaven its dome above?
Doth not the firm-set earth beneath us lie?
And beaming tenderly with looks of love
Climb not the everlasting stars on high?
Do I not gaze into thine eyes?
Nature's impenetrable agencies,
Are they not thronging on thy heart and brain,
Viewless, or visible to mortal ken,
Around thee weaving their mysterious chain?
Fill thence thy heart, how large soe'er it be;
And in the feeling when thou utterly art blest,
Then call it what thou wilt—
Call it Bliss! Heart! Love! God!
I have no name for it!
Feeling is all;
Name is but sound and smoke
Shrouding the glow of heaven.[24]

The upshot of this enthusiasm that overflows all boundaries and spurns definition as mere smoke that veils its heavenly glow is the seduction of a poor peasant girl. Such is the romantic contrast between the "ideal" and the "real."

Those to whom I may seem to be treating the nature cult with undue severity should remember that I am treating it only in its pseudo-religious aspect. In its proper place all this refining on man's relation to the "outworld" may be legitimate and delightful; but that place is secondary. My quarrel is only with the æsthete who assumes an apocalyptic pose and gives forth as a profound philosophy what is at best only a holiday or week-end view of existence. No distinction is more important for any one who wishes to maintain a correct scale of values than that between what is merely recreative and what ministers to leisure. There are times when we may properly seek solace and renewal in nature, when we may invite both our souls and our bodies to loaf. The error is to look on these moments of recreation and relief from concentration on some definite end as in themselves the consummation of wisdom. Rousseau indeed assumes that his art of mixing himself up with the landscape is identical with leisure; like innumerable disciples he confuses revery with meditation—a confusion so grave that I shall need to revert to it later. He parodies subtly what is above the ordinary rational level in terms of what is below it. He thus brings under suspicion the most necessary of all truths—that the kingdom of heaven is within us.

The first place always belongs to action and purpose and not to mere idling, even if it be like that of the Rousseauist transcendental idling. The man who makes a deliberate choice and then plans his life with reference to it is less likely than the aimless man to be swayed by every impulse and impression. The figures of Raphael according to Hazlitt have always "a set, determined, voluntary character," they "want that wild uncertainty of expression which is connected with the accidents of nature and the changes of the elements." And Hazlitt therefore concludes rightly that Raphael has "nothing romantic about him." The distinction is so important that it might be made the basis for a comparison between the painting of the Renaissance and some of the important schools of the nineteenth century. Here again no sensible person would maintain that the advantage is all on one side. Romanticism gave a great impulse to landscape painting and to the painting of man in the landscape. Few romantic gains are more indubitable. One may prefer the best work of the Barbizon school for example to the contemporary product in French literature. But even here it must be insisted that painting from which man is absent or in which he is more or less subordinated to the landscape is not the highest type of painting. Turner, one of the greatest masters of landscape, was almost incapable of painting the human figure. Ruskin is therefore indulging in romantic paradox when he puts Turner in the same class as Shakespeare. Turner's vision of life as compared with that of Shakespeare is not central but peripheral.

The revolution that has resulted from the triumph of naturalistic over humanistic tendencies in painting extends down to the minutest details of technique; it has meant the subordination of design—the imposition, that is, on one's material of a firm central purpose—to light and color; and this in painting corresponds to the literary pursuit of glamour and illusion for their own sake. It has meant in general a tendency to sacrifice all the other elements of painting to the capture of the vivid and immediate impression. And this corresponds to the readiness of the writer to forego decorum in favor of intensity. The choice that is involved, including a choice of technique, according as one is a naturalist or a humanist, is brought out by Mr. Kenyon Cox in his comparison of two paintings of hermits,[25] one by Titian and one by John Sargent: the impressionistic and pantheistic hermit of Sargent is almost entirely merged in the landscape; he is little more than a pretext for a study of the accidents of light. The conception of Titian's St. Jerome in the Desert is perhaps even more humanistic than religious. The figure of the saint on which everything converges is not merely robust, it is even a bit robustious. The picture affirms in its every detail the superior importance of man and his purposes to his natural environment. So far as their inner life is concerned the two hermits are plainly moving in opposite directions. An appropriate motto for Sargent's hermit would be the following lines that I take from a French symbolist, but the equivalent of which can be found in innumerable other Rousseauists:

> *Je voudrais me confondre avec les choses, tordre*
> *Mes bras contre la pierre et les fraîches écorces,*
> *Etre l'arbre, le mur, le pollen et le sel,*
> *Et me dissoudre au fond de l'être universel.*

This is to push the reciprocity between man and nature to a point where the landscape is not only a state of the soul but the soul is a state of the landscape; just as in Shelley's Ode, Shelley becomes the West Wind and the West Wind becomes Shelley.[26] The changes in the romantic soul are appropriately mirrored in the change of the seasons. In Tieck's "Genoveva," for example, Golo's love blossoms in the springtime, the sultry summer impels him to sinful passion, the autumn brings grief and repentance, and in winter avenging judgment overtakes the offender and casts him into the grave.[27] Autumn is perhaps even more than springtime the favorite season of the Rousseau-ist. The movement is filled with souls who like the hero of Poe's "Ulalume" have reached the October of their sensations. Some traces of this sympathetic relation between man and nature may indeed be found in the literature of the past. The appropriateness of the setting in the "Prometheus Bound" of Æschylus would scarcely seem to be an accident. The storm in "Lear" may also be instanced. But as I have already said occidental man did not before Rousseau show much inclination to mingle with the landscape. The parallelism that Pater establishes in "Marius the Epicurean" between the moods of the hero and the shifting aspects of nature is felt as a distinct anachronism. If we wish to find any early approximations to the subtleties and refinements of the Rousseauist in his dealings with nature we need to turn to the Far East—especially to the Taoist movement in China.[28] As a result of the Taoist influence China had from a very early period poets and painters for whom the landscape is very plainly a state of the soul.

Pantheistic revery of the kind I have been describing leads inevitably to a special type of symbolism. The Rousseauist reads into nature unutterable love. He sees shining through its finite forms the light of the infinite. The Germans especially set out to express symbolically the relationship between the love and infinitude that they saw in nature and the kindred elements in themselves. Any one who has attempted to thread his way through the German theories of the symbol will feel that he has, like Wordsworth's shepherd, "been in the heart of many thousand mists." But in view of the importance of the subject it is necessary to venture for a moment into this metaphysical murk. Schelling's "Nature Philosophy" is perhaps the most ambitious of all the German attempts to run together symbolically the human spirit and phenomenal nature. "What we call nature," says Schelling, "is a poem that lies hidden in a secret wondrous writing"; if the riddle could be revealed we should recognize in nature "the Odyssey of the Spirit." "There looks out through sensuous objects as through a half-transparent mist the world of phantasy for which we long." "All things are only a garment of the world of spirit." "To be romantic," says Uhland, "is to have an inkling of the infinite in appearances." "Beauty," says Schelling in similar vein, "is a finite rendering of the infinite." Now the infinite and the finite can only be thus brought together through the medium of the symbol. Therefore, as A. W. Schlegel says, "beauty is a symbolical representation of the infinite. All poetry is an everlasting symbolizing."

This assertion is in an important sense true. Unfortunately there remains the ambiguity that I have already pointed out in the word "infinite." No one would give a high rating to a certain type of allegory that flourished in neo-classical times as also in a somewhat different form during the Middle Ages. It is a cold intellectual contrivance in which the imagination has little part and which therefore fails to suggest the infinite in any sense. But to universalize the particular in the classical sense is to give access imaginatively to the human infinite that is set above nature. Every successful humanistic creation is more or less symbolical. Othello is not merely a jealous man; he is also a symbol of jealousy. Some of the myths of Plato again are imaginative renderings of a supersensuous realm to which man has no direct access. They are symbolical representations of an infinite that the romanticist leaves out of his reckoning. The humanistic and spiritual symbols that abound in the religion and poetry of the past are then, it would seem, very different from the merely æsthetic symbolizing of a Schelling. For Schelling is one of the chief of those who from Shaftesbury down have tended to identify beauty and truth and to make both purely æsthetic. But a symbol that is purely æsthetic, that is in other words purely a matter of feeling, rests on what is constantly changing not only from man to man but in the same man. Romantic symbolism, therefore, though it claims at one moment to be scientific (especially in Germany) and at another moment to have a religious value, is at bottom the symbolizing of mood. Both the imagination and the emotion that enter into the romantic symbol are undisciplined The results of such a symbolism do not meet the demand of the genuine man of science for experimental proof, they do not again satisfy the test of universality imposed by those who believe in a distinctively human realm that is set above nature. The nature philosophy of a Schelling leads therefore on the one hand to sham science and on the other to sham philosophy and religion.

The genuine man of science has as a matter of fact repudiated the speculations of Schelling and other romantic physicists as fantastic. He may also be counted on to look with suspicion on the speculations of a Bergson who, more perhaps than any living Rousseauist, reminds one of the German romantic philosophers. One idea has however lingered in the mind even of the genuine man of science as a result of all this romantic theorizing—namely that man has access to the infinite only through nature. Thus Professor Henry Fairfield Osborn said in a recent address to the students of Columbia University:

I would not for a moment take advantage of the present opportunity to discourage the study of human nature and of the humanities, but for what is called the best opening for a constructive career give me nature. The ground for my preference is that human nature is an exhaustible fountain of research; Homer understood it well; Solomon fathomed it; Shakespeare divined it, both normal and abnormal; the modernists have been squeezing out the last drops of abnormality. Nature, studied since Aristotle's time, is still full to the brim; no perceptible falling of its tides is evident from any point at which it is attacked, from nebulæ to protoplasm; it is always wholesome, refreshing and invigorating. Of the two most creative literary artists of our time, Maeterlinck, jaded with human abnormality, comes back to the bee and the flowers and the "blue bird," with a delicious renewal of youth, while Rostand turns to the barnyard.

The romanticists acted from the start, following here in the wake of the pseudo-classicists, on Professor Osborn's assumption that normal human nature is something that may be bottled up once for all and put by on a shelf, though they would have been pained to learn from him that even abnormal human nature may also be bottled up and put by in the same fashion. Sophistries of this kind should perhaps be pardoned in the man of science when so many men who are supposed to stand for letters have shown him the way. Great literature is an imaginative and symbolical interpretation of an infinite that is accessible only to those who possess in some degree the same type of imagination. A writer like Maeterlinck, whom Professor Osborn takes to be representative of literature in general, is merely a late exponent of a movement that from the start turned away from this human infinite towards pantheistic revery.

The imagination is, as Coleridge says, the great unifying power; it draws together things that are apparently remote. But its analogies to be of value should surely have validity apart from the mere shifting mood of the man who perceives them. Otherwise he simply wrests some outer object from the chain of cause and effect of which it is actually a part, and incorporates it arbitrarily into his own private dream. Wordsworth is not sparing of homely detail in his account of his leech-gatherer; but at a given moment in this poem the leech-gatherer undergoes a strange transformation; he loses all verisimilitude as a leech-gatherer and becomes a romantic symbol, a mere projection, that is, of the poet's own broodings. To push this symbolizing of mood beyond a certain point is incipient hallucination. We are told that when the asylum at Charenton was shelled in the Franco-Prussian War of 1870, the lunatics saw reflected in the bursting bombs, each in a different way, his own madness. One took the bombs to be a link in the plot of his enemies against him, etc. It is hard to consider the symbolizing and visions of the extreme romanticist, such as those of William Blake, without thinking at times of Charenton.

What I have said of the romantic symbol is true in some degree of the romantic metaphor, for the symbol and even the myth are often only a developed metaphor. The first part of the romantic metaphor, the image or impression that has been received from the outer world, is often admirably fresh and vivid.[29] But the second part of the metaphor when the analogy involved is that between some fact of outer perception and the inner life of man is often vague and misty; for the inner life in which the romanticist takes interest is not the life he possesses in common with other men but what is most unique in his own emotions—his mood in short. That is why the metaphor and still more the symbol in so far as they are romantic are always in danger of becoming unintelligible, since it is not easy for one man to enter into another's mood. Men accord a ready welcome to metaphors and symbols that instead of expressing something more or less individual have a real relevancy to their common nature. Tribulation, for example, means literally the beating out of grain on the threshing floor. The man who first saw the analogy between this process and certain spiritual experiences established a legitimate link between nature and human nature, between sense and the supersensuous. Language is filled with words and expressions of this kind which have become so current that their metaphorical and symbolical character has been forgotten and which have at the same time ceased to be vivid and concrete and become abstract.

The primitivistic fallacies of the German romanticists in their dealings with the symbol and metaphor appear in various forms in French romanticism and even more markedly in its continuation known as the symbolistic movement. What is exasperating in many of the poets of this school is that they combine the pretence to a vast illumination with the utmost degree of spiritual and intellectual emptiness and vagueness. Like the early German romanticists they mix up flesh and spirit in nympholeptic longing and break down and blur all the boundaries of being in the name of the infinite. Of this inner formlessness and anarchy the chaos of the *vers libre* (in which they were also anticipated by the Germans) is only an outer symptom.[30]

If the Rousseauistic primitivist recognizes the futility of his symbolizing, and consents to become a passive register of outer perception, if for example he proclaims himself an imagist, he at least has the merit of frankness, but in that case he advertises by the very name he has assumed the bankruptcy of all that is most worth while in poetry.

But to return to romanticism and nature. It should be plain from what has already been said that the romanticist tends to make of nature the mere plaything of his mood. When Werther's mood is cheerful, nature smiles at him benignly. When his mood darkens, she becomes for him "a devouring monster." When it grows evident to the romanticist that nature does not alter with his alteration, he chides her at times for her impassibility; or again he seeks to be impassible like her, even if he can be so only at the expense of his humanity. This latter attitude is closely connected with the dehumanizing of man by science that is reflected in a whole literature during the last half of the nineteenth century—for instance, in so-called "impassive" writers like Flaubert and Leconte de Lisle.

The causal sequences that had been observed in the physical realm were developed more and more during this period with the aid of pure mathematics and the mathematical reason (*es-prit de géométrie*) into an all-embracing system. For the earlier romanticists nature had at least been a living presence whether benign or sinister. For the mathematical determinist she tends to become a soulless, pitiless mechanism against which man is helpless.[31] This conception of nature is so important that I shall need to revert to it in my treatment of melancholy.

The man who has accepted the universe of the mechanist or determinist is not always gloomy. But men in general felt the need of some relief from the deterministic obsession. Hence the success of the philosophy of Bergson and similar philosophies. The glorification of impulse (*élan vital*) that Bergson opposes to the mechanizing of life is in its main aspects, as I have already indicated, simply a return to the spontaneity of Rousseau. His plan of escape from deterministic science is at bottom very much like Rousseau's plan of escape from the undue rationalism of the Enlightenment. As a result of these eighteenth-century influences, nature had, according to Carlyle, become a mere engine, a system of cogs and pulleys. He therefore hails Novalis as an "anti-mechanist," a "deep man," because of the way of deliverance that he teaches from this nightmare. "I owe him somewhat." What Carlyle owed to Novalis many moderns have owed to Bergson, but it is not yet clear that either Novalis or Bergson are "deep men."

The mechanistic view of nature, whether held pessimistically or optimistically, involving as it does factors that are infinite and therefore beyond calculation, cannot furnish proofs that will satisfy the true positivist: he is inclined to dismiss it as a mere phantasmagoria of the intellect. The Rousseau-istic view of nature, on the other hand, whether held optimistically or pessimistically, is even less capable of satisfying the standards of the positivist and must be dismissed as a mere phantasmagoria of the emotions. The fact is that we do not know and can never know what nature is in herself. The mysterious mother has shrouded herself from us in an impenetrable veil of illusion. But though we cannot know nature absolutely we can pick up a practical and piecemeal knowledge of nature not by dreaming but by doing. The man of action can within certain limits have his way with nature. Now the men who have acted during the past century have been the men of science and the utilitarians who have been turning to account the discoveries of science. The utilitarians have indeed derived such potent aid from science that they have been able to stamp their efforts on the very face of the landscape. The romanticists have not ceased to protest against this scientific utilizing of nature as a profanation. But inasmuch as these protests have come from men who have stood not for work but for revery they have for the most part been futile. This is not the least of the ironic contrasts that abound in this movement between the ideal and the real. No age ever grew so ecstatic over natural beauty as the nineteenth century, at the same time no age ever did so much to deface nature. No age ever so exalted the country over the town, and no age ever witnessed such a crowding into urban centres.

A curious study might be made of this ironic contrast as it appears in the early romantic crusade against railways. One of the romantic grievances against the railway is that it does not encourage vagabondage: it has a definite goal and gets to it so far as possible in a straight line. Yet in spite of Wordsworth's protesting sonnet the Windermere railway was built. Ruskin's wrath at railways was equally vain. In general, sentiment is not of much avail when pitted against industrial advance. The papers announced recently that one of the loveliest cascades in the California Sierras had suddenly disappeared as a result of the diversion of its water to a neighboring power-plant. The same fate is overtaking Niagara itself. It is perhaps symbolic that a quarry has made a hideous gash in the hillside on the shores of Rydal Mere right opposite Wordsworth's house.

If the man of science and the utilitarian do not learn what nature is in herself they learn at least to adjust themselves to forces outside themselves. The Rousseauist, on the other hand, does not in his "communion" with nature adjust himself to anything. He is simply communing with his own mood. Rousseau chose appropriately as title for the comedy that was his first literary effort "Narcissus or the Lover of Himself." The nature over which the Rousseauist is bent in such rapt contemplation plays the part of the pool in the legend of Narcissus. It renders back to him his own image. He sees in nature what he himself has put there. The Rousseauist transfuses himself into nature in much the same way that Pygmalion transfuses himself into his statue. Nature is dead, as Rousseau says, unless animated by the fires of love. "Make no mistake," says M. Masson, "the nature that Jean-Jacques worships is only a projection of Jean-Jacques. He has poured himself forth so complacently upon it that he can always find himself and cherish himself in it." And M. Masson goes on and quotes from a curious and little-known fragment of Rousseau: "Beloved solitude," Rousseau sighs, "beloved solitude, where I still pass with pleasure the remains of a life given over to suffering. Forest with stunted trees, marshes without water, broom, reeds, melancholy heather, inanimate objects, you who can neither speak to me nor hear me, what secret charm brings me back constantly into your midst? Unfeeling and dead things, this charm is not in you; it could not be there. It is in my own heart which wishes to refer back everything to itself." [32] Coleridge plainly only continues Rousseau when he writes:

> *O Lady! we receive but what we give,*
> *And in our life alone does nature live:* [33]
> *Ours is her wedding-garment, ours her shroud!*

> *And would we aught behold, of higher worth,*
> *Than that inanimate cold world allow'd*
> *To the poor loveless ever-anxious crowd,*
> *Ah! from the soul itself must issue forth*
> *A light, a glory, a fair luminous cloud*
> *Enveloping the Earth.*

The fair luminous cloud is no other than the Arcadian imagination. "The light that never was on sea or land, the consecration and the poet's dream" of which Wordsworth speaks, is likewise as appears very plainly from the context,[34] Arcadian. He should once, Wordsworth writes, have wished to see Peele Castle bathed in the Arcadian light, but now that he has escaped by sympathy for his fellow-men from the Arcadian aloofness, he is willing that it should be painted in storm. Mere storminess, one should recollect, is not in itself an assurance that one has turned from the romantic dream to reality. One finds in this movement, if nowhere else, as I remarked apropos of Chateaubriand, the stormy Arcadia.

It is not through the Arcadian imagination that one moves towards reality. This does not much matter if what one seeks in a "return to nature" is merely recreation. I cannot repeat too often that I have no quarrel with the nature cult when it remains recreative but only when it sets up as a substitute for philosophy and religion. This involves a confusion between the two main directions of the human spirit, a confusion as I have said in a previous chapter between the realm of awe and the region of wonder. Pascal exaggerates somewhat when he says the Bible never seeks to prove religion from the "wonders" of nature. But this remark is true to the total spirit of the Bible. A knowledge of the flowers of the Holy Land is less necessary for an understanding of the gospel narrative than one might suppose from Renan.[35] Renan is simply seeking to envelop Jesus so far as possible in an Arcadian atmosphere. In so doing he is following in the footsteps of the great father of sentimentalists. According to M. Masson, Jesus, as depicted by Jean-Jacques, becomes "a sort of grand master of the Golden Age."

Here as elsewhere the Rousseauist is seeking to identify the Arcadian view of life with wisdom. The result is a series of extraordinarily subtle disguises for egoism. We think we see the Rousseauist prostrate before the ideal woman or before nature or before God himself, but when we look more closely we see that he is only (as Sainte-Beuve said of Alfred de Vigny) "in perpetual adoration before the holy sacrament of himself." The fact that he finds in nature only what he has put there seems to be for Rousseau himself a source of satisfaction. But the poem of Coleridge I have just quoted, in which he proclaims that so far as nature is concerned "we receive but what we give," is entitled "Ode to Dejection." One of man's deepest needs would seem to be for genuine communion, for a genuine escape, that is, from his ordinary self. The hollowness of the Rousseauistic communion with nature as well as other Rousseauistic substitutes for genuine communion is indissolubly bound up with the subject of romantic melancholy.

CHAPTER NINE

ROMANTIC MELANCHOLY

Rousseau and his early followers—especially perhaps his early French followers—were very much preoccupied with the problem of happiness. Now in a sense all men—even those who renounce the world and mortify the flesh—aim at happiness. The important point to determine is what any particular person means by happiness and how he hopes to attain it. It should be plain from all that has been said that the Rousseauist seeks happiness in the free play of the emotions. The "Influence of the Passions on Happiness" is the significant title of one of Madame de Staël's early treatises. The happiness that the Rousseauist seeks involves not merely a free play of feeling but—what is even more important—a free play of the imagination. Feeling acquires a sort of infinitude as a result of this coöperation of the imagination, and so the romanticist goes, as we have seen, in quest of the thrill superlative, as appears so clearly in his nympholepsy, his pursuit of the "impossible she." But the more imaginative this quest for emotional happiness grows the more it tends to become a mere nostalgia. Happiness is achieved so far as it is achieved at all in dreamland. Rousseau says of himself: *Mon plus constant bonheur fut en songe.* Every finite satisfaction by the very fact that it is finite leaves him unsatisfied. René says that he had exhausted soli-

tude as he had exhausted society: they had both failed to satisfy his insatiable desires. René plainly takes his insatiableness
to be the badge of his spiritual distinction. To submit to any
circumscribing of one's desires is to show that one has no sense
of infinitude and so to sink to the level of the philistine.

But does one become happy by being nostalgic and hyperæsthetic, by burning with infinite indeterminate desire? We
have here perhaps the chief irony and contradiction in the
whole movement. The Rousseauist seeks happiness and yet on
his own showing, his mode of seeking it results, not in happiness but in wretchedness. One finds indeed figures in the
nineteenth century, a Browning, for example, who see in life
first of all an emotional adventure and then carry this adventure through to the end with an apparently unflagging
gusto. On may affirm nevertheless that a movement which
began by asserting the goodness of man and the loveliness
of nature ended by producing the greatest literature of despair
the world has ever seen. No movement has perhaps been so
prolific of melancholy as emotional romanticism. To follow it
from Rousseau down to the present day is to run through the
whole gamut of gloom.[1]

> *Infections of unutterable sadness,*
> *Infections of incalculable madness,*
> *Infections of incurable despair.*

According to a somewhat doubtful authority, Ninon de
Lenclos, "the joy of the spirit measures its force." When the
romanticist on the other hand discovers that his ideal of happiness works out into actual unhappiness he does not blame his
ideal. He simply assumes that the world is unworthy of a being so exquisitely organized as himself, and so shrinks back
from it and enfolds himself in his sorrow as he would in a
mantle. Since the superlative bliss that he craves eludes him, he
will at least be superlative in woe. So far from being a mark
of failure this woe measures his spiritual grandeur. "A great
soul," as René says, "must contain more grief than a small
one." The romantic poets enter into a veritable competition
with one another as to who shall be accounted the most for-

lorn. The victor in this competition is awarded the palm not merely for poetry but for wisdom. In the words of Arnold:

> *Amongst us one*
> *Who most has suffered, takes dejectedly*
> *His seat upon the intellectual throne;*
> *And all his store of sad experience he*
> *Lays bare of wretched days.*
> *Tells us his misery's birth and growth and signs,*
> *And how the dying spark of hope was fed,*
> *And how the breast was soothed, and how the head,*
> *And all his hourly varied anodynes.*
>
> *This for our wisest! and we others pine,*
> *And wish the long unhappy dream would end,*
> *And waive all claim to bliss, and try to bear;*
> *With close-lipped patience for our only friend,*
> *Sad patience, too near neighbor to despair.*

Though Arnold may in this poem, as some one has complained, reduce the muse to the rôle of hospital nurse, he is, like his master Senancour, free from the taint of theatricality. He does not, as he said of Byron, make "a pageant of his bleeding heart"; and the Byronic pose has a close parallel in the pose of Chateaubriand. An Irish girl at London once told Chateaubriand that "he carried his heart in a sling." He himself said that he had a soul of the kind "the ancients called a sacred malady."

Chateaubriand, to be sure, had his cheerful moments and many of them. His sorrows he bestowed upon the public. Herein he was a true child of Jean-Jacques. We are told by eye-witnesses how heartily Rousseau enjoyed many aspects of his life at Motiers-Travers. On his own showing, he was plunged during this period in almost unalloyed misery. Froude writes of Carlyle: "It was his peculiarity that if matters were well with himself, it never occurred to him that they could be going ill with any one else; and, on the other hand, if he was uncomfortable, he required everybody to be uncomfortable along with him." We can follow clear down to Gissing the assumption in some form or other that "art must be the mouth-piece of misery." This whole question as to the proper function of art goes to the root of the debate between the classicist and the Rousseauist. "All these poets," Goethe complains to Eckermann of the romanticists of 1830, "write as though they were ill, and as though the whole world were a hospital. . . . Every one of them in writing tries to be more desolate than all the others. This is really an abuse of poetry which has been given to make man satisfied with the world and with his lot. But the present generation is afraid of all solid energy; its mind is at ease and sees poetry only in weakness. I have found a good expression to vex these gentlemen. I am going to call their poetry hospital poetry." [2]

Now Goethe is here, like Chateaubriand, mocking to some degree his own followers. When he suffered from a spiritual ailment of any kind he got rid of it by inoculating others with it; and it was in this way, as we learn from his Autobiography, that he got relief from the *Weltschmerz* of "Werther." But later in life Goethe was classical not merely in precept like Chateaubriand, but to some extent in practice. The best of the poetry of his maturity tends like that of the ancients to elevate and console.

The contrast between classic and romantic poetry in this matter of melancholy is closely bound up with the larger contrast between imitation and spontaneity. Homer is the greatest of poets, according to Aristotle, because he does not entertain us with his own person but is more than any other poet an imitator. The romantic poet writes, on the other hand, as Lamartine says he wrote, solely for the "relief of his heart." He pours forth himself—his most intimate and private self; above all, his anguish and his tears. In his relation to his reader, as Musset tells us in a celebrated image,[3] he is like the pelican who rends and lacerates his own flesh to provide nourishment for his young (*Pour toute nourriture il apporte son cœur*):

> *Les plus désespérés sont les chants les plus beaux,*
> *Et j'en sais d'immortels qui sont de purs sanglots.*[4]

To make of poetry a spontaneous overflow of powerful emotion, usually of sorrowful emotion, is what the French understand by lyricism (*le lyrisme*); and it may be objected that it is not fair to compare an epic poet like Homer with a lyricist like Musset. Let us then take for our comparison the poet whom the ancients themselves looked upon as the supreme type of the lyricist—Pindar. He is superbly imaginative, "sailing," as Gray tells us, "with supreme dominion through the azure deep of air," but his imagination is not like that of Musset in the service of sensibility. He does not bestow his own emotions upon us but is rather in the Aristotelian sense an imitator. He is indeed at the very opposite pole from Rousseau and the "apostles of affliction." "Let a man," he says, "not darken delight in his life." "Disclose not to strangers our burden of care; this at least shall I advise thee. Therefore is it fitting to show openly to all the folk the fair and pleasant things allotted us; but if any baneful misfortune sent of heaven befalleth man, it is seemly to shroud this in darkness." [5] And one should also note Pindar's hostility towards that other great source of romantic lyricism—nostalgia ("The desire of the moth for the star"), and the closely allied pursuit of the strange and the exotic. He tells of the condign punishment visited by Apollo upon the girl Coronis who became enamoured of "a strange man from Arcadia," and adds: "She was in love with things remote—that passion which many ere now have felt. For among men, there is a foolish company of those who, putting shame on what they have at home, cast their glances afar, and pursue idle dreams in hopes that shall not be fulfilled." [6]

We are not to suppose that Pindar was that most tiresome and superficial of all types—the professional optimist who insists on inflicting his "gladness" upon us. "The immortals," he says, "apportion to man two sorrows for every boon they grant." [7] In general the Greek whom Kipling sings and whom we already find in Schiller—the Greek who is an incarnation of the "joy of life unquestioned, the everlasting wondersong of youth" [8]—is a romantic myth. We read in the Iliad:[9] "Of all the creatures that breathe or crawl upon the earth, none is more wretched than man." Here is the "joy of life unquestioned" in Homer. Like Homer the best of the later Greeks and Romans face unflinchingly the facts of life and these facts do not encourage a thoughtless elation. Their melancholy is even more concerned with the lot of man in general than with their personal and private grief. The quality of this melancholy is rendered in Tennyson's line on Virgil, one of the finest in nineteenth-century English poetry:

> *Thou majestic in thy sadness at the doubtful doom*
> *of human kind.*[10]

One should indeed not fail to distinguish between the note of melancholy in a Homer or a Virgil and the melancholy of the ancients, whether Stoic or Epicurean, who had experienced the hopelessness and helplessness of a pure naturalism in dealing with ultimate problems. The melancholy of the Stoic is the melancholy of the man who associates with the natural order a "virtue" that the natural order does not give, and so is tempted to exclaim at last with Brutus, that he had thought virtue a thing and had found that it was only a word. The melancholy of the Epicurean is that of the man who has tasted the bitter sediment (*amari aliquid*) in the cup of pleasure. It is not difficult to discover modern equivalents of both Stoic and Epicurean melancholy. "One should seek," says Sainte-Beuve, "in the pleasures of René the secret of his *ennuis*," and so far as this is true Chateaubriand is on much the same level as some Roman voluptuary who suffered from the *Tædium vitæ* in the time of Tiberius or Nero.[11] But though the Roman decadent gave himself up to the pursuit of sensation and often of violent and abnormal sensation, he was less prone than a Chateaubriand to associate this pursuit with the "infinite"; and so he was less nostalgic and hyperæsthetic. His Epicureanism was therefore less poetical no doubt, but on the other hand he did not set up mere romantic restlessness as a sort of substitute for religion. It was probably easier therefore for him to feel the divine discontent and so turn to real religion than it would have been if he had, like the Rousseauist, complicated his Epicureanism with sham spirituality.

To say that the melancholy even of the decadent ancient is less nostalgic is perhaps only another way of saying what I have said about the melancholy of the ancients in general—that it is not so purely personal. It derives less from his very private and personal illusions and still less from his very private and personal disillusions. In its purely personal quality romantic melancholy is indeed inseparable from the whole conception of original genius. The genius sets out not merely to be unique but unique in feeling, and the sense of uniqueness in feeling speedily passes over into that of uniqueness in suffering—on the principle no doubt laid down by Horace Walpole that life, which is a comedy for those who think, is a tragedy for those who feel. To be a beautiful soul, to preserve one's native goodness of feeling among men who have been perverted by society, is to be the elect of nature and yet this election turns out as Rousseau tells us to be a "fatal gift of heaven." It is only the disillusioned romanticist, however, who assumes this elegiac tone. We need to consider what he means by happiness while he still seeks for it in the actual world and not in the *pays des chimères*. Rousseau tells us that he based the sense of his own worth on the fineness of his powers of perception. Why should nature have endowed him with such exquisite faculties[12] if he was not to have a satisfaction commensurate with them, if he was "to die without having lived"? We have here the psychological origins of the right to happiness that the romanticists were to proclaim. "We spend on the passions," says Joubert, "the stuff that has been given us for happiness." The Rousseauist hopes to find his happiness in the passions themselves. Romantic happiness does not involve any moral effort and has been defined in its extreme forms as a "monstrous dream of passive enjoyment." Flaubert has made a study of the right to happiness thus understood in his "Madame Bovary." Madame Bovary, who is very commonplace in other respects, feels exquisitely; and inasmuch as her husband had no such fineness the right to happiness meant for her, as it did for so many other "misunderstood" women, the right to extramarital adventure. One should note the germs of melancholy that lurk in the quest of the superlative moment even if the quest is relatively successful. Suppose Saint-Preux had succeeded in compressing into a single instant "the delights of a thousand centuries"; and so far as outer circumstances are concerned had had to pay no penalty. The nearer the approach to a superhuman intensity of feeling the greater is likely to be the ensuing languor. The ordinary round of life seems pale and insipid compared with the exquisite and fugitive moment. One seems to one's self to have drained the cup of life at a draught and save perhaps for impassioned recollection of the perfect moment to have no reason for continuing to live. One's heart is "empty and swollen" [13] and one is haunted by thoughts of suicide.

This sense of having exhausted life[14] and the accompanying temptation to suicide that are such striking features of the malady of the age are not necessarily associated with any outer enjoyment at all. One may devour life in revery and then the melancholy arises from the disproportion between the dream and the fact. The revery that thus consumes life in advance is not necessarily erotic. What may be termed the cosmic revery of a Senancour or an Amiel [15] has very much the same effect.

The atony and aridity of which the sufferer from romantic melancholy complains may have other sources besides the depression that follows upon the achieving of emotional intensity whether in revery or in fact; it may also be an incident in the warfare between head and heart that assumes so many forms among the spiritual posterity of Jean-Jacques. The Rousseauist seeks happiness in emotional spontaneity and this spontaneity seems to be killed by the head which stands aloof and dissects and analyzes. Perhaps the best picture of the emotionalist who is thus incapacitated for a frank surrender to his own emotions is the "Adolphe" of Benjamin Constant (a book largely reminiscent of Constant's actual affair with Madame de Staël).

Whether the victim of romantic melancholy feels or analyzes he is equally incapable of action. He who faces resolutely the rude buffetings of the world is gradually hardened against them. The romantic movement is filled with the groans of those who have evaded action and at the same time become highly sensitive and highly self-conscious. The man who thrills more exquisitely to pleasure than another will also thrill more exquisitely to pain; nay, pleasure itself in its extreme is allied to pain;[16] so that to be hyperæsthetic is not an unmixed advantage especially if it be true, as Pindar says, that the Gods bestow two trials on a man for every boon. Perhaps the deepest bitterness is found not in those who make a pageant of their bleeding hearts, but in those who, like Leconte de Lisle[17] and others *(les impassibles)*, disdain to make a show of themselves to the mob, and so dissimulate their quivering sensibility under an appearance of impassibility; or, like Stendhal, under a mask of irony that "is imperceptible to the vulgar."

Stendhal aims not at emotional intensity only, but also glorifies the lust for power. He did as much as any one in his time to promote the ideal of the superman. Yet even if the superman has nerves of steel, as seems to have been the case with Stendhal's favorite, Napoleon, and acts on the outer world with a force of which the man in search of a sensation is quite incapable, he does not act upon himself, he remains ethically passive. This ethical passivity is the trait common to all those who incline to live purely on the naturalistic level—whether they sacrifice the human law and its demands for measure to the lust of knowledge or the lust of sensation or the lust of power. The man who neglects his ethical self and withdraws into his temperamental or private self must almost necessarily have the sense of isolation, of remoteness from other men. We return here to the psychology or the original genius to whom it was a tame and uninteresting thing to be simply human and who, disdaining to seem to others a being of the same clay as themselves, wished to be in their eyes either an angel or a demon— above all a demon.[18] René does not, as I have said,[19] want even the woman who loves him to feel at one with him, but rather to be at once astonished and appalled. He exercises upon those who approach him a malign fascination; for he not only lives in misery himself as in his natural element, but communicates this misery to those who approach him. He is like one of those fair trees under which one cannot sit without perishing. Moreover René disavows all responsibility for thus being a human Upas-tree. Moral effort is unavailing, for it was all written in the book of fate. The victim of romantic melancholy is at times tender and elegiac, at other times he sets up as a heaven-defying Titan. This latter pose became especially common in France around 1830 when the influence of Byron had been added to that of Chateaubriand. Under the influence of these two writers a whole generation of youth became "things of dark imaginings," [20] predestined to a blight that was at the same time the badge of their superiority. One wished like René to have an "immense, solitary and stormy soul," and also, like a Byronic hero, to have a diabolical glint in the eye and a corpse-like complexion,[21] and so seem the "blind and deaf agent of funereal mysteries." [22] "It was possible to believe everything about René except the truth." The person who delights in being as mysterious as this easily falls into mystification. Byron himself we are told was rather flattered by the rumor that he had committed at least one murder. Baudelaire, it has been said, displayed his moral gangrene as a warrior might display honorable wounds. This flaunting of his own perversity was part of the literary attitude he had inherited from the "Satanic School."

When the romanticist is not posing as the victim of fate he poses as the victim of society. Both ways of dodging moral responsibility enter into the romantic legend of the *poète maudit*. Nobody loves a poet. His own mother, according to Baudelaire, utters a malediction upon him.[23] That is because the poet feels so exquisitely that he is at once odious and unintelligible to the ordinary human pachyderm. Inasmuch as the philistine is not too sensitive to act he has a great advantage over the poet in the real world and often succeeds in driving him from it and indeed from the life itself. This inferiority in action is a proof of the poet's ideality. "His gigantic wings," as Baudelaire says, "keep him from walking." He has, in Coleridgean phrase, fed on "honey dew and drunk the milk of paradise," [24] and so can scarcely be expected to submit to a diet of plain prose. It is hardly necessary to say that great poets of the past have not been at war with their public in this way. The reason is that they were less taken up with the uttering of their own uniqueness; they were, without ceasing to be themselves, servants of the general sense.

Chatterton became for the romanticists a favorite type of the *poète maudit,* and his suicide a symbol of the inevitable defeat of the "ideal" by the "real." The first performance of Vigny's "Chatterton" (1835) with its picture of the implacable hatred of the philistine for the artist was received by the romantic youth of Paris with something akin to delirium. As Gautier says in his well-known account of this performance one could almost hear in the night the crack of the solitary pistols. The ordinary man of letters, says Vigny in his preface to this play, is sure of success, even the great writer may get a hearing, but the poet, a being who is on a far higher level than either, can look forward only to "perpetual martyrdom and immolation." He comes into the world to be a burden to others; his native sensibility is so intimate and profound that it "has plunged him from childhood into involuntary ecstasies, interminable reveries, infinite inventions. Imagination possesses him above all . . . it sweeps his faculties heavenward as irresistibly as the balloon carries up its car." From that time forth he is more or less cut off from normal contact with his fellowmen. "His sensibility has become too keen; what only grazes other men wounds him until he bleeds." He is thrown back more and more upon himself and becomes a sort of living volcano, "consumed by secret ardors and inexplicable languors," and incapable of self-guidance. Such is the poet. From his first appearance he is an outlaw. Let all your tears and all your pity be for him. If he is finally forced to suicide not he but society is to blame. He is like the scorpion that cruel boys surround with live coals and that is finally forced to turn his sting upon himself. Society therefore owes it to itself to see that this exquisite being is properly pensioned and protected by government, to the end that idealism may not perish from the earth. M. Thiers who was prime minister at that time is said to have received a number of letters from young poets, the general tenor of which was: "A position or I'll kill myself." [25]

A circumstance that should interest Americans is that Poe as interpreted by Baudelaire came to hold for a later generation of romanticists the place that Chatterton had held for the romanticists of 1830. Poe was actually murdered, says Baudelaire— and there is an element of truth in the assertion along with much exaggeration—by this great gas-lighted barbarity (i.e., America). All his inner and spiritual life, whether drunkard's or poet's, was one constant effort to escape from this antipathetic atmosphere "in which," Baudelaire goes on to say, "the impious love of liberty has given birth to a new tyranny, the tyranny of the beasts, a zoöcracy"; and in this human zoo a being with such a superhuman fineness of sensibility as Poe was of course at a hopeless disadvantage. In general our elation at Poe's recognition in Europe should be tempered by the reflection that this recognition is usually taken as a point of departure for insulting America. Poe is about the only hyperæsthetic romanticist we have had, and he therefore fell in with the main European tendency that comes down from the eighteenth century. Villiers de l'Isle-Adam, whom I have already cited as an extreme example of romantic idealism, was one of Poe's avowed followers; but Villiers is also related by his æsthetic and "diabolic" Catholicism to Chateaubriand; and the religiosity of Chateaubriand itself derives from the religiosity of Rousseau.

Hitherto I have been studying for the most part only one main type of modern melancholy. This type even in a Chateaubriand or a Byron and still more in their innumerable followers may seem at once superficial and theatrical. It often does not get beyond that Epicurean toying with sorrow, that luxury of grief, which was not unknown even to classical antiquity.[26] The despair of Chateaubriand is frequently only a disguise of his love of literary glory, and Chesterton is inclined to see in the Byronic gloom an incident of youth and high spirits.[27] But this is not the whole story even in Byron and Chateaubriand. To find what is both genuine and distinctive in romantic melancholy we need to enlarge a little further on the underlying difference between the classicist and the Rousseauist. The Rousseauist, as indeed the modern man in general, is more preoccupied with his separate and private self than the classicist. Modern melancholy has practically always this touch of isolation not merely because of the proneness of the "genius" to dwell on his own uniqueness, but also because of the undermining of the traditional communions by critical analysis. The noblest form of the "malady of the age" is surely that which supervened upon the loss of religious faith. This is what distinguishes the sadness of an Arnold or a Senancour from that of a Gray. The "Elegy" belongs to the modern movement by the humanitarian note, the sympathetic interest in the lowly, but in its melancholy it does not go much beyond the milder forms of classical meditation on the inevitable sadness of life— what one may term pensiveness. Like the other productions of the so-called graveyard school, it bears a direct relation to Milton's "Il Penseroso." It is well to retain Gray's own distinction. "Mine is a white Melancholy, or rather Leucocholy for the most part," he wrote to Richard West in 1742, "but there is another sort, black indeed, which I have now and then felt." Gray did not experience the more poignant sadness, one may suspect, without some loss of the "trembling hope" that is the final note of the "Elegy." No forlornness is greater than that of the man who has known faith and then lost it. Renan writes of his own break with the Church:

> The fish of Lake Baikal, we are told, have spent thousands of years in becoming fresh-water fish after being salt-water fish. I had to go through my transition in a few weeks. Like an enchanted circle Catholicism embraces the whole of life with so much strength that when one is deprived of it everything seems insipid. I was terribly lost. The universe produced upon me the impression of a cold and arid desert. For the moment that Christianity was not the truth, all the rest appeared to me indifferent, frivolous, barely worthy of interest. The collapse of my life upon itself left in me a feeling of emptiness like that which follows an attack of fever or an unhappy love-affair.[28]

The forlornness at the loss of faith is curiously combined in many of the romanticists with the mood of revolt. This type of romanticist heaps reproaches on a God in whose existence he no longer believes (as in Leconte de Lisle's "Quaïn," itself related to Byron's "Cain"). He shakes his fist at an empty heaven, or like Alfred de Vigny (in his *Jardin des Oliviers*) assumes towards this emptiness an attitude of proud disdain. He is loath to give up this grandiose defiance of divinity if only because it helps to save him from subsiding into platitude. A somewhat similar mood appears in the "Satanic" Catholics who continue to cling to religion simply because it adds to the gusto of sinning.[29] A Barbey succeeded in combining the rôle of Byronic Titan with that of champion of the Church. But in general the romantic Prometheus spurns the traditional forms of communion whether classical or Christian. He is so far as everything established is concerned enormously centrifugal, but he hopes to erect on the ruins of the past the new religion of human brotherhood. Everything in this movement from Shaftesbury down hinges on the rôle that is thus assigned to sympathy: if it can really unite men who are at the same

time indulging each to the utmost his own "genius" or idiosyncrasy there is no reason why one should not accept romanticism as a philosophy of life.

But nowhere else perhaps is the clash more violent between
the theory and the fact. No movement is so profuse in professions of brotherhood and none is so filled with the aching sense
of solitude. "Behold me then alone upon the earth," is the sentence with which Rousseau begins his last book;[30] and he goes
on to marvel that he, the "most loving of men," had been
forced more and more into solitude. "I am in the world as
though in a strange planet upon which I have fallen from the
one that I inhabited."[31] When no longer subordinated to something higher than themselves both the head and the heart (in
the romantic sense) not only tend to be opposed to one another, but also, each in its own way, to isolate. Empedocles was
used not only by Arnold but by other victims[32] of romantic
melancholy as a symbol of intellectual isolation: by his indulgence in the "imperious lonely thinking power" Empedocles
has broken the warm bonds of sympathy with his fellows:

> *thou art*
> *A living man no more, Empedocles!*
> *Nothing but a devouring flame of thought,—*
> *But a naked eternally restless mind!*

His leaping into Ætna typifies his attempt to escape from his
loneliness by a fiery union with nature herself.

According to religion one should seek to unite with a something that is set above both man and nature, whether this
something is called God as in Christianity or simply the Law
as in various philosophies of the Far East.[33] The most severe
penalty visited on the man who transgresses is that he tends
to fall away from this union. This is the element of truth in
the sentence of Diderot that Rousseau took as a personal affront: "Only the wicked man is alone." Rousseau asserted in
reply, anticipating Mark Twain,[34] that "on the contrary only
the good man is alone." Now in a sense Rousseau is right.
"Most men are bad," as one of the seven sages of Greece remarked, and any one who sets out to follow a very strenuous
virtue is likely to have few companions on the way. Rousseau

is also right in a sense when he says that the wicked man needs to live in society so that he may have opportunity to practice his wickedness. Yet Rousseau fails to face the main issue: solitude is above all a psychic thing. A man may frequent his fellows and suffer none the less acutely, like Poe's "Man of the Crowd," from a ghastly isolation. And conversely one may be like the ancient who said that he was never less alone than when he was alone.

Hawthorne, who was himself a victim of solitude, brooded a great deal on this whole problem, especially, as may be seen in the "Scarlet Letter" and elsewhere, on the isolating effects of sin. He perceived the relation of the problem to the whole trend of religious life in New England. The older Puritans had a sense of intimacy with God and craved no other companionship. With the weakening of their faith the later Puritans lost the sense of a divine companionship, but retained their aloofness from men. Hawthorne's own solution of the problem of solitude, so far as he offers any, is humanitarian. Quicken your sympathies. Let the man who has taken as his motto *Excelsior*[35] be warned. Nothing will console him on the bleak heights either of knowledge or of power for the warm contact with the dwellers in the valley. Faust, who is a symbol of the solitude of knowledge, seeks to escape from his forlornness by recovering this warm contact. That the inordinate quest of power also leads to solitude is beyond question. Napoleon, the very type of the superman, must in the nature of the case have been very solitary.[36] His admirer Nietzsche wrote one day: "I have forty-three years behind me and am as alone as if I were a child." Carlyle, whose "hero" derives like the superman from the original genius[37] of the eighteenth century, makes the following entry in his diary: "My isolation, my feeling of loneliness, unlimitedness (much meant by this) what tongue shall say? Alone, alone!" [38]

It cannot be granted, however, that one may escape by love, as the Rousseauist understands the word, from the loneliness that arises from the unlimited quest either of knowledge or power. For Rousseauistic love is also unlimited whether one understands by love either passion or a diffusive sympathy for mankind at large. "What solitudes are these human bodies,"

Musset exclaimed when fresh from his affair with George Sand. Wordsworth cultivated a love for the lowly that quite overflowed the bounds of neo-classic selection. It is a well-known fact that the lowly did not altogether reciprocate. "A desolate-minded man, ye kna," said an old inn-keeper of the Lakes to Canon Rawnsley, " 'T was potry as did it." If Wordsworth writes so poignantly of solitude one may infer that it is because he himself had experienced it.[39] Nor would it be difficult to show that the very philanthropic Ruskin was at least as solitary as Carlyle with his tirades against philanthropy.

I have spoken of the isolating effects of sin, but sin is scarcely the right word to apply to most of the romanticists. The solitude of which so many of them complain does, however, imply a good deal of spiritual inertia. Now to be spiritually inert, as I have said elsewhere, is to be temperamental, to indulge unduly the lust for knowledge or sensation or power without imposing on these lusts some centre or principle of control set above the ordinary self. The man who wishes to fly off on the tangent of his own temperament and at the same time enjoy communion on any except the purely material level is harboring incompatible desires. For temperament is what separates. A sense of unlimitedness ("much meant by this" as Carlyle says) and of solitude are simply the penalties visited upon the eccentric individualist. If we are to unite on the higher levels with other men we must look in another direction than the expansive outward striving of temperament: we must in either the humanistic or religious sense undergo conversion. We must pull back our temperaments with reference to the model that we are imitating, just as, in Aristotle's phrase, one might pull back and straighten out a crooked stick.[40] Usually the brake on temperament is supplied by the ethos, the convention of one's age and country. I have tried to show elsewhere that the whole programme of the eccentric individualist is to get rid of this convention, whatever it may be, without developing some new principle of control. The eccentric individualist argues that to accept control, to defer to some centre as the classicist demands, is to cease to be himself. But are restrictions upcn temperament so fatal to a man's being himself? The reply hinges upon the definition of the word self, inasmuch as man is a dual being. If a man is to escape from his isolation he must, I have said, aim at some goal set above his ordinary self which is at the same time his unique and separate self. But because this goal is set above his ordinary self, it is not therefore necessarily set above his total personality. The limitations that he imposes on his ordinary self may be the necessary condition of his entering into posession of his ethical self, the self that he possesses in common with other men. Aristotle says that if a man wishes to achieve happiness he must be a true lover of himself. It goes without saying that he means the ethical self. The author of a recent book on Ibsen says that Ibsen's message to the world is summed up in the line:

This above all,—to thine own selft be true.

It is abundantly plain from the context, however, that Polonius is a decayed Aristotelian and not a precursor of Ibsen. The self to which Aristotle would have a man be true is at the opposite pole from the self that Ibsen and the original geniuses are so eager to get uttered.

To impose the yoke of one's human self upon one's temperamental self is, in the Aristotelian sense, to work. Aristotle conceives of happiness in terms of work. All types of temperamentalists, on the other hand, are from the human point of view, passive. The happiness that they crave is a passive happiness. A man may pursue power with the energy of a Napoleon and yet remain ethically passive. He may absorb whole encyclopædias and remain ethically passive. He may expand his sympathies until, like Schiller, he is ready to "bestow a kiss upon the whole world" and yet remain ethically passive. A man ceases to be ethically passive only when he begins to work in the Aristotelian sense, that is when he begins to put the brake on temperament and impulse, and in the same degree he tends to become ethically efficient. By his denial of the dualism of the spirit, Rousseau discredited this inner working, so that inwardness has come to seem synonymous with mere subjectivity; and to be subjective in the Rousseauistic sense is to be diffusive, to lack purpose and concentration, to lose one's self in a shoreless sea of revery.

The utilitarian intervenes at this point and urges the romanticist, since he has failed to work inwardly, at least to work outwardly. Having missed the happiness of ethical efficiency he may in this way find the happiness of material efficiency, and at the same time serve the world. This is the solution of the problem of happiness that Goethe offers at the end of the Second Faust, and we may affirm without hesitation that it is a sham solution. To work outwardly and in the utilitarian sense, without the inner working that can alone save from ethical anarchy is to stimulate rather than repress the most urgent of all the lusts—the lust of power. It is only too plain that the unselective sympathy or joy in service with which Goethe would complete Faust's utilitarian activity is not in itself a sufficient counterpoise to the will to power, unless indeed we assume with Rousseau that one may control expansive impulses by opposing them to one another.

A terrible danger thus lurks in the whole modern programme: it is a programme that makes for a formidable mechanical efficiency and so tends to bring into an ever closer material contact men who remain ethically centrifugal. The reason why the humanitarian and other schemes of communion that have been set up during the last century have failed is that they do not, like the traditional schemes, set any bounds to mere expansiveness, or, if one prefers, they do not involve any conversion. And so it is not surprising that the feeling of emptiness[41] or unlimitedness and isolation should be the special mark of the melancholy of this period. René complains of his "moral solitude";[42] but strictly speaking his solitude is the reverse of moral. Only by cultivating his human self and by the unceasing effort that this cultivation involves does a man escape from his nightmare of separateness and so move in some measure towards happiness. But the happiness of which René dreams is unethical—something very private and personal and egoistic. Nothing is easier than to draw the line from René to Baudelaire and later decadents—for instance to Des Esseintes, the hero of Huysmans's novel "A Rebours,"[43] who is typical of the last exaggerations of the movement. Des Esseintes cuts himself off as completely as possible from other men and in the artificial paradise he has devised gives himself up to the quest of strange and violent sensation; but his dream of happiness along egoistic lines turns into a nightmare,[44] his palace of art becomes a hell. Lemaître is quite justified in saying of Des Esseintes that he is only René or Werther brought up to date—"a played-out and broken-down Werther who has a malady of the nerves, a deranged stomach and eighty years more of literature to the bad."[45]

Emotional romanticism was headed from the start towards this bankruptcy because of its substitution for ethical effort of a mere lazy floating on the stream of mood and temperament. I have said that Buddhism saw in this ethical indolence the root of all evil. Christianity in its great days was preoccupied with the same problem. To make this point clear it will be necessary to add to what I have said about classical and romantic melancholy a few words about melancholy in the Middle Ages. In a celebrated chapter of his "Genius of Christianity" (*Le Vague des passions*) Chateaubriand seeks to give to the malady of the age Christian and mediæval origins. This was his pretext, indeed, for introducing René into an apology for Christianity and so, as Sainte-Beuve complained, administering poison in a sacred wafer. Chateaubriand begins by saying that the modern man is melancholy because, without having had experience himself, he is at the same time overwhelmed by the second-hand experience that has been heaped up in the books and other records of an advanced civilization; and so he suffers from a precocious disillusion; he has the sense of having exhausted life before he has enjoyed it. There is nothing specifically Christian in this disillusion and above all nothing mediæval. But Chateaubriand goes on to say that from the decay of the pagan world and the barbarian invasions the human spirit received an impression of sadness and possibly a tinge of misanthropy which has never been completely effaced. Those that were thus wounded and estranged from their fellowmen took refuge formerly in monasteries, but now that this resource has failed them, they are left in the world without being of it and so they "become the prey of a thousand chimeras." Then is seen the rise of that guilty melancholy which the passions engender when, left without definite object, they prey upon themselves in a solitary heart.[46]

The *vague des passions,* the expansion of infinite indeterminate desire, that Chateaubriand here describes may very well
be related to certain sides of Christianity—especially to what
may be termed its neo-Platonic side. Yet Christianity at its
best has shown itself a genuine religion, in other words, it
has dealt sternly and veraciously with the facts of human nature. It has perceived clearly how a man may move towards
happiness and how on the other hand he tends to sink into
despair; or what amounts to the same thing, it has seen the
supreme importance of spiritual effort and the supreme danger
of spiritual sloth. The man who looked on himself as cut off
from God and so ceased to strive was according to the mediæval Christian the victim of *acedia.* This sluggishness and slack-
ness of spirit, this mere drifting and abdication of will, may,
as Chaucer's parson suggests, be the crime against the Holy
Ghost itself. It would in fact not be hard to show that what
was taken by the Rousseauist to be the badge of spiritual distinction was held by the mediæval Christian to be the chief of
all the deadly sins.

The victim of *acedia* often looked upon himself, like the
victim of the malady of the age, as foredoomed. But though
the idea of fate enters at times into mediæval melancholy,
the man of the Middle Ages could scarcely so detach himself
from the community as to suffer from that sense of loneliness
which is the main symptom of romantic melancholy. This forlornness was due not merely to the abrupt disappearance of the
older forms of communion, but to the failure of the new attempts at communion. When one gets beneath the surface of
the nineteenth century one finds that it was above all a period
of violent disillusions, and it is especially after violent disillusion that a man feels himself solitary and forlorn. I have said
that the special mark of the half-educated man is his harboring of incompatible desires. The new religions or unifications
of life that appeared during the nineteenth century made an
especially strong appeal to the half-educated man because it
seemed to him that by accepting some one of these he could
enjoy the benefits of communion and at the same time not
have to take on the yoke of any serious discipline; that he
could, in the language of religion, achieve salvation without

conversion. When a communion on these lines turns out to be not a reality, but a sham, and its disillusioned votary feels solitary and forlorn, he is ready to blame everybody and everything except himself.

A few specific illustrations will help us to understand how romantic solitude, which was created by the weakening of the traditional communions, was enhanced by the collapse of various sham communions. Let us return for a moment to that eminent example of romantic melancholy and disillusion, Alfred de Vigny. His "Chatterton" deals with the fatal misunderstanding of the original genius by other men. "Moïse" deals more specifically with the problem of his solitude. The genius is so eminent and unique, says Vigny, speaking for himself from behind the mask of the Hebrew prophet, that he is quite cut off from ordinary folk who feel that they have nothing in common with him.[47] This forlornness of the genius is not the sign of some capital error in his philosophy. On the contrary it is the sign of his divine election, and so Moses blames God for his failure to find happiness.[48] If the genius is cut off from communion with men he cannot hope for companionship with God because he has grown too sceptical. Heaven is empty and in any case dumb; and so in the poem to which I have already referred (*Le Mont des Oliviers*) Vigny assumes the mask of Jesus himself to express this desolateness, and concludes that the just man will oppose a haughty and Stoic disdain to the divine silence.[49]

All that is left for the genius is to retire into his ivory tower—a phrase appropriately applied for the first time to Vigny.[50] In the ivory tower he can at least commune with nature and the ideal woman. But Vigny came at a time when Arcadian glamour was being dissipated from nature. Partly under scientific influence she was coming to seem not a benign but a cold and impassive power, a collection of cruel and inexorable laws. I have already mentioned this mood that might be further illustrated from Taine and so many others towards the middle of the nineteenth century.[51] "I am called a 'mother,'" Vigny makes Nature say, "and I am a tomb" [52] ("La Maison du Berger"); and so in the *Maison roulante,* or sort of Arcadia on wheels that he has imagined, he must seek his chief solace with the ideal feminine companion. But woman herself turns out to be treacherous; and, assuming the mask of Samson ("La Colère de Samson"), Vigny utters a solemn malediction upon the eternal Delilah (*Et, plus ou moins, la Femme est toujours Dalila*). Such is the disillusion that comes from having sought an ideal communion in a liaison with a Parisian actress.[53]

Now that every form of communion has failed, all that is left it would seem is to die in silence and solitude like the wolf ("La Mort du Loup"). Vigny continues to hold, however, like the author of the "City of Dreadful Night," that though men may not meet in their joys, they may commune after a fashion in their woe. He opposes to heartless nature and her "vain splendors" the religion of pity, "the majesty of human sufferings." [54] Towards the end when Vigny feels the growing prestige of science, he holds out the hope that a man may to a certain extent escape from the solitude of his own ego into some larger whole by contributing his mite to "progress." But the symbol of this communion[55] that he has chosen—that of the shipwrecked and sinking mariner who consigns his geographical discoveries to a bottle in the hope that it may be washed up on some civilized shore—is itself of a singular forlornness.

Vigny has a concentration and power of philosophical reflection that is rare among the romanticists. George Sand is inferior to him in this respect but she had a richer and more generous nature, and is perhaps even more instructive in her life and writings for the student of romantic melancholy. After the loss of the religious faith of her childhood she became an avowed Rousseauist. She attacks a society that seems to her to stand in the way of the happiness of which she dreams—the supreme emotional intensity to be achieved in an ideal love. In celebrating passion and the rights of passion she is lyrical in the two main modes of the Rousseauist—she is either tender and elegiac, or else stormy and Titanic. But when she attempts to practice with Musset this religion of love, the result is violent disillusion. In the forlornness that follows upon the collapse of her sham communion she meditates suicide. "Ten years ago," she wrote in 1845 to Mazzini, "I was in Switzer-

land; I was still in the age of tempests; I made up my mind
even then to meet you, if I should resist the temptation to suicide which pursued me upon the glaciers." And then gradually
a new faith dawned upon her; she substituted for the religion
of love the religion of human brotherhood. She set up as an
object of worship humanity in its future progress; and then,
like so many other dreamers, she suffered a violent disillusion
in the Revolution of 1848. The radiant abstraction she had
been worshipping had been put to the test and she discovered
that there entered into the actual make-up of the humanity
she had so idealized "a large number of knaves, a very large
number of lunatics, and an immense number of fools." What
is noteworthy in George Sand is that she not only saved the
precious principle of faith from these repeated shipwrecks but
towards the end of her life began to put it on a firmer footing. Like Goethe she worked out to some extent, in opposition
to romanticism, a genuinely ethical point of view.

This latter development can best be studied in her correspondence with Flaubert. She urges him to exercise his will, and
he replies that he is as "fatalistic as a Turk." His fatalism,
however, was not oriental but scientific or pseudo-scientific. I
have already cited his demand that man be studied "ob-
jectively" just as one would study "a mastodon or a crocodile." Flaubert refused to see any connection between this determinism and his own gloom or between George Sand's assertion of will and her cheerfulness. It was simply, he held, a
matter of temperament, and there is no doubt some truth in
this contention. "You at the first leap mount to heaven," he
says, "while I, poor devil, am glued to the earth as though
by leaden soles." And again: "In spite of your great sphinx eyes
you have always seen the world as through a golden mist,"
whereas "I am constantly dissecting; and when I have finally
discovered the corruption in anything that is supposed to be
pure, the gangrene in its fairest parts, then I raise my head
and laugh." Yet George Sand's cheerfulness is also related to
her perception of a power in man to work upon himself—a
power that sets him apart from other animals. To enter into
this region of ethical effort is to escape from the whole fatal
circle of naturalism, and at the same time to show some ca-

pacity to mature—a rare achievement among the romanticists. The contrast is striking here between George Sand and Hugo, who, as the ripe fruit of his meditations, yields nothing better than the apotheosis of Robespierre and Marat. "I wish to see man as he is," she writes to Flaubert. "He is not good or bad: he is good and bad. But he is something else besides: being good and bad he has an inner force which leads him to be very bad and a little good, or very good and a little bad. I have often wondered," she adds, "why your 'Education Sentimen- tale' was so ill received by the public, and the reason, as it seems to me, is that its characters are passive—that they do not act upon themselves." But the Titaness of the period of "Lélia" can scarcely be said to have acted upon herself, so that she is justified in writing: "I cannot forget that my personal victory over despair is the work of my will, and of a new way of understanding life which is the exact opposite of the one I held formerly." How different is the weary cry of Flaubert: "I am like a piece of clock work, what I am doing to-day I shall be doing to-morrow; I did exactly the same thing yesterday; I was exactly the same man ten years ago."

The correspondence of Flaubert and George Sand bears in- terestingly on another of the sham religions of the nineteenth century—the religion of art. Art is for Flaubert not merely a religion but a fanaticism. He preaches abstinence, renunciation and mortification of the flesh in the name of art. He excommu- nicates those who depart from artistic orthodoxy and speaks of heretics and disbelievers in art with a ferocity worthy of a Spanish inquisitor. Ethical beauty such as one finds in the Greeks at their best resides in order and proportion; it is not a thing apart but the outcome of some harmonious whole. Beauty in the purely æsthetic and unethical sense that Flau- bert gives to the word is little more than the pursuit of illusion. The man who thus treats beauty as a thing apart, who does not refer back his quest of the exquisite to some ethical cen- tre will spend his life Ixion-like embracing phantoms. "O Art, Art," exclaims Flaubert, "bitter deception, nameless phan- tom, which gleams and lures us to our ruin!" He speaks else- where of "the chimera of style which is wearing him out soul and body." Attaching as he did an almost religious importance to his quest of the exquisite he became like so many other Rousseauists not merely æsthetic but hyperæsthetic. He complains in his old age: "My sensibility is sharper than a razor's edge; the creaking of a door, the face of a bourgeois, an absurd statement set my heart to throbbing and completely upset me." Hardly anywhere else, indeed, will one find such accents of bitterness, such melancholy welling up unbidden from the very depths of the heart, as in the devotees of art for art's sake—Flaubert, Leconte de Lisle, Théophile Gautier.

George Sand takes Flaubert to task with admirable tact for his failure to subordinate art to something higher than itself. "Talent imposes duties; and art for art's sake is an empty word." As she grew older, she says, she came more and more to put truth above beauty, and goodness before strength. "I have reflected a great deal on what is *true,* and in this search for truth, the sentiment of my ego has gradually disappeared." The truth on which she had reflected was what she herself calls total truth (*le vrai total*), not merely truth according to the natural law, which received such exclusive emphasis towards the middle of the nineteenth century as to lead to the rise of another sham religion—the religion of science. "You have a better sense for total truth," she tells one of her correspondents "than Sainte-Beuve, Renan and Littré. They have fallen into the German rut: therein lies their weakness." And Flaubert writes to George Sand: "What amazes and delights me is the strength of your whole personality, not that of the brain alone."

Furthermore the holding of the human law that made possible this rounded development, this growth towards total truth, was a matter not of tradition but of immediate perception. George Sand had succeeded, as Taine says, in making the difficult transition from an hereditary faith to a personal conviction. Now this perception of the human law is something very different from the pantheistic revery in which George Sand was also an adept. To look on revery as the equivalent of vision in the Aristotelian sense, as Rousseau and so many of his followers have done, is to fall into sham spirituality. Maurice de Guérin falls into sham spirituality when he exclaims "Oh! this contact of nature and the soul would engender an ineffable voluptuousness, a prodigious love of heaven and of God." I am not asserting that George Sand herself discriminated sharply between ethical and æsthetic perception or that she is to be rated as a very great sage at any time. Yet she owes her recovery of serenity after suffering shock upon shock of disillusion to her having exercised in some degree what she terms "the contemplative sense wherein resides invincible faith" (*le sens contemplatif où réside la foi invincible*), and the passages that bear witness to her use of this well-nigh obsolete sense are found in her correspondence.

Wordsworth lauds in true Rousseauistic fashion a "wise passiveness." But to be truly contemplative is not to be passive at all, but to be "energetic" in Aristotle's sense, or strenuous in Buddha's sense. It is a matter of no small import that the master analyst of the East and the master analyst of the West are at one in their solution of the supreme problem of ethics— the problem of happiness. For there can be no doubt that the energy[56] in which the doctrine of Aristotle culminates is the same as the "strenuousness" [57] on which Buddha puts his final emphasis. The highest good they both agree is a contemplative *working*. It is by thus working according to the human law that one rises above the naturalistic level. The scientific rationalists of the nineteenth century left no place for this true human spontaneity when they sought to subject man entirely to the "law of thing." This scientific determinism was responsible for a great deal of spiritual depression and *acedia*, especially in France during the second half of the nineteenth century.[58] But even if science is less dogmatic and absolute one needs to consider why it does not deserve to be given the supreme and central place in life, why it cannot in short take the place of humanism and religion, and the working according to the human law that they both enjoin.

A man may indeed effect through science a certain escape from himself, and this is very salutary so far as it goes; he has to discipline himself to an order that is quite independent of his own fancies and emotions. He becomes objective in short, but objective according to the natural and not according to the human law. Objectivity of this kind gives control over natural forces but it does not supply the purpose for which these forces are to be used. It gives the airship, for instance, but does not determine whether the airship is to go on some beneficent errrand or is to scatter bombs on women and children. Science does not even set right limits to the faculty that it chiefly exercises—the intellect. In itself it stimulates rather than curbs one of the three main lusts to which human nature is subject—the lust of knowledge. Renan, who makes a religion of science, speaks of "sacred curiosity." But this is even more dangerous than the opposite excess of the ascetic Christian who denounces all curiosity as vain. The man of science avers indeed that he does subordinate his knowledge to an adequate aim, namely the progress of humanity. But the humanity of the Baconian is only an intellectual abstraction just as the humanity of the Rousseauist is only an emotional dream. George Sand found, as we have seen, that the passage from one's dream of humanity to humanity in the concrete involved a certain disillusion. The scientific or rationalistic humanitarian is subject to similar disillusions.[59] Science not only fails to set proper limits to the activity of the intellect, but one must also note a curious paradox in its relation to the second of the main lusts to which man is subject, the lust for emotion (*libido sentiendi*). The prime virtue of science is to be unemotional and at the same time keenly analytical. Now protracted and unemotional analysis finally creates a desire, as Renan says, for the opposite pole, "the kisses of the naïve being," and in general for a frank surrender to the emotions. Science thus actually prepares clients for the Rousseauist.[60] The man of science is also flattered by the Rousseauistic notion that conscience and virtue are themselves only forms of emotion. He is thus saved from anything so distasteful as having to subordinate his own scientific discipline to some superior religious or humanistic discipline. He often oscillates between the rationalistic and emotional pole not only in other things but also in his cult of humanity. But if conscience is merely an emotion there is a cult that makes a more potent appeal to conscience than the cult of humanity itself and that is the cult of country. One is here at the root of the most dangerous of all the sham religions of the modern age—the religion of country, the frenzied nationalism that is now threatening to make an end of civilization itself.

Both emotional nationalism and emotional internationalism go back to Rousseau, but in his final emphasis he is an emotional nationalist;[61] and that is because he saw that patriotic "virtue" is a more potent intoxicant than the love of humanity. The demonstration came in the French Revolution which began as a great international movement on emotional lines and ended in imperialism and Napoleon Bonaparte. It is here that the terrible peril of a science that is pursued as an end it itself becomes manifest. It disciplines man and makes him efficient on the naturalistic level, but leaves him ethically undisciplined. Now in the absence of ethical discipline the lust for knowledge and the lust for feeling count very little, at least practically, compared with the third main lust of human nature —the lust for power. Hence the emergence of that most sinister of all types, the efficient megalomaniac. The final use of a science that has thus become a tool of the lust for power is in Burke's phrase to "improve the mystery of murder."

This union of material efficiency and ethical unrestraint, though in a way the upshot of the whole movement we have been studying, is especially marked in the modern German. Goethe as I have pointed out is ready to pardon Faust for grave violations of the moral law because of work which, so far from being ethical, is, in view of the ruin in which it involves the rustic pair, Baucis and Philemon, under suspicion of being positively unethical. Yet Goethe was far from being a pure utilitarian and he had reacted more than most Germans of his time from Rousseauism. Rousseau is glorified by Germans as a chief source of their *Kultur,* as I have already pointed out. Now *Kultur* when analyzed breaks up into two very different things—scientific efficiency and emotionalism or what the Germans (and unfortunately not the Germans alone) term "idealism." There is no question about the relation of this idealism to the stream of tendency of which Rousseau is the chief representative. By his corruption of conscience Rousseau made it possible to identify character with temperament. It was easy for Fichte and others to take the next step and identify national character with national temperament. The Germans according to Fichte are all beautiful souls, the elect of nature. If they have no special word for character it is because to be a German and have character are synonymous. Character is something that gushes up from the primordial depths of the German's being without any conscious effort on his part.[62] The members of a whole national group may thus flatter one another and inbreed their national "genius" in the romantic sense, and feel all the while that they are ecstatic "idealists"; yet as a result of the failure to refer their genius back to some ethical centre, to work, in other words, according to the human law, they may, so far as the members of other national groups are concerned, remain in a state of moral solitude.

Everything thus hinges on the meaning of the word work. In the abstract and metaphysical sense man can know nothing of unity. He may, however, by working in the human sense, by imposing, that is, due limits on his expansive desires, close up in some measure the gap in his own nature (the "civil war in the cave") and so tend to become inwardly one. He may hope in the same way to escape from the solitude of his own ego, for the inner unity that he achieves through work is only an entering into possession of his ethical self, the self that he possesses in common with other men. Thus to work ethically is not only to become more unified and happy but also to move away from what is less permanent towards what is more permanent and therefore more peaceful in his total nature; so that the problem of happiness and the problem of peace turn out at last to be inseparable.

Souls, says Emerson, never meet; and it is true that a man never quite escapes from his solitude. That does not make the choice of direction any the less important. An infinite beckons to him on either hand. The one inspires the divine discontent, the other romantic restlessness. If instead of following the romantic lure he heeds the call from the opposite direction, he will not indeed attain to any perfect communion but he will be less solitary. Strictly speaking a man is never happy in the sense of being completely satisfied with the passing moment,[63] or never, Dr. Johnson would add, except when he is drunk. The happiness of the sober and waking man resides, it may be, not in his content with the present moment but in the very effort that marks his passage from a lower to a higher ethical level.

The happiness of which Rousseau dreamed, it has been made plain, was not this active and ethical happiness, but rather the passive enjoyment of the beautiful moment—the moment that he would like to have last forever. After seeking for the beautiful moment in the intoxication of love, he turned as we have seen to pantheistic revery. "As long as it lasts," he says of a moment of this kind, "one is self-sufficing like God." Yes, but it does not last, and when he wakes from his dream of communion with nature, he is still solitary, still the prisoner of his ego. The pantheistic dreamer is passive in every sense. He is not working either according to the human or according to the natural law, and so is not gaining either in material or in ethical efficiency. In a world such as that in which we live this seems too much like picnicking on a battlefield. Rousseau could on occasion speak shrewdly on this point. He wrote to a youthful enthusiast who wished to come and live with him at Montmorency: "The first bit of advice I should like to give you is not to indulge in the taste you say you have for the contemplative life and which is only an indolence of the spirit reprehensible at every age and especially at yours. Man is not made to meditate but to act."

The contemplative life is then, according to Rousseau, the opposite of action. But to contemplate is according to an Aristotle or a Buddha to engage in the most important form of action, the form that leads to happiness. To identify leisure and the contemplative life with pantheistic revery, as Rousseau does, is to fall into one of the most vicious of confusions. Perhaps indeed the most important contrast one can reach in a subject of this kind is that between a wise strenuousness and a more or less wise passiveness, between the spiritual athlete and the cosmic loafer, between a Saint Paul, let us say, and a Walt Whitman.

The spiritual idling and drifting of the Rousseauist would be less sinister if it did not coexist in the world of to-day with an intense material activity. The man who seeks happiness by work according to the natural law is to be rated higher than

the man who seeks happiness in some form of emotional intox
ication (including pantheistic revery). He is not left unarmed,
a helpless dreamer in the battle of life. The type of efficiency he
is acquiring also helps him to keep at bay man's great enemy,
ennui. An Edison, we may suppose, who is drawn ever onward
by the lure of wonder and curiosity and power, has little time
to be bored. It is surely better to escape from the boredom of
life after the fashion of Edison than after the fashion of Baudelaire.[64]

I have already pointed out, however, the peril in a one-sided
working of this kind. It makes man efficient without making
him ethical. It stimulates rather than corrects a fearless, formless expansion on the human level. This inordinate reaching out
beyond bounds is, as the great Greek poets saw with such clearness, an invitation to Nemesis. The misery that results from
unrestraint, from failure to work according to the human law,
is something different from mere pain and far more to be
dreaded; just as the happiness that results from a right working
according to the human law is something different from mere
pleasure and far more worthy of pursuit.

The present alliance between emotional romanticists and utilitarians[65] is a veritable menace to civilization itself. It does not
follow, as I said in a previous chapter, because revery or "intuition of the creative flux" cannot take the place of leisure or
meditation, that one must therefore condemn it utterly. It may
like other forms of romanticism have a place on the recreative
side of life. What finally counts is work according to either the
human or the natural law, but man cannot always be working.
He needs moments of relief from tension and concentration
and even, it should seem, of semi-oblivion of his conscious self.
As one of the ways of winning such moments of relaxation and
partial forgetfulness much may be said for revery. In general
one must grant the solace and rich source of poetry that is
found in communion with nature even though the final emphasis be put on communion with man. It is no small thing to be,
as Arnold says Wordsworth was, a "priest of the wonder and
bloom of the world." One cannot however grant the Wordsworthian that to be a priest of wonder is necessarily to be also
a priest of wisdom. Thus to promote to the supreme and cen-

tral place something that is legitimate in its own degree, but secondary, is to risk starting a sham religion.

Those who have sought to set up a cult of love or beauty or science or humanity or country are open to the same objections as the votaries of nature. However important each of these things may be in its own place, it cannot properly be put in the supreme and central place for the simple reason that it does not involve any adequate conversion or discipline of man's ordinary self to some ethical centre. I have tried to show that the sense of solitude or forlornness that is so striking a feature of romantic melancholy arises not only from a loss of hold on the traditional centres, but also from the failure of these new attempts at communion to keep their promises. The number of discomfitures of this kind in the period that has elapsed since the late eighteenth century suggests that this period was even more than most periods an age of sophistry. Every age has had its false teachers, but possibly no age ever had so many dubious moralists as this, an incomparable series of false prophets from Rousseau himself down to Nietzsche and Tolstoy. It remains to sum up in a closing chapter the results of my whole inquiry and at the same time to discuss somewhat more specifically the bearing of my whole point of view, especially the idea of work according to the human law, upon the present situation.

CHAPTER TEN

THE PRESENT OUTLOOK

It has been my endeavor throughout this book to show that classic and romantic art, though both at their best highly imaginative, differ in the quality of the imagination. I pointed out in my first chapter that in his recoil from the intellectual romanticism of the Renaissance and the mediæval romanticism of actual adventure the neo-classicist came to rest his literary faith on "reason" (by which he meant either ordinary good sense or abstract reasoning), and then opposed this reason or judgment to imagination. This supposed opposition between reason and imagination was accepted by the romantic rebels against neo-classicism and has been an endless source of confusion to the present day. Though both neo-classicists and romanticists achieved much admirable work, work which is likely to have a permanent appeal, it is surely no small matter that they both failed on the whole to deal adequately with the imagination and its rôle whether in literature or life. Thus Dryden attributes the immortality of the Æneid to its being "a well-weighed judicious poem. Whereas poems which are produced by the vigor of imagination only have a gloss upon them at the first which time wears off, the works of judgment are like the diamond; the more they are polished, the more lustre they receive." [1] Read on and you will find that Dryden thus stresses judgment by way of protest against the Cavalier Marini and the imaginative unrestraint that he and other intellectual romanticists display. Dryden thus obscures the fact that what gives the immortalizing touch to the Æneid is not mere judgment but imagination—a certain quality of imagination. Even the reader who is to enter properly into the spirit of Virgil needs more than judgment—he needs to possess in some measure the same quality of imagination. The romantic answer to the neo-classic distrust of the imagination was the apotheosis of the imagination, but without sufficient discrimination as to its quality, and this led only too often to an anarchy of the imagination—an anarchy associated, as we have seen, in the case of the Rousseauist, with emotion rather than with thought or action.

The modern world has thus tended to oscillate between extremes in its attitude towards the imagination, so that we still have to turn to ancient Greece for the best examples of works in which the imagination is at once disciplined and supreme. Aristotle, I pointed out, is doing little more than give an account of this Greek practice when he says that the poet ranks higher than the historian because he achieves a more general truth, but that he can achieve this more general truth only by being a master of illusion. Art in which the illusion is not disciplined to the higher reality counts at best on the recreative side of life. "Imagination," says Poe, "feeling herself for once unshackled, roamed at will among the ever-changing wonders of a shadowy and unstable land." [2] To take seriously the creations of this type of imagination is to be on the way towards madness. Every madhouse, indeed, has inmates who are very imaginative in the fashion Poe here describes. We must not confuse the concentric or ethical with the eccentric imagination if we are to define rightly the terms classic and romantic or indeed to attain to sound criticism at all. My whole aim has been to show that a main stream of emotional sophistry that takes its rise in the eighteenth century and flows down through the nineteenth involves just such a confusion.

The general distinction between the two types of imagination would seem sufficiently clear. To apply the distinction concretely is, it must be admitted, a task infinitely difficult and delicate, a task that calls for the utmost degree of the *esprit de finesse.* In any particular case there enters an element of vital novelty. The relation of this vital novelty to the ethical or permanent element in life is something that cannot be determined by any process of abstract reasoning or by any rule of thumb; it is a matter of immediate perception. The art of the critic is thus hedged about with peculiar difficulties. It does not follow that Aristotle himself because he has laid down sound principles in his "Poetics" would always have been right in applying them. Our evidence on this point is as a matter of fact somewhat scanty.

Having thus admitted the difficulty of the undertaking we may ourselves attempt a few concrete illustrations of how sound critical standards tended to suffer in connection with the romantic movement. Leaving aside for the moment certain larger aspects of the ethical imagination that I am going to discuss presently, let us confine ourselves to poetry. Inasmuch as the ethical imagination does not in itself give poetry but wisdom, various cases may evidently arise: a man may be wise without being poetical; he may be poetical without being wise; he may be both wise and poetical.

We may take as an example of the person who was wise without being poetical Dr. Johnson. Though most persons would grant that Dr. Johnson was not poetical, it is well to remember that this generalization has only the approximate truth that a literary generalization can have. The lines on Levet have been inserted and rightly in anthologies. If not on the whole poetical, Johnson was, as Boswell says, eminently fitted to be a "majestic teacher of moral and religious wisdom." Few men have had a firmer grasp on the moral law or been freer from the various forms of sophistry that tend to obscure it. Unlike Socrates, however, of whom he reminds us at times by his ethical realism, Johnson rests his insight not on a positive but on a traditional basis. To say that Johnson was truly religious is only another way of saying that he was truly humble, and one of the reasons for his humility was his perception of the ease with which illusion in man passes over into delusion, and even into madness. His chapter on the "Dangerous Prevalence of Imagination" in "Rasselas" not only gives the key to that work but to much else in his writings. What he opposes to this dangerous prevalence of imagination is not a different type of imagination but the usual neo-classical reason or judgment or "sober probability." His defence of wisdom against the gathering naturalistic sophistries of his time is therefore somewhat lacking in imaginative prestige. He seemed to be opposing innovation on purely formalistic and traditional grounds in an age which was more and more resolutely untraditional and which was determined above all to emancipate the imagination from its strait-jacket of formalism. Keats would not have hesitated to rank Johnson among those who "blasphemed the bright Lyrist to his face."

Keats himself may serve as a type of the new imaginative spontaneity and of the new fullness and freshness of sensuous perception. If Johnson is wise without being poetical, Keats is poetical without being wise, and here again we need to remember that distinctions of this kind are only approximately true. Keats has written lines that have high seriousness. He has written other lines which without being wise seem to lay claim to wisdom—notably the lines in which, following Shaftesbury and other æsthetes, he identifies truth and beauty; an identification that was disproved for practical purposes at least as far back as the Trojan War. Helen was beautiful, but was neither good nor true. In general, however, Keats's poetry is not sophistical. It is simply delightfully recreative. There are signs that Keats himself would not have been content in the long run with a purely recreative rôle—to be "the idle singer of an empty day." Whether he would ever have achieved genuine ethical purpose is a question. In working out a wise view of life he did not, like Dante, have the support of a great and generally accepted tradition. It is not certain again that he would ever have developed the critical keenness that enabled a Sophocles to work out a wise view of life in a less traditional age than that of Dante. The evidence is rather that Keats would have succumbed, to his own poetical detriment, to some of the forms of sham wisdom current in his day, especially the new humanitarian evangel.[3]

In any case we may contrast Sophocles and Dante with Keats as examples of poets who were not merely poetical but wise—wise in the relative and imperfect sense in which it is vouchsafed to mortals to achieve wisdom. Sophocles and Dante are not perhaps more poetical than Keats—it is not easy to be more poetical than Keats. As Tennyson says, "there is something magic and of the innermost soul of poetry in almost everything he wrote." Yet Sophocles and Dante are not only superior to Keats, but in virtue of the presence of the ethical imagination in their work, superior not merely in degree but in kind. Not that even Sophocles and Dante maintain themselves uniformly on the level of the ethical imagination. There are passages in Dante which are less imaginative than theological. Passages of this kind are even more numerous in Milton, a poet who on the whole is highly serious.[4] It is in general easy to be didactic, hard to achieve ethical insight.

If Keats is highly imaginative and poetic without on the whole rising to high seriousness or sinking to sophistry, Shelley, on the other hand, illustrates in his imaginative activity the confusion of values that was so fostered by romanticism. Here again I do not wish to be too absolute. Shelley has passages especially in his "Adonais" that are on a high level. Yet nothing is more certain than that the quality of his imagination is on the whole not ethical but Arcadian or pastoral. In the name of his Arcadia conceived as the "ideal" he refuses to face the facts of life. I have already spoken of the flimsiness of his "Prometheus Unbound" as a solution of the problem of evil. What is found in this play is the exact opposite of imaginative concentration on the human law. The imagination wanders irresponsibly in a region quite outside of normal human experience. We are hindered from enjoying the gorgeous iridescences of Shelley's cloudland by Shelley's own evident conviction that it is not a cloudland, an "intense inane," but a true empyrean of the spirit. And our irritation at Shelley's own confusion is further increased by the long train of his indiscreet admirers. Thus Professor C. H. Herford writes in the "Cambridge History of English Literature" that what Shelley has done in the "Prometheus Unbound" is to give "magnificent expression to the faith of Plato and of Christ"![5] Such a statement in such a place is a veritable danger signal, an indication of some grave spiritual bewilderment in the present age. To show the inanity of these attempts to make a wise man of Shelley it is enough to compare him not with Plato and Christ, but with the poet whom he set out at once to continue and contradict—with Æschylus. The "Prometheus Bound" has the informing ethical imagination that the "Prometheus Unbound" lacks, and so in its total structure belongs to an entirely different order of art. Shelley, indeed, has admirable details. The romanticism of nympholeptic longing may almost be said to culminate, at least in England, in the passage I have already cited ("My soul is an enchanted boat"). There is no reason why in recreative moods one should not imagine one's soul an enchanted boat and float away in a musical rapture with the ideal dream companion towards Arcady. But to suppose that revery of this kind has anything to do with the faith of Plato and of Christ is to fall from illusion into dangerous delusion.

We may doubt whether if Shelley had lived longer he would ever have risen above emotional sophistry and become more ethical in the quality of his imagination. Such a progress from emotional sophistry to ethical insight we actually find in Goethe; and this is the last and most complex case we have to consider. Johnson, I have said, is wise without being poetical and Keats poetical without being wise; Sophocles is both poetical and wise, whereas Shelley is poetical, but with a taint of sophistry or sham wisdom. No such clear-cut generalization can be ventured about Goethe. I have already quoted Goethe's own judgment on his "Werther" as weakness seeking to give itself the prestige of strength, and perhaps it would be possible to instance from his early writings even worse examples of a morbid emotionalism (e.g. "Stella"). How about "Faust" itself? Most Germans will simply dismiss such a question as profane. With Hermann Grimm they are ready to pronounce "Faust" the greatest work of the greatest poet of all times, and of all peoples. Yet it is not easy to overlook the sophistical element in both parts of "Faust." I have already commented on those passages that would seem especially sophistical: the passage in which the devil is defined as the spirit that always says no strikes at the very root of any proper distinction between good and evil. The passage again in which Faust breaks down all precise discrimination in favor of mere emotional intoxication is an extreme example of the Rousseauistic art of "making madness beautiful." The very conclusion of the whole poem, with its setting up of work according to the natural law as a substitute for work according to the human law, is an egregious piece of sham wisdom. The result of work according to the human law, of ethical efficiency in short, is an increasing serenity; and it is not clear that Faust is much calmer at the end of the poem than he is at the beginning. According to Dr. Santayana he is ready to carry into heaven itself his romantic restlessness—his desperate and feverish attempts to escape from ennui.[6] Perhaps this is not the whole truth even in regard to "Faust"; and still less can we follow Dr. Santayana when he seems to discover in the whole work of Goethe only romantic restlessness. At the very time when Goethe was infecting others with the wild expansiveness of the new movement, he himself was beginning to strike out along an entirely different path. He writes in his Journal as early as 1778: "A more definite feeling of limitation and in consequence of true broadening." Goethe here glimpses the truth that lies at the base of both humanism and religion. He saw that the romantic disease was the imaginative and emotional straining towards the unlimited (*Hang zum Unbegrenzten*), and in opposition to this unrestraint he was never tired of preaching the need of working within boundaries. It may be objected that Goethe is in somewhat the same case here as Rousseau: that the side of his work which has imaginative and emotional driving power and has therefore moved the world is of an entirely different order. We may reply that Goethe is at times both poetical and wise. Furthermore in his maxims and conversations where he does not rise to the poetical level, he displays a higher quality of wisdom than Rousseau. At his best he shows an ethical realism worthy of Dr. Johnson, though in his attitude towards tradition he is less Johnsonian than Socratic. Like Socrates he saw on what terms a break with the past may be safely attempted. "Anything that emancipates the spirit," he says, "without a corresponding growth in self-mastery is pernicious." We may be sure that if the whole modern experiment fails it will be because of the neglect of the truth contained in this maxim. Goethe also saw that a sound individualism must be rightly imaginative. He has occasional hints on the rôle of illusion in literature and life that go far beneath the surface.

Though the mature Goethe, then, always stands for salvation by work, it is not strictly correct to say that it is work only according to the natural law. In Goethe at his best the imagination accepts the limitations imposed not merely by the natural, but also by the human law. However, we must admit that the humanistic Goethe has had few followers either in Germany or elsewhere, whereas innumerable persons have escaped from the imaginative unrestraint of the emotional romanticist, as Goethe himself likewise did, by the discipline of science.

The examples I have chosen should suffice to show how my distinction between two main types of imagination—the ethical type that gives high seriousness to creative writing and the Arcadian or dalliant type that does not raise it above the recreative level—works out in practice. Some such distinction is necessary if we are to understand the imagination in its relation to the human law. But in order to grasp the present situation firmly we need also to consider the imagination in its relation to the natural law. I have just said that most men have escaped from the imaginative anarchy of the emotional romanticist through science. Now the man of science at his best is like the humanist at his best, at once highly imaginative and highly critical. By this coöperation of imagination and intellect they are both enabled to concentrate effectively on the facts, though on facts of a very different order. The imagination reaches out and perceives likenesses and analogies whereas the power in man that separates and discriminates and traces causes and effects tests in turn these likenesses and analogies as to their reality: for we can scarcely repeat too often that though the imagination gives unity it does not give reality. If we were all Aristotles or even Goethes we might concentrate imaginatively on both laws, and so be both scientific and humanistic: but as a matter of fact the ordinary man's capacity for concentration is limited. After a spell of concentration on either law he aspires to what Aristotle calls "relief from tension." Now the very conditions of modern life require an almost tyrannical concentration on the natural law. The problems that have been engaging

more and more the attention of the Occident since the rise of
the great Baconian movement have been the problems of power
and speed and utility. The enormous mass of machinery that
has been accumulated in the pursuit of these ends requires the
closest attention and concentration if it is to be worked effi-
ciently. At the same time the man of the West is not willing to
admit that he is growing in power alone, he likes to think that
he is growing also in wisdom. Only by keeping this situation in
mind can we hope to understand how emotional romanticism
has been able to develop into a vast system of sham spirituality.
I have said that the Rousseauist wants unity without reality. If
we are to move towards reality, the imagination must be controlled by the power of discrimination and the Rousseauist has
repudiated this power as "false and secondary." But a unity
that lacks reality can scarcely be accounted wise. The Baconian,
however, accepts this unity gladly. He has spent so much energy
in working according to the natural law that he has no energy
left for work according to the human law. By turning to the
Rousseauist he can get the "relief from tension" that he needs
and at the same time enjoy the illusion of receiving a vast spiritual illumination. Neither Rousseauist nor Baconian carry into
the realm of the human law the keen analysis that is necessary
to distinguish between genuine insight and some mere phantasmagoria of the emotions. I am speaking especially, of course, of
the interplay of Rousseauistic and Baconian elements that appear in certain recent philosophies like that of Bergson. According to Bergson one becomes spiritual by throwing overboard
both thought and action, and this is a very convenient notion
of spirituality for those who wish to devote both thought and
action to utilitarian and material ends. It is hard to see in
Bergson's intuition of the creative flux and perception of real
duration anything more than the latest form of Rousseau's
transcendental idling. To work with something approaching
frenzy according to the natural law and to be idle according to
the human law must be accounted a rather one-sided view of
life. The price the man of to-day has paid for his increase in
power is, it should seem, an appalling superficiality in dealing
with the law of his own nature. What brings together Baconian
and Rousseauist in spite of their surface differences is that they

are both intent on the element of novelty. But if wonder is associated with the Many, wisdom is associated with the One. Wisdom and wonder are moving not in the same but in opposite directions. The nineteenth century may very well prove to have been the most wonderful and the least wise of centuries. The men of this period—and I am speaking of course of the main drift—were so busy being wonderful that they had no time, apparently, to be wise. Yet their extreme absorption in wonder and the manifoldness of things can scarcely be commended unless it can be shown that happiness also results from all this revelling in the element of change. The Rousseauist is not quite consistent on this point. At times he bids us boldly set our hearts on the transitory. *Aimez*, says Vigny, *ce que jamais on ne verra deux fois.* But the Rousseauist strikes perhaps a deeper chord when looking forth on a world of flux he utters the anguished exclamation of Leconte de Lisle: *Qu'est-ce que tout cela qui n'est pas éternel?* Even as one swallow, says Aristotle, does not make a spring, so no short time is enough to determine whether a man deserves to be called happy. The weakness of the romantic pursuit of novelty and wonder and in general of the philosophy of the beautiful moment—whether the erotic moment[7] or the moment of cosmic revery—is that it does not reckon sufficiently with the something deep down in the human breast that craves the abiding. To pin one's hope to happiness to the fact that "the world is so full of a number of things" is an appropriate sentiment for a "Child's Garden of Verse." For the adult to maintain an exclusive Bergsonian interest in "the perpetual gushing forth of novelties" would seem to betray an inability to mature. The effect on a mature observer of an age so entirely turned from the One to the Many as that in which we are living must be that of a prodigious peripheral richness joined to a great central void.

What leads the man of to-day to work with such energy according to the natural law and to be idle according to the human law is his intoxication with material success. A consideration that should therefore touch him is that in the long run not merely spiritual success or happiness, but material prosperity depend on an entirely different working. Let me revert here for a moment to my previous analysis: to work according to the hu-

man law is simply to rein in one's impulses. Now the strongest
of all the impulses is the will to power. The man who does not
rein in his will to power and is at the same time very active according to the natural law is in a fair way to become an efficient megalomaniac. Efficient megalomania, whether developed
in individuals of the same group or in whole national groups in
their relations with one another, must lead sooner or later to
war. The efficient megalomaniacs will proceed to destroy one
another along with the material wealth to which they have sacrificed everything else; and then the meek, if there are any
meek left, will inherit the earth.

"If I am to judge by myself," said an eighteenth-century
Frenchman, "man is a stupid animal." Man is not only a stupid
animal in spite of his conceit of his own cleverness, but we are
here at the source of his stupidity. The source is the moral indolence that Buddha with his almost infallible sagacity defined
long ago. In spite of the fact that his spiritual and in the long
run his material success hinge on his ethical effort, man persists
in dodging this effort, in seeking to follow the line of least or
lesser resistance. An energetic material working does not mend
but aggravate the failure to work ethically and is therefore especially stupid. Just this combination has in fact led to the
crowning stupidity of the ages—the Great War. No more delirious spectacle has ever been witnessed than that of hundreds of
millions of human beings using a vast machinery of scientific
efficiency to turn life into a hell for one another. It is hard to
avoid concluding that we are living in a world that has gone
wrong on first principles, a world that, in spite of all the warnings of the past, has allowed itself to be caught once more in the
terrible naturalistic trap. The dissolution of civilization with
which we are threatened is likely to be worse in some respects
than that of Greece or Rome in view of the success that has
been attained in "perfecting the mystery of murder." Various
traditional agencies are indeed still doing much to chain up the
beast in man. Of these the chief is no doubt the Church. But
the leadership of the Occident is no longer here. The leaders
have succumbed in greater or less degree to naturalism[8] and so
have been tampering with the moral law. That the brutal im-
perialist who brooks no obstacle to his lust for dominion has

been tampering with this law goes without saying; but the humanitarian, all adrip with brotherhood and profoundly convinced of the loveliness of his own soul, has been tampering with it also, and in a more dangerous way for the very reason that it is less obvious. This tampering with the moral law, or what amounts to the same thing, this overriding of the veto power in man, has been largely a result, though not a necessary result, of the rupture with the traditional forms of wisdom. The Baconian naturalist repudiated the past because he wished to be more positive and critical, to plant himself upon the facts. Yet the veto power is itself a fact—the weightiest with which man has to reckon. The Rousseauistic naturalist threw off traditional control because he wished to be more imaginative. Yet without the veto power the imagination falls into sheer anarchy. Both Baconian and Rousseauist were very impatient of any outer authority that seemed to stand between them and their own perceptions. Yet the veto power is nothing abstract, nothing that one needs to take on hearsay, but is very immediate. The naturalistic leaders may be proved wrong without going beyond their own principles, and their wrongness is of a kind to wreck civilization.

I have no quarrel, it is scarcely necessary to add, either with the man of science or the romanticist when they keep in their proper place. As soon however as they try, whether separately or in unison, to set up some substitute for humanism or religion, they should be at once attacked, the man of science for not being sufficiently positive and critical, the romanticist for not being rightly imaginative.

This brings us back to the problem of the ethical imagination —the imagination that has accepted the veto power—which I promised a moment ago to treat in its larger aspects. This problem is indeed in a peculiar sense the problem of civilization itself. A curious circumstance should be noted here: a civilization that rests on dogma and outer authority cannot afford to face the whole truth about the imagination and its rôle. A civilization in which dogma and outer authority have been undermined by the critical spirit, not only can but must do this very thing if it is to continue at all. Man, a being ever changing and living in a world of change, is, as I said at the outset, cut off from immediate access to anything abiding and therefore worthy to be called real, and condemned to live in an element of fiction or illusion. Yet civilization must rest on the recognition of something abiding. It follows that the truths on the survival of which civilization depends cannot be conveyed to man directly but only through imaginative symbols. It seems hard, however, for man to analyze critically this disability under which he labors, and, facing courageously the results of his analysis, to submit his imagination to the necessary control. He consents to limit his expansive desires only when the truths that are symbolically true are presented to him as literally true. The salutary check upon his imagination is thus won at the expense of the critical spirit. The pure gold of faith needs, it should seem, if it is to gain currency, to be alloyed with credulity. But the civilization that results from humanistic or religious control tends to produce the critical spirit. Sooner or later some Voltaire utters his fatal message:

> *Les prêtres ne sont pas ce qu'un vain peuple pense;*
> *Notre crédulité fait toute leur science.*

The emancipation from credulous belief leads to an anarchic individualism that tends in turn to destroy civilization. There is some evidence in the past that it is not quite necessary to run through this cycle. Buddha, for example, was very critical; he had a sense of the flux and evanescence of all things and so of universal illusion keener by far than that of Anatole France; at the same time he had ethical standards even sterner than those of Dr. Johnson. This is a combination that the Occident has rarely seen and that it perhaps needs to see. At the very end of his life Buddha uttered words that deserve to be the Magna Charta of the true individualist: "Therefore, O Ananda, be ye lamps unto yourselves. Be ye refuges unto yourselves. Look to no outer refuge. Hold fast as a refuge unto the Law (*Dhamma*)." [9] A man may safely go into himself if what he finds there is not, like Rousseau, his own emotions, but like Buddha, the law of righteousness.

Men were induced to follow Rousseau in his surrender to the emotions, it will be remembered, because that seemed the only alternative to a hard and dry rationalism. The rationalists of the Enlightenment were for the most part Cartesians, but Kant himself is in his main trend a rationalist. The epithet critical usually applied to his philosophy is therefore a misnomer. For to solve the critical problem—the relation between appearance and reality—it is necessary to deal adequately with the rôle of the imagination and this Kant has quite failed to do.[10] Modern philosophy is in general so unsatisfactory because it has raised the critical problem without carrying it through; it is too critical to receive wisdom through the traditional channels and not critical enough to achieve insight, and so has been losing more and more its human relevancy, becoming in the words of one of its recent votaries, a "narrow and unfruitful eccentricity." The professional philosophers need to mend their ways and that speedily if the great world is not to pass them disdainfully by and leave them to play their mysterious little game among themselves. We see one of the most recent groups, the new realists, flat on their faces before the man of science—surely an undignified attitude for a philosopher. It is possible to look on the kind of knowledge that science gives as alone real only by dodging the critical problem—the problem as to the trustworthiness of the human instrument through which all knowledge is received—and it would be easy to show, if this were the place to go into the more technical aspects of the question, that the new realists have been doing just this—whether through sheer naïveté or metaphysical despair I am unable to say. The truly critical observer is unable to discover anything real in the absolute sense since everything is mixed with illusion. In this absolute sense the man of science must ever be ignorant of the reality behind the shows of nature. The new realist is, however, justified relatively in thinking that the only thing real in the view of life that has prevailed of late has been its working according to the natural law and the fruits of this working. The self-deception begins when he assumes that there can be no other working. What I have myself been opposing to naturalistic excess, such as appears in the new realism, is insight; but insight is in itself only a word, and unless it can be shown to have its own working and its own fruits, entirely different from those of work according to the natural law, the positivist at all events will have none of it.

The positivist will not only insist upon fruits, but will rate these fruits themselves according to their bearing upon his main purpose. Life, says Bergson, can have no purpose in the human sense of the word.[11] The positivist will reply to Bergson and to the Rousseauistic drifter in general, in the words of Aristotle, that the end is the chief thing of all and that the end of ends is happiness. To the Baconian who wants work and purpose but according to the natural law alone, the complete positivist will reply that happiness cannot be shown to result from this one-sided working; that in itself it affords no escape from the misery of moral solitude, that we move towards true communion and so towards peace and happiness only by work according to the human law. Now the more individualistic we are, I have been saying, the more we must depend for the apprehension of this law on the imagination, the imagination, let me hasten to add, supplemented by the intellect. It is not enough to put the brakes on the natural man—and that is what work according to the human law means—we must do it intelligently. Right knowing must here as elsewhere precede right doing. Even a Buddha admitted that at one period in his life he had not been intelligent in his self-discipline. I need only to amplify here what I have said in a previous chapter about the proper use of the "false secondary power" by those who wish to be either religious or humanistic in a positive fashion. They will employ their analytical faculties, not in building up some abstract system, but in discriminating between the actual data of experience with a view to happiness, just as the man of science at his best employs the same faculties in discriminating between the data of experience with a view to power and utility.

I have pointed out another important use of the analytical intellect in its relation to the imagination. Since the imagination by itself gives unity but does not give reality, it is possible to discover whether a unification of life has reality only by subjecting it to the keenest analysis. Otherwise what we take to be wisdom may turn out to be only an empty dream. To take as wise something that is unreal is to fall into sophistry. For a man like Rousseau whose imagination was in its ultimate quality not ethical at all but overwhelmingly idyllic to set up as an inspired teacher was to become an arch-sophist. Whether or not he was sincere in his sophistry is a question which the emotionalist is very fond of discussing, but which the sensible person will dismiss as somewhat secondary. Sophistry of all kinds always has a powerful ally in man's moral indolence. It is so pleasant to let one's self go and at the same time deem one's self on the way to wisdom. We need to keep in mind the special quality of Rousseau's sophistry if we wish to understand a very extraordinary circumstance during the past century. During this period men were moving steadily toward the naturalistic level, where the law of cunning and the law of force prevail, and at the same time had the illusion—or at least multitudes had the illusion—that they were moving towards peace and brotherhood. The explanation is found in the endless tricks played upon the uncritical and still more upon the half-critical by the Arcadian imagination.

The remedy is not only a more stringent criticism, but, as I have tried to make plain in this whole work, in an age of sophistry, like the present, criticism itself amounts largely to that art of inductive defining which it is the great merit of Socrates, according to Aristotle,[12] to have devised and brought to perfection. Sophistry flourishes, as Socrates saw, on the confused and ambiguous use of general terms; and there is an inexhaustible source of such ambiguities and confusions in the very duality of human nature. The word nature itself may serve as an illustration. We may take as a closely allied example the word progress. Man may progress according to either the human or the natural law. Progress according to the natural law has been so rapid since the rise of the Baconian movement that it has quite captivated man's imagination and stimulated him to still further concentration and effort along naturalistic lines. The very magic of the word progress seems to blind him to the failure to progress according to the human law. The more a word refers to what is above the strictly material level, the more it is subject to the imagination and therefore to sophistication. It is not easy to sophisticate the word horse, it is only too easy to sophisticate the word justice. One may affirm, indeed, not only that man is governed by his imagination but that in all that belongs to his own special domain *the imagination itself is governed by words.*[13]

We should not therefore surrender our imaginations to a general term until it has been carefully defined, and to define it carefully we need usually to practice upon it what Socrates would call a dichotomy. I have just been dichotomizing or "cutting in two" the word progress. When the two main types of progress, material and moral, have been discriminated in their fruits, the positivist will proceed to rate these fruits according to their relevancy to his main goal—the goal of happiness. The person who is thus fortified by a Socratic dialectic will be less ready to surrender his imagination to the first sophist who urges him to be "progressive." He will wish to make sure first that he is not progressing towards the edge of a precipice.

Rousseau would have us get rid of analysis in favor of the "heart." No small part of my endeavor in this work and elsewhere has been to show the different meanings that may attach to the term heart (and the closely allied terms "soul" and "intuition")—meanings that are a world apart, when tested by their fruits. Heart may refer to outer perception and the emotional self or to inner perception and the ethical self. The heart of Pascal is not the heart of Rousseau. With this distinction once obliterated the way is open for the Rousseauistic corruption of such words as virtue and conscience, and this is to fling wide the door to every manner of confusion. The whole vocabulary that is properly applicable only to the super-sensuous realm is then transferred to the region of the subrational. The impulsive self proceeds to cover its nakedness with all these fair phrases as it would with a garment. A recent student of wartime psychology asks: "Is it that the natural man in us has been masquerading as the spiritual man by hiding himself under splendid words—courage, patriotism, justice—and now he rises up and glares at us with blood-red eyes?" That is precisely what has been happening.

But after all the heart in any sense of the word is controlled by the imagination, so that a still more fundamental dichotomy, perhaps the most fundamental of all, is that of the imagination itself. We have seen how often the Arcadian dreaming of the emotional naturalist has been labelled the "ideal." Our views of this type of imagination will therefore determine our views of much that now passes current as idealism. Now the term idealist may have a sound meaning: it may designate the man who is realistic according to the human law. But to be an idealist in Shelley's sense or that of innumerable other Rousseauists is to fall into sheer unreality. This type of idealist shrinks from the sharp discriminations of the critic: they are like the descent of a douche of ice-water upon hot illusions. But it is pleasanter, after all, to be awakened by a douche of ice-water than by an explosion of dynamite under the bed; and that has been the frequent fate of the romantic idealist. It is scarcely safe to neglect any important aspect of reality in favor of one's private dream, even if this dream be dubbed the ideal. The aspect of reality that one is seeking to exclude finally comes crashing through the walls of the ivory tower and abolishes the dream and at times the dreamer.

The transformation of the Arcadian dreamer into the Utopist is a veritable menace to civilization. The ends that the Utopist proposes are often in themselves desirable and the evils that he denounces are real. But when we come to scrutinize critically his means, what we find is not a firm grip on the ascertained facts of human nature but what Bagehot calls the feeble idealities of the romantic imagination. Moreover various Utopists may come together as to what they wish to destroy, which is likely to include the whole existing social order; but what they wish to erect on the ruins of this order will be found to be not only in dreamland, but in different dreamlands. For with the elimination of the veto power from personality—the only power that can pull men back to some common centre—the ideal will amount to little more than the projection of this or that man's temperament upon the void. In a purely temperamental world an affirmative reply may be given to the question of Euryalus in Virgil: "Is each man's God but his own fell desire?" (*An sua cuique deus fit dira cupido?*)

The task of the Socratic critic at the present time is, then, seen to consist largely in stripping idealistic disguises from egoism, in exposing what I have called sham spirituality. If the word spirituality means anything, it must imply, it should seem, some degree of escape from the ordinary self, an escape that calls in turn for effort according to the human law. Even when he is not an open and avowed advocate of a "wise passiveness," the Rousseauistic idealist is only too manifestly not making any such effort—it would interfere with his passion for self-expression which is even more deeply rooted in him than his passion for saving society. He inclines like Rousseau to look upon every constraint[14] whether from within or from without as incompatible with liberty. A right definition of liberty is almost as important as a right definition of imagination and derives from it very directly. Where in our anarchical age will such a definition be found, a definition that is at once modern and in accord with the psychological facts? "A man has only to declare himself free," says Goethe, "and he will at once feel himself dependent. If he ventures to declare himself dependent, he will feel himself free." In other words he is not free to do whatever he pleases unless he wishes to enjoy the freedom of the lunatic, but only to adjust himself to the reality of either the natural or the human law. A progressive adjustment to the human law gives ethical efficiency, and this is the proper corrective of material efficiency, and not love alone as the sentimentalist is so fond of preaching. Love is another word that cries aloud for Socratic treatment.

A liberty that means only emancipation from outer control will result, I have tried to show, in the most dangerous form of anarchy—anarchy of the imagination. On the degree of our perception of this fact will hinge the soundness of our use of another general term—democracy. We should beware above all of surrendering our imaginations to this word until it has been hedged about on every side with discriminations that have behind them all the experience of the past with this form of government. Only in this way may the democrat know whether he is aiming at anything real or merely dreaming of the golden age. Here as elsewhere there are pitfalls manifold for the uncritical enthusiast. A democracy that produces in sufficient numbers sound individualists who look up imaginatively to standards set above their ordinary selves, may well deserve enthusiasm. A democracy, on the other hand, that is not rightly imaginative, but is impelled by vague emotional intoxications, may mean all kinds of lovely things in dreamland, but in the real world it will prove an especially unpleasant way of returning to barbarism. It is a bad sign that Rousseau, who is more than any other one person the father of radical democracy, is also the first of the great anti-intellectualists.

Enough has been said to show the proper rôle of the secondary power of analysis that the Rousseauist looks upon with so much disfavor. It is the necessary auxiliary of the art of defining that can alone save us in an untraditional age from receiving some mere phantasmagoria of the intellect or emotions as a radiant idealism. A Socratic dialectic of this kind is needed at such a time not only to dissipate sophistry but as a positive support to wisdom. I have raised the question in my Introduction whether the wisdom that is needed just now should be primarily humanistic or religious. The preference I have expressed for a positive and critical humanism I wish to be regarded as very tentative. In the dark situation that is growing up in the Occident, all genuine humanism and religion, whether on a traditional or a critical basis, should be welcome. I have pointed out that traditional humanism and religion conflict in certain respects, that it is difficult to combine the imitation of Horace with the imitation of Christ. This problem does not disappear entirely when humanism and religion are dealt with critically and is indeed one of the most obscure that the thinker has to face. The honest thinker, whatever his own preference, must begin by admitting that though religion can get along without humanism, humanism cannot get along without religion. The reason has been given by Burke in pointing out the radical defect of Rousseau: the whole ethical life of man has its root in humility. As humility diminishes, conceit or vain imagining rushes in almost automatically to take its place. Under these circumstances decorum, the supreme virtue of the humanist, is in danger of degenerating into some art of going through the motions. Such was only too often the decorum of the French drawing-room, and such we are told, has frequently been the decorum of the Chinese humanist. Yet the decorum of Confucius himself was not only genuine but he has put the case for the humanist with his usual shrewdness. "I venture to ask about death," one of his disciples said to him. "While you do not know life," Confucius replied, "how can you know about death?" [15]

The solution of this problem as to the relation between humanism and religion, so far as a solution can be found, lies in looking upon them both as only different stages in the same path. Humanism should have in it an element of religious insight: it is possible to be a humble and meditative humanist. The type of the man of the world who is not a mere worldling is not only attractive in itself but has actually been achieved in the West, though not perhaps very often, from the Greeks down. Chinese who should be in a position to know affirm again that, alongside many corrupt mandarins, a certain number of true Confucians[16] have been scattered through the centuries from the time of the sage to the present.

If humanism may be religious, religion may have its humanistic side. I have said, following Aristotle, that the law of measure does not apply to the religious life, but this saying is not to be understood in an absolute sense. Buddha is continually insisting on the middle path in the religious life itself. The resulting urbanity in Buddha and his early followers in India is perhaps the closest approach that that very unhumanistic land has ever made to humanism.

It is right here in this joining of humanism and religion that Aristotle, at least the Aristotle that has come down to us, does not seem altogether adequate. He fails to bring out sufficiently the bond between the meditative or religious life that he describes at the end of his "Ethics" and the humanistic life or life of meditation to which most of this work is devoted. An eminent French authority on Aristotle [17] complains that this separation of the two lives encouraged the ascetic excess of the Middle Ages, the undue spurning of the world in favor of mystic contemplation. I am struck rather by the danger of leaving the humanistic life without any support in religion. In a celebrated passage,[18] Aristotle says that the "magnanimous" man or ideal gentleman sees all things including himself proportionately: he puts himself neither too high nor too low. And this is no doubt true so far as other men are concerned. But does the magnanimous man put human nature itself in its proper place? Does he feel sufficiently its nothingness and helplessness, its dependence on a higher power? No one, indeed, who gets beyond words and outer forms would maintain that humility is a Christian monopoly. Pindar is far more humble[19] than Aristotle, as humble, one might almost maintain, as the austere Christian.

A humanism sufficiently grounded in humility is not only desirable at all times but there are reasons for thinking that it would be especially desirable to-day. In the first place, it would so far as the emotional naturalist is concerned raise a clear-cut issue. The naturalist of this type denies rather than corrupts humanism. He is the foe of compromise and inclines to identify meditation and mediocrity. On the other hand, he corrupts rather than denies religion, turning meditation into pantheistic revery and in general setting up a subtle parody of what is above the ordinary rational level in terms of the subrational. On their own showing Rousseau and his followers are extremists,[20] and even more effective perhaps than to attack them directly for their sham religion would be to maintain against them that thus to violate the law of measure is to cease to be human.

Furthermore, a critical humanism would appear to be the proper corrective of the other main forms of naturalistic excess at the present time—the one-sided devotion to physical science. What keeps the man of science from being himself a humanist is not his science but his pseudo-science, and also the secret push for power and prestige that he shares with other men. The reasons for putting humanistic truth above scientific truth are not metaphysical but very practical: the discipline that helps a man to self-mastery is found to have a more important bearing on his happiness than the discipline that helps him to a mastery of physical nature. If scientific discipline is not supplemented by a truly humanistic or religious discipline the result is unethical science, and unethical science is perhaps the worst monster that has yet been turned loose on the race. Man in spite of what I have termed his stupidity, his persistent evasion of the main issue, the issue of his own happiness, will awaken sooner or later to the fearful evil he has already suffered from a science that has arrogated to itself what does not properly belong to it; and then science may be as unduly depreciated as it has, for the past century or two, been unduly magnified; so that in the long run it is in the interest of science itself to keep in its proper place, which is below both humanism and religion.

It would be possible to frame in the name of insight an indictment against science that would make the indictment Rousseau has framed against it in the name of instinct seem mild. The critical humanist, however, will leave it to others to frame such an indictment. Nothing is more foreign to his nature than every form of obscurantism. He is ready indeed to point out that the man of science has in common with him at least one important idea—the idea of habit, though its scientific form seems to him very incomplete. One may illustrate from perhaps the best known recent treatment of the subject, that of James in his "Psychology." It is equally significant that the humanist can agree with nearly every line of James's chapter on habit and that he disagrees very gravely with James in his total tendency. That is because James shows himself, as soon as he passes from the naturalistic to the humanistic level, wildly romantic. Even when dealing with the "Varieties of Religious Experience" he is plainly more preoccupied with the intensity than with the centrality of this experience.[21] He is obsessed with the idea that comes down to him straight from the age of original genius that to be at the centre is to be commonplace. In a letter to C. E. Norton (June 30, 1904) James praises Ruskin's Letters and adds: "Mere sanity is the most philistine and at bottom unessential of a man's attributes." "Mere sanity" is not to be thus dismissed, because to lack sanity is to be headed towards misery and even madness. "Ruskin's," says Norton, who was in a position to know, "was essentially one of the saddest of lives." [22] Is a man to live one of the saddest of lives merely to gratify romantic lovers of the vivid and picturesque like James?

However, if the man of science holds fast to the results reached by James and others regarding habit and at the same time avoids James's romantic fallacies he might perceive the possibility of extending the idea of habit beyond the naturalistic level; and the way would then be open for an important coöperation between him and the humanist. Humanists themselves, it must be admitted, even critical humanists, have diverged somewhat in their attitude towards habit, and that from the time of Socrates and Aristotle. I have been dwelling thus far on the indispensableness of a keen Socratic dialectic

and of the right knowledge it brings for those who aspire to
be critical humanists. But does right knowing in itself suffice
to ensure right doing? Socrates and Plato with their famous
identification of knowledge and virtue would seem to reply
in the affirmative. Aristotle has the immediate testimony of
consciousness on his side when he remarks simply regarding
this identification: "The facts are otherwise.²³ No experience is
sadder or more universal than that of the failure of right knowledge to secure right performance: so much so that the austere
Christian has been able to maintain with some plausibility that
all the knowledge in the world is of no avail without a special
divine succor. Now the Aristotelian agrees with the Christian
that mere knowledge is insufficient: conversion is also necessary.
He does not incline, however, like the austere Christian to look
for conversion to "thunderclaps and visible upsets of grace."
Without denying necessarily these pistol-shot transformations of
human nature he conceives of man's turning away from his ordinary self—and here he is much nearer in temper to the man
of science—as a gradual process. This gradual conversion the
Aristotelian hopes to achieve by work according to the human
law. Now right knowledge though it supplies the norm is not
in itself this working, which consists in the actual pulling back
of impulse. But an act of this kind to be effective must be repeated. A habit is thus formed until at last the new direction
given to the natural man becomes automatic and unconscious.
The humanistic worker may thus acquire at last the spontaneity
in right doing that the beautiful soul professes to have received
as a free gift from "nature." Confucius narrates the various
stages of knowledge and moral effort through which he had
passed from the age of fifteen and concludes: "At seventy I
could follow what my heart desired without transgressing the
law of measure." ²⁴

The keener the observer the more likely he is to be struck
by the empire of habit. Habit, as Wellington said, is ten times
nature, and is indeed so obviously a second nature that many
of the wise have suspected that nature herself is only a first
habit.²⁵ Now Aristotle who is open to criticism, it may be, on
the side of humility, still remains incomparable among the philosophers of the world for his treatment of habit on the human-

istic level. Any one who wishes to learn how to become moderate and sensible and decent can do no better even at this late day than to steep himself in the "Nicomachean Ethics."

One of the ultimate contrasts that presents itself in a subject of this kind is that between habit as conceived by Aristotle and nature as conceived by Rousseau. The first great grievance of the critical humanist against Rousseau is that he set out to be an individualist and at the same time attacked analysis, which is indispensable if one is to be a sound individualist. The second great grievance of the humanist is that Rousseau sought to discredit habit which is necessary if right analysis is to be made effective. "The only habit the child should be allowed to form," says Rousseau, "is that of forming no habit." 26 How else is the child to follow his bent or genius and so arrive at full self-expression? The point I am bringing up is of the utmost gravity, for Rousseau is by common consent the father of modern education. To eliminate from education the idea of a progressive adjustment to a human law, quite apart from temperament, may be to imperil civilization itself. For civilization (another word that is sadly in need of Socratic defining) may be found to consist above all in an orderly transmission of right habits; and the chief agency for securing such a transmission must always be education, by which I mean far more of course than mere formal schooling.

Rousseau's repudiation of habit is first of all, it should be pointed out, perfectly chimerical. The trait of the child to which the sensible educator will give chief attention is not his spontaneity, but his proneness to imitate. In the absence of good models the child will imitate bad ones, and so, long before the age of intelligent choice and self-determination, become the prisoner of bad habits. Men, therefore, who aim at being civilized must come together, work out a convention in short, regarding the habits they wish transmitted to the young. A great civilization is in a sense only a great convention. A sane individualist does not wish to escape from convention in itself; he merely remembers that no convention is final—that it is always possible to improve the quality of the convention in the midst of which he is living, and that it should therefore be held flexibly. He would oppose no obstacles to those who are rising above the conventional level, but would resist firmly those who are sinking beneath it. It is much easier to determine practically whether one has to do with an ascent or a descent (even though the descent be rapturous like that of the Rousseauist) than our anarchical individualists are willing to acknowledge.

The notion that in spite of the enormous mass of experience that has been accumulated in both East and West we are still without light as to the habits that make for moderation and good sense and decency, and that education is therefore still purely a matter of exploration and experiment is one that may be left to those who are suffering from an advanced stage of naturalistic intoxication—for example, to Professor John Dewey and his followers. From an ethical point of view a child has the right to be born into a cosmos, and not, as is coming to be more and more the case under such influences, pitchforked into chaos. But the educational radical, it may be replied, does stress the idea of habit; and it is true that he would have the young acquire the habits that make for material efficiency. This, however, does not go beyond Rousseau who came out very strongly for what we should call nowadays vocational training.[27] It is the adjustment to the human law against which Rousseau and all the Rousseauists are recalcitrant.

Self-expression and vocational training combined in various proportions and tempered by the spirit of "service" are nearly the whole of the new education. But I have already said that it is not possible to extract from any such compounding of utilitarian and romantic elements, with the resulting material efficiency and ethical inefficiency, a civilized view of life. It is right here indeed in the educational field that concerted opposition to the naturalistic conspiracy against civilization is most likely to be fruitful. If the present generation—and I have in mind especially American conditions—cannot come to a working agreement about the ethical training it wishes given the young, if it allows the drift towards anarchy on the human level to continue, it will show itself, however ecstatic it may be over its own progressiveness and idealism, both cowardly and degenerate. It is very stupid, assuming that it is not very hypocritical, to denounce *Kultur,* and then to adopt educational ideas that work out in much the same fashion as *Kultur,* and have indeed the same historical derivation.

The dehumanizing influences I have been tracing are especially to be deprecated in higher education. The design of higher education, so far as it deserves the name, is to produce leaders, and on the quality of the leadership must depend more than on any other single factor the success or failure of democracy. I have already quoted Aristotle's saying that "most men would rather live in a disorderly than in a sober manner." This does not mean much more than that most men would like to live temperamentally, to follow each his own bent and then put the best face on the matter possible. Most men, says Goethe in a similar vein, prefer error to truth because truth imposes limitations and error does not. It is well also to recall Aristotle's saying that "the multitude is incapable of making distinctions." [28] Now my whole argument is that to be sound individualists we must not only make the right distinctions but submit to them until they become habitual. Does it follow that the whole experiment in which we are engaged is foredoomed to failure? Not quite—though the obstacles to success are somewhat greater than our democratic enthusiasts suspect. The most disreputable aspect of human nature, I have said, is its proneness to look for scapegoats; and my chief objection to the movement I have been studying is that more perhaps than any other in history it has encouraged the evasion of moral responsibility and the setting up of scapegoats. But as an offset to this disreputable aspect of man, one may note a creditable trait: he is very sensitive to the force of a right example. If the leaders of a community look up to a sound model and work humanistically with reference to it, all the evidence goes to show that they will be looked up to and imitated in turn by enough of the rank and file to keep that community from lapsing into barbarism. Societies always decay from the top. It is therefore not enough, as the humanitarian would have us believe, that our leaders should act vigorously on the outer world and at the same time be filled with the spirit of "service." Purely expansive leaders of this kind we have seen who have the word humanity always on their lips and are at the same time ceasing to be human. "That wherein the superior man cannot be equalled," says Confucius, "is simply this—his work which other men cannot see." [29] It is this inner work and the habits that result from it that above all humanize a man and make him exemplary to the multitude. To perform this work he needs to look to a centre and model.

We are brought back here to the final gap that opens between classicist and romanticist. To look to a centre according to the romanticist is at the best to display "reason," at the worst to be smug and philistine. To look to a true centre is, on the contrary, according to the classicist, to grasp the abiding human element through all the change in which it is implicated, and this calls for the highest use of the imagination. The abiding human element exists, even though it cannot be exhausted by dogmas and creeds, is not subject to rules and refuses to be locked up in formulæ. A knowledge of it results from experience—experience vivified by the imagination. To do justice to writing which has this note of centrality we ourselves need to be in some measure experienced and imaginative. Writing that is romantic, writing in which the imagination is not disciplined to a true centre is best enjoyed while we are young. The person who is as much taken by Shelley at forty as he was at twenty has, one may surmise, failed to grow up. Shelley himself wrote to John Gisborne (October 22, 1821): "As to real flesh and blood, you know that I do not deal in those articles; you might as well go to a ginshop for a leg of mutton as expect anything human or earthly from me." The mature man is likely to be dissatisfied with poetry so unsubstantial as this even as an intoxicant and still more when it is offered to him as the "ideal." The very mark of genuinely classical work, on the other hand, is that it yields its full meaning only to the mature. Young and old are, as Cardinal Newman says, affected very differently by the words of some classic author, such as Homer or Horace. "Passages, which to a boy are but rhetorical commonplaces, neither better nor worse than a hundred others which any clever writer might supply . . . at length come home to him, when long years have passed, and he has had experience of life, and pierce him, as if he had never before known them, with their sad earnestness and vivid exactness. Then he comes to understand how it is that lines, the birth of some chance morning or evening at an Ionian festival or among the Sabine hills, have lasted generation after generation for thousands of years, with a power over the mind and a charm which the current literature of his own day, with all its obvious advantages, is utterly unable to rival."

In the poets whom Newman praises the imagination is, as it were, centripetal. The neo-classic proneness to oppose good sense to imagination, and the romantic proneness to oppose imagination to good sense, have at least this justification, that in many persons, perhaps in most persons, the two actually conflict, but surely the point to emphasize is that they may come together, that good sense may be imaginative and imagination sensible. If imagination is not sensible, as is plainly the case in Victor Hugo, for example, we may suspect a lack of the universal and ethical quality. All men, even great poets, are more or less immersed in their personal conceit and in the zones of illusion peculiar to their age. But there is the question of degree. The poets to whom the world has finally accorded its suffrage have not been megalomaniacs; they have not threatened like Hugo to outbellow the thunder or pull comets around by the tail.[30] Bossuet's saying that "good sense is the master of human life" does not contradict but complete Pascal's saying that "the imagination disposes of everything," provided only due stress be laid on the word human. It would not be easy to live a more imaginative life than Hugo, but his imagination was so unrestrained that we may ask whether he lived a very human life, whether he was not rather, in Tennyson's phrase, a "weird Titan." Man realizes that immensity of his being of which Joubert speaks only in so far as he ceases to be the thrall of his own ego. This human breadth he achieves not by throwing off but by taking on limitations, and what he limits is above all his imagination. The reason why he should strive for a life that is thus increasingly full and complete is simply, as Joubert suggests, that it is more delectable, that it is found practically to make for happiness.

CHINESE PRIMITIVISM

Perhaps the closest approach in the past to the movement of
which Rousseau is the most important single figure is the early
Taoist movement in China. Taoism, especially in its popular
aspects, became later something very different, and what I say
is meant to apply above all to the period from about 550 to
200 B.C. The material for the Taoism of this period will be
found in convenient form in the volume of Léon Wieger
(1913)—*Les Pères du Système taoïste* (Chinese texts with
French translation of Lao-tzŭ, Lieh-tzŭ and Chuang-tzŭ.
The Tao Tê King of Lao-tzŭ is a somewhat enigmatical docu-
ment of only a few thousand words, but plainly primitivistic in
its general trend. The phrase that best sums up its general
spirit is that of Wordsworth—a "wise passiveness." The unity
at which it aims is clearly of the pantheistic variety, the unity
that is obtained by breaking down discrimination and affirming
the "identity of contradictories," and that encourages a rever-
sion to origins, to the state of nature and the simple life. According to the Taoist the Chinese fell from the simple life into
artificiality about the time of the legendary Yellow Emperor,
Hoang-ti (27th century B.C.). The individual also should
look back to beginnings and seek to be once more like the
new-born child [1] or, according to Chuang-tzŭ, like the new-

born calf.[2] It is in Chuang-tzŭ indeed that the doctrine develops its full naturalistic and primitivistic implications. Few writers in either East or West have set forth more entertainingly what one may term the Bohemian attitude towards life. He heaps ridicule upon Confucius and in the name of spontaneity attacks his doctrine of humanistic imitation.[3] He sings the praises of the unconscious,[4] even when obtained through intoxication,[5] and extols the morality of the beautiful self.[6] He traces the fall of mankind from nature into artifice in a fashion that anticipates very completely both Rousseau's Discourse on the Arts and Sciences [7] and that on the Origin of Inequality.[8] See also the amusing passage in which the brigand Chi, child of nature and champion of the weak against the oppressions of government, paints a highly Rousseauistic picture of man's fall from his primitive felicity.[9] Among the things that are contrary to nature and purely conventional, according to Chuang-tzŭ and the Taoists, are, not only the sciences and arts and attempts to discriminate between good and bad taste,[10] but likewise government and statecraft,[11] virtue and moral standards.[12] To the artificial music of the Confucians, the Taoists oppose a natural music that offers startling analogies to the most recent programmatic and descriptive tendencies of Occidental music.[13] See especially Chuang-tzŭ's programme for a cosmic symphony in three movements[14]—the *Pipes of Pan* as one is tempted to call it. This music that is supposed to reflect in all its mystery and magic the infinite creative processes of nature is very close to the primitivistic music ("L'arbre vu du côté des racines") with which Hugo's satyr strikes panic into the breasts of the Olympians.

The Taoist notion of following nature is closely related, as in other naturalistic movements, to the idea of fate whether in its stoical or epicurean form.[15] From the references in Chuang-tzŭ [16] and elsewhere to various sects and schools we see that Taoism was only a part of a great stream of naturalistic and primitivistic tendency. China abounded at that time in pacifists,[17] in apostles of brotherly love, and as we should say nowadays Tolstoyans. A true opposite to the egoistic Yang-chu was the preacher of pure altruism and indiscriminate sympathy, Mei-ti. Mencius said that if the ideas of either of these extremists prevailed the time would come, not only when wolves would devour men, but men would devour one another.[18] In opposing discrimination and ethical standards to the naturalists, Mencius and the Confucian humanists were fighting for civilization. Unfortunately there is some truth in the Taoist charge that the standards of the Confucians are too literal, that in their defence of the principle of imitation they did not allow sufficiently for the element of flux and relativity and illusion in things—an element for which the Taoists had so keen a sense that they even went to the point of suppressing the difference between sleeping and waking[19] and life and death.[20] To reply properly to the Taoist relativist the Confucians would have needed to work out a sound conception of the rôle of the imagination—the universal key to human nature—and this they do not seem to have done. One is inclined to ask whether this is the reason for China's failure to achieve a great ethical art like that of the drama and the epic of the Occident at their best. The Taoists were richly imaginative but along romantic lines. We should not fail to note the Taoist influence upon Li Po and other Bohemian and bibulous poets of the Tang dynasty, or the relation of Taoism to the rise of a great school of landscape painting at about the same time. We should note also the Taoist element in "Ch'an" Buddhism (the "Zen" Buddhism[21] of Japan), some knowledge of which is needed for an understanding of whole periods of Japanese and Chinese art.

In these later stages, however, the issues are less clear-cut than in the original struggle between Taoists and Confucians. The total impression one has of early Taoism is that it is a main manifestation of an age of somewhat sophistical individualism. Ancient Chinese individualism ended like that of Greece at about the same time in disaster. After a period of terrible convulsions (the era of the "Fighting States"), the inevitable man on horseback appeared from the most barbaric of these states and "put the lid" on everybody. Shi Hwang-ti, the new emperor, had many of the scholars put to death and issued an edict that the writings of the past, especially the Confucian writings, should be destroyed (213 B.C.). Though the emperor behaved like a man who took literally the Taoist views as to the blessings of ignorance, it is not clear from our chief authority, the historian Ssŭ-ma Ch'ien, that he acted entirely or indeed mainly under Taoist influence.

It is proper to add that though Lao-tzŭ proclaims that the soft is superior to the hard, a doctrine that should appeal to the Occidental sentimentalist, one does not find in him or in the other Taoists the equivalent of the extreme emotional expansiveness of the Rousseauist. There are passages, especially in Lao-tzŭ, that in their emphasis on concentration and calm are in line with the ordinary wisdom of the East; and even where the doctrine is unmistakably primitivistic the emotional quality is often different from that of the corresponding movement in the West.

INTRODUCTION

1 See, for example, in vol. IX of the *Annales de la Société Jean-Jacques Rousseau* the bibliography (pp. 87-276) for 1912—the year of the bicentenary.

2 *Literature and the American College* (1908); *The New Laokoon* (1910); *The Masters of Modern French Criticism* (1912).

3 See his Oxford address *On the Modern Element in Literature.*

4 These two tendencies in Occidental thought go back respectively at least as far as Parmenides and Heraclitus.

5 In his *World as Imagination* (1916) E. D. Fawcett, though ultraromantic and unoriental in his point of view, deals with a problem that has always been the special preoccupation of the Hindu. A Hindu, however, would have entitled a similar volume *The World as Illusion* (māyā). Aristotle has much to say of fiction in his *Poetics* but does not even use the word imagination ($\phi a\nu\tau a\sigma\iota a$). In the *Psychology*, where he discusses the imagination, he assigns not to it, but to mind or reason the active and creative rôle ($\nu o\hat{\nu}s\ \pi o\iota\eta\tau\iota\kappa\acute{o}s$). It is especially the notion of the *creative* imagination that is recent. The earliest example of the phrase that I have noted in French is in Rousseau's description of his erotic reveries at the Hermitage (*Confessions*, Livre IX).

6 Essay on Flaubert in *Essais de Psychologie contemporaine.*

7 *Le Romantisme et les mœurs* (1910).

8 *Annales de la Société Jean-Jacques Rousseau*, VIII, 30-31.

9 I should perhaps say that in the case of Buddha I have been able to consult the original Pāli documents. In the case of Confucius and the Chinese I have had to depend on translations.

10 See appendix on Chinese primitivism.

11 See, for example, *Majjhima* (Pāli Text Society), I, 265. Later Buddhism, especially Mahāyāna Buddhism, fell away from the positive and critical spirit of the founder into mythology and metaphysics.

12 Buddha expressed on many occasions his disdain for the *Vedas*, the great traditional authority of the Hindus.

13 I have explained the reasons for giving this place to Bacon in chapter II of *Literature and the American College.*

14 *Eth. Nic.*, 1179 a.

15 I scarcely need remind the reader that the extant Aristotelian writings which have repelled so many by their form were almost certainly not meant for publication. For the problems raised by these writings as well as for the mystery in the method of their early transmission see R. Shute, *History of the Aristotelian Writings* (1888). The writings which Aristotle prepared for publication and which Cicero describes as a "golden stream of speech" (*Acad.* II,

301

38, 119) have, with the possible exception of the recently recovered
Constitution of Athens, been lost.

THE TERMS CLASSIC AND ROMANTIC

[1] See his *Essai sur le genre dramatique sérieux.*

[2] Quoted in Grimm's Dictionary.

[3] Ex lectione quorundam romanticorum, i.e. librorum compositorum
in gallico poeticorum de gestis militaribus, in quibus maxima pars
fabulosa est.

[4] Perhaps the most romantic lines in English are found in one of
Camillo's speeches in *The Winter's Tale* (IV, 4):

> a wild dedication of yourselves
> To unpath'd waters, undream'd shores.

This "wild dedication" is, it should be noted, looked upon by
Camillo with disfavor.

[5] *Pepys's Diary,* 13 June, 1666.

[6] Thomas Shadwell, Preface to the *Sullen Lovers,* 1668.

[7] *Spectator,* 142, by Steele.

[8] Pope, 2d Epistle, *Of the Character of Women.*

[9] Cf. *Revue d'hist. litt.,* XVIII, 440. For the Early French history of the
word, see also the article *Romantique* by A. François in *Annales de
la Soc. J.-J. Rousseau,* V, 199-236.

[10] First edition, 1698; second edition, 1732.

[11] Cf. his *Elégie à une dame.*

> Mon âme, imaginant, n'a point la patience
> De bien polir les vers et ranger la science.
> La règle me déplaît, j'écris confusément:
> Jamais un bon esprit ne fait rien qu'aisément.
>
> .   .   .   .
>
> Je veux faire des vers qui ne soient pas contraints
>
> .   .   .   .
>
> Chercher des lieux secrets où rien ne me déplaise,
> Méditer à loisir, rêver tout à mon aise,
> Employer toute une heure à me mirer dans l'eau,
> Ouïr, comme en songeant, la course d'un ruisseau,
> Ecrire dans un bois, m'interrompre, me taire,
> Composer un quatrain sans songer à le faire.

[12] *Caractères,* ch. v.

[13] His psychology of the memory and imagination is still Aristotelian.
Cf. E. Wallace, *Aristotle's Psychology,* Intr., lxxxvi-cvii.

[14] *An Essay upon Poetry* (1682).

[15] The French Academy discriminates in its *Sentiments sur le Cid*
between two types of probability, "ordinary" and "extraordinary."
Probability in general is more especially reserved for action. In the
domain of action "ordinary" probability and decorum run very

close together. It is, for example, both indecorous and improbable that Chimène in the *Cid* should marry her father's murderer.

[16] In his *Preface* to Shakespeare.

[17] For a similar distinction in Aristotle see *Eth. Nic.*, 1143 b.

[18] The Platonic and Aristotelian reason or mind (νοῦς) contains an element of intuition.

[19] In his *Lettre à d'Alembert sur les spectacles.*

[20] *Rousseau contre Molière*, 238.

[21] *Letters on Chivalry and Romance.*

ROMANTIC GENIUS

[1] See verses prefixed to Congreve's *Double-Dealer.*

[2] Change l'état douteux dans lequel tu nous ranges,
Nature! élève-nous à la clarté des anges,
Ou nous abaisse au sens des simples animaux.

Sonnet (1657?).

[3] See, for example, A. Gerard's *Essay on Genius* (1774), *passim.*

[4] The English translation of this part of the *Critique of Judgment*, edited by J. C. Meredith, is useful for its numerous illustrative passages from these theorists (Young, Gerard, Duff, etc.).

[5] Mrs. Katharine Fullerton Gerould has dealt interestingly with this point in an article in the *Unpopular Review* (October, 1914) entitled *Tabu and Temperament.*

[6] See *Biographia literaria*, ch. xxii.

[7] This message came to him in any case straight from German romanticism. See Walzel, *Deutsche Romantik*, 22, 151.

[8] "De tous les corps et esprits, on n'en saurait tirer un mouvement de vraie charité; cela est impossible, et d'un autre ordre, surnaturel." *Pensées*, Article xvii. "Charité," one should recollect, here has its traditional meaning—the love, not of man, but of God.

[9] See poem, *Ce siècle avait deux ans* in the *Feuilles d'Automne.*

[10] For amusing details, see L. Maigron, *Le Romantisme et la mode* (1911), ch. v.

[11] For Disraeli see Wilfrid Ward, *Men and Matters*, 54 ff. Of Bulwer-Lytton at Nice about 1850 Princess von Racowitza writes as follows in her *Autobiography* (p. 46): "His fame was at its zenith. He seemed to me antediluvian, with his long dyed curls and his old-fashioned dress . . . with long coats reaching to the ankles, knee-breeches, and long colored waistcoats. Also, he appeared always with a young lady who adored him, and who was followed by a man servant carrying a harp. She sat at his feet and appeared as he did in the costume of 1830, with long flowing curls called *Anglaises*. . . . In society, however, people ran after him tremendously, and spoilt him in every possible way. He read aloud from his own works, and, in especially poetic passages, his 'Alice' accompanied him with arpeggios on the harp."

[12] See essay by Kenyon Cox on *The Illusion of Progress*, in his *Artist and Public.*

[13] See *Creative Criticism* by J. E. Spingarn, and my article on *Genius and Taste*, reviewing this book, in the *Nation* (New York), 7 Feb., 1918.

[14] One should note here as elsewhere points of contact between scientific and emotional naturalism. Take, for example, the educational theory that has led to the setting up of the elective system. The general human discipline embodied in the fixed curriculum is to be discarded in order that the individual may be free to work along the lines of his bent or "genius." In a somewhat similar way scientific naturalism encourages the individual to sacrifice the general human discipline to a specialty.

[15] See his poem *L'Art* in *Emaux et Camées.*

ROMANTIC IMAGINATION

[1] Quel esprit ne bat la campagne?
  Qui ne fait châteaux en Espagne?
  Picrochole, Pyrrhus, la laitière, enfin tous,
    Autant les sages que les fous
  Chacun songe en veillant; il n'est rien de plus doux.
  Une flatteuse erreur emporte alors nos âmes;
    Tout le bien du monde est à nous,
    Tous les honneurs, toutes les femmes.
  Quand je suis seul, je fais au plus brave un défi,
  Je m'écarte, je vais détrôner le sophi;
    On m'élit roi, mon peuple m'aime;
  Les diadèmes vont sur ma tête pleuvant:
  Quelque accident fait-il que je rentre en moi-même,
    Je suis gros Jean comme devant.

[2] *Rasselas*, ch. XLIV.

[3] *Nouvelle Héloïse*, Pt. II, Lettre XVII.

[4] Rostand has hit off this change in the Balcony Scene of his *Cyrano de Bergerac.*

[5] Essay on *Simple and Sentimental Poetry.*

[6] The life of Rousseau by Gerhard Gran is written from this point of view.

[7] The world's great age begins anew,
    The golden years return, etc.
                    Hellas, vv. 1060 ff.

[8] For an excellent analysis of Shelley's idealism see Leslie Stephen's *Godwin and Shelley* in his *Hours in a Library.*

[9] *Letters*, II, 292.

[10] See his letter to Wordsworth, 30 January, 1801.

[11] *Dramatic Art and Literature*, ch. I.

[12] Cf. Voltaire: On ne peut désirer ce qu'on ne connaît pas. (*Zaïre.*)

[13] Cf. Sainte-Beuve, *Causeries du lundi*, xv, 371: "Le romantique a la nostalgie, comme Hamlet; il cherche ce qu'il n'a pas, et jusque par delà les nuages; il rêve, il vit dans les songes. Au dix-neuvième siècle, il adore le moyen âge; au dix-huitième, il est déjà révolutionnaire avec Rousseau," etc. Cf. also T. Gautier as quoted in the *Journal des Goncourt*, II, 51: "Nous ne sommes pas Français, nous autres, nous tenons à d'autres races. Nous sommes pleins de nostalgies. Et puis quand à la nostalgie d'un pays se joint la nostalgie d'un temps . . . comme vous par exemple du dix-huitième siècle . . . comme moi de la Venise de Casanova, avec embranchement sur Chypre, oh! alors, c'est complet."

[14] See article *Goût* in *Postscriptum de ma vie*.

[15] Schlegel's *Dramatic Art and Literature*, Lecture XXII.

[16] For a discussion of this point see I. Rouge: *F. Schlegel et la Genèse du romantisme allemand*, 48 ff.

[17] For a development of this point of view see the essay of Novalis: *Christianity or Europe*.

[18] *Confessions*, Livre IX (1756).

[19] This is Goethe's very classical definition of genius: Du nur, Genius, mehrst in der Natur die Natur.

[20] Greek literature, after it had lost the secret of selection and the grand manner, as was the case during the Alexandrian period, also tended to oscillate from the pole of romance to the pole of so-called realism—from the *Argonautica* of Apollonius of Rhodes, let us say, to the *Mimes* of Herondas.

[21] *Emile*, Livre II.

ROMANTIC MORALITY: THE IDEAL

[1] *Etudes de la nature.*

[2] See, for example, *Tatler*, 17 November, 31 December, 1709 (by Steele).

[3] See her letter to Gustavus III, King of Sweden, cited in *Gustave III et la cour de France*, II, 402, par A. Geoffroy.

[4] See Hastings Rashdall: *Is Conscience an Emotion?* (1914), especially ch. I. Cf. *Nouvelle Héloïse*. (Pt. VI, Lettre VII): "Saint-Preux fait de la conscience morale un sentiment, et non pas un jugement."

[5] *Nouvelle Héloïse*, Pt. V, Lettre II.

[6] *Ibid.*

[7] *Ibid.*, Pt. IV, Lettre XII.

[8] Schiller's definition is well known: "A beautiful soul we call a state where the moral sentiment has taken possession of all the emotions to such a degree that it may unhesitatingly commit the guidance of life to instinct," etc. (*On Grace and Dignity.*) Cf. Madame de Staël: "La vertu devient alors une impulsion involontaire, un mouvement qui passe dans le sang, et vous entraîne irrésistiblement comme les

passions les plus impérieuses." (*De la Littérature: Discours préliminaire.*)

[9] *Avenir de la Science*, 354.

[10] *Ibid.*, 179-180.

[11] *Avenir de la Science*, 476.

[12] Madame de Warens felt the influence of German pietism in her youth. See *La Jeunesse de J.-J. Rousseau* par E. Ritter; ch. XIII.

[13] *Lettre à M. Molé* (21 October, 1803).

[14] *Le romantisme français*, 215.

[15] See *Les Amours de Milord Bomston* at the end of *La Nouvelle Héloïse*.

[16] *Sultan Mourad* in *La Légende des Siècles*.

[17] *Correspondence*, III, 213 (June, 1791). The date of this letter should be noted. Several of the worst terrorists of the French Revolution began by introducing bills for the abolition of capital punishment.

[18] See Burton's *Hume*, II, 309 (note 2).

This sentimental trait did not escape the authors of the *Anti-Jacobin:*

> Sweet child of sickly Fancy—Her of yore
> From her lov'd France Rousseau to exile bore;
> And while midst lakes and mountains wild he ran
> Full of himself and shunn'd the haunts of man,
> Taught her o'er each lone vale and Alpine steep
> To lisp the stories of his wrongs and weep;
> Taught her to cherish still in either eye
> Of tender tears a plentiful supply,
> And pour them in the brooks that babbled by—
> Taught her to mete by rule her feelings strong,
> False by degrees and delicately wrong,
> For the crush'd Beetle, *first*—the widow'd Dove,
> And all the warbled sorrows of the grove,
> *Next* for poor suff'ring Guilt—and *last* of all,
> For Parents, Friends, or King and Country's fall.

[19] Shepherds, dwellers in the valleys, men
> Whom I already loved;—not verily
> For their own sakes, but for the fields and hills
> Where was their occupation and abode.
>   *Michael*

[20] Once more the Ass, with motion dull,
> Upon the pivot of his skull
> Turned round his long left ear.

"The bard who soars to elegize an ass" and the "laureate of the long-eared kind" (*English Bards and Scotch Reviewers*) is, however, not Wordsworth but Coleridge. See his poem *To a Young Ass, its mother being tethered near it.*

[21] See the poem *Acte d'accusation* in *Les Contemplations*.

[22] *Le Crapaud* in *La Légende des Siècles*.

²³ See *Apology* 31D.

²⁴ His *Language and Wisdom of the Hindus* appeared in 1808.

²⁵ See *Jugendschriften,* ed. by J. Minor, II, 362.

²⁶ *Dhammapada.*

²⁷ *Sutta-Nipāta,* v. 149 (*Metta-sutta*).

²⁸ *Second Dialogue.*

²⁹ *Letters,* II, 298. For Ruskin and Rousseau see *Ibid.* I, 360: "[Ruskin] said that great parts of *Les Confessions* were so true to himself that he felt as if Rousseau must have transmigrated into his body."

³⁰ "If a poet wishes an atmosphere of indistinct illusion and of moving shadow, he must use the romantic style. . . . Women, such as we know them, such as they are likely to be, ever prefer a delicate unreality to a true or firm art." Essay on *Pure, Ornate, and Grotesque Art in English Poetry* (1864).

³¹ "Die Romanze auf einem Pferde" utters the following lines in the Prologue to Tieck's *Kaiser Octavianus:*

> Mondbeglänzte Zaubernacht,
> Die den Sinn gefangen hält,
> Wundervolle Märchenwelt
> Steig' auf in der alten Pracht.

A special study might be made of the rôle of the moon in Chateaubriand and Coleridge—even if one is not prepared like Carlyle to dismiss Coleridge's philosophy as "bottled moonshine."

³² O. Walzel points out that as soon as the women in H. von Kleist's plays become conscious they fall into error (*Deutsche Romantik,* 3. Auflage, 147).

³³ Byron, *Sardanapalus,* IV, 5. Cf. Rousseau, *Neuvième Promenade:* "Dominé par mes sens, quoi que je puisse faire, je n'ai jamais pu résister à leurs impressions, et, tant que l'objet agit sur eux, mon cœur ne cesse d'en être affecté." Cf. also Musset, *Rolla:*

> Ce n'était pas Rolla qui gouvernait sa vie,
> C'étaient ses passions; il les laissait aller
> Comme un pâtre assoupi regarde l'eau couler.

³⁴ *Modern Painters,* Part V, ch. xx.

³⁵ *Confessions,* Pt. II, Livre IX (1756).

³⁶ With nature never do *they* wage
A foolish strife; they see
A happy youth and their old age
Is beautiful and free.
Wordsworth: *The Fountain.*

³⁷ The phrase imaginative insight is, I believe, true to the spirit of Plato at his best, but it is certainly not true to his terminology. Plato puts the imagination (φαντασία) not only below intuitive reason (νοῦς) and discursive reason or understanding (διάνοια), but even below outer perception (πίστις). He recognizes indeed that it may reflect the operations of the understanding and even the higher reason as well as the impressions of sense. This notion of a

superior intellectual imagination was carried much further by Plotinus and the neo-Platonists. Even the intellectual imagination is, however, conceived of as passive. Perhaps no Greek thinker, not even Plato, makes as clear as he might that reason gets its intuition of reality and the One with the aid of the imagination and, as it were, through a veil of illusion, that, in Joubert's phrase, "l'illusion est une partie intégrante de la réalité" (*Pensées,* Titre xi, xxxix). Joubert again distinguishes (*ibid.,* Titre iii, xlvii, li) between "l'imaginative" which is passive and "l'imagination" which is active and creative ("l'œil de l'âme"). In its failure to bring out with sufficient explicitness this *creative* rôle of the imagination and in the stubborn intellectualism that this failure implies is to be found, if anywhere, the weak point in the cuirass of Greek philosophy.

[38] See Xenophon, *Memorabilia,* iv, 16, 3.

[39] Σωφροσύνη.

[40] See his *Lettre à d'Alembert.*

[41] *Varieties of Religious Experience,* 387.

[42] *Blütezeit der Romantik,* 126.

[43] "Parfaite illusion, réalité parfaite" (Alfred de Vigny). "Die Welt wird Traum, der Traum wird Welt" (Novalis). "This sort of dreaming existence is the best; he who quits it to go in search of realities generally barters repose for repeated disappointments and vain regrets" (Hazlitt).

ROMANTIC MORALITY: THE REAL

[1] *Lit. Ang.,* iv, 130.

[2] About 1885.

[3] *Le Théâtre en France,* 304.

[4] Je suis une force qui va!
Agent aveugle et sourd de mystères funèbres.

[5] E.g., Lillo's *Fatal Curiosity* (1736) had a marked influence on the rise of the German fate tragedy.

[6] Wo ist der, der sagen dürfe,
So will ich's, so sei's gemacht,
Unsre Taten sind nur Würfe
In des Zufalls blinde Nacht.
Die Ahnfrau.

[7] "So that in the first place, I put for a general inclination of all mankind, a perpetual and restless desire of Power after power, that ceaseth only in Death." *Leviathan,* Part i, ch. xi.

[8] See *Unpopular Review,* October, 1915.

[9] E. Seillière has been tracing, in *Le Mal romantique* and other volumes, the relation between Rousseauism and what he terms an "irrational imperialism." His point of view is on the constructive side very different from mine.

[10] The best account of Rousseau's German influence is still that of H. Hettner in his *Literaturgeschichte des 18. Jahrhunderts.* Compared with Rousseau's German influence, says Professor Paul Hensel in his *Rousseau* (1907), "his influence in France seems almost trifling." In Germany "Rousseau became the basis not of a guillotine but of a new culture (Kultur). . . . We have drawn his spirit over to us, we have made it our own." (121.) See also Professor Eugen Kühnemann, *Vom Weltreich des deutschen Geistes* (1914), 54-62, and *passim.* German idealism is, according to Kühnemann, the monument that does the greatest honor to Rousseau.

[11] A robin redbreast in a cage
Puts all Heaven in a rage.

. . . . . .

He who shall hurt the little wren
Shall never be belov'd by men.
He who the ox to wrath has mov'd
Shall never be by woman lov'd.

. . . . . .

Kill not the moth nor butterfly,
For the Last Judgment draweth nigh.
     Auguries of Innocence.

[12] See *Hart-Leap Well.*

[13] *Beyond Good and Evil,* ch. iv.

[14] "Out into distant futures, which no dream hath yet seen, into warmer souths than ever sculptor conceived . . . Let this love be your new nobility,—the undiscovered in the remotest seas," etc. (*Thus Spake Zarathustra,* translated by Thomas Common, 240, 248.)

[15] "On trouverait, en rétablissant les anneaux intermédiares de la chaîne, qu'à Pascal se rattachent les doctrines modernes qui font passer en première ligne la connaissance immédiate, l'intuition, la vie intérieure, comme à Descartes . . . se rattachent plus particulièrement les philosophies de la raison pure." *La Science française* (1915), I, 17.

[16] Cf. Tennyson:

Fantastic beauty, such as lurks
In some wild poet when he works
Without a conscience or an aim—

[17] Addison writes:

'T was then great Marlbro's mighty soul was proved,
That, in the shock of changing hosts unmoved,
Amidst confusion, horror, and despair,
Examin'd all the dreadful scenes of war;
In peaceful thought the field of death survey'd.

So far as Marlborough deserved this praise he was a general in the grand manner.

[18] "Beauty resides in due proportion and order," says Aristotle (*Poetics,* ch. vii).

[19] *A Survey of English Literature, 1780-1830* (1912), II, 191.

[20] Confucius and the Chinese sages were if anything even more concerned than Plato or Aristotle with the ethical quality of music.

[21] Like Bishop Blougram's his "interest's on the dangerous edge of things."

[22] Does he take inspiration from the church,
Directly make her rule his law of life?
Not he: his own mere impulse guides the man.

. . . .

Such is, for the Augustine that was once,
This Canon Caponsacchi we see now.

X, 1911-28.

[23] See X, 1367-68.

[24] Letter to Joseph d'Ortigue, January 19, 1833.

[25] Here is an extreme example from Maigron's manuscript collection (*Le Romantisme et les mœurs*, 153). A youth forced to be absent three weeks from the woman he loves writes to her as follows: "Trois semaines, mon amour, trois semaines loin de toi! . . . Oh! Dieu m'a maudit! . . . Hier j'ai erré toute l'après-midi comme une bête fauve, une bête traquée. . . . Dans la forêt, j'ai hurlé, hurlé comme un démon . . . je me suis roulé par terre . . . j'ai broyé sous mes dents des branches que mes mains avaient arrachées. . . . Alors, de rage, j'ai pris ma main entre mes dents; j'ai serré, serré convulsivement; le sang a jailli et j'ai craché au ciel le morceau de chair vive . . . j'aurais voulu lui cracher mon cœur."

[26] Maxime Du Camp asserts in his *Souvenirs littéraires* (I, 118) that this anæmia was due in part to the copious blood-letting to which the physicians of the time, disciples of Broussais, were addicted.

[27] This perversion was not unknown to classical antiquity. Cf. Seneca, *To Lucilius*, XCIX: "Quid turpius quam captare in ipso luctu voluptatem; et inter lacrymas quoque, quod juvet, quaerere?"

[28] *Nouvelle Héloïse*, Pt. III, Lettre VI.

ROMANTIC LOVE

[1] *Confessions*, Livre IV.

[2] *The New Laokoon*, ch. V.

[3] *Franciscae meae laudes*, in *Les Fleurs du mal*.

[4] *Architecture and Painting*, Lecture II. This diatribe may have been suggested by Byron's *Don Juan*, Canto XIII, IX-XI:

Cervantes smiled Spain's chivalry away:
A single laugh demolished the right arm
Of his own country, etc.

[5] "Nondum amabam, et amare amabam, quærebam quid amarem, amans amare."

[6] Cf. Shelley's *Alastor:*

> Two eyes,
> Two starry eyes, hung in the gloom of thought
> And seemed with their serene and azure smiles
> To beckon.

[7] "Some of us have in a prior existence been in love with an Antigone, and that makes us find no full content in any mortal tie." Shelley to John Gisborne, October 22, 1821.

[8] *Confessions*, Livre XI (1761).

[9] *Mémoires d'Outre-Tombe*, November, 1817.

[10] "Je me faisais une félicité de réaliser avec ma sylphide mes courses fantastiques dans les forêts du Nouveau Monde."

> *Mémoires d'Outre-Tombe*, December, 1821.

[11] Peacock has in mind *Childe Harold*, canto IV, CXXI ff.

[12] Rousseau plans to make a nympholept of his ideal pupil, Emile: "Il faut que je sois le plus maladroit des hommes si je ne le rends d'avance passionné sans savoir de quoi," etc. *Emile*, Liv. IV.

[13] Cf. René's letter to Céluta in *Les Natchez*: "Je vous ai tenue sur ma poitrine au milieu du désert, dans les vents de l'orage, lorsque, après vous avoir portée de l'autre côté d'un torrent, j'aurais voulu vous poignarder pour fixer le bonheur dans votre sein, et pour me punir de vous avoir donné ce bonheur."

[14] The romantic lover, it should be observed, creates his dream companion even less that he may adore her than that she may adore him.

[15] Walter Bagehot has made an interesting study of the romantic imagination in his essay on a figure who reminds one in some respects of Gérard de Nerval—Hartley Coleridge.

[16] Don Juan bids his servant give a coin to the beggar not for the love of God but for the love of humanity.

[17] Demandant aux forêts, à la mer, à la plaine,
> Aux brises du matin, à toute heure, à tout lieu,
> La femme de son âme et de son premier voeu!
> Prenant pour fiancée un rêve, une ombre vaine,
> Et fouillant dans le cœur d'une hécatombe humaine,
> Prêtre désespéré, pour y trouver son Dieu.

> A. de Musset, *Namouna*.

"Don Juan avait en lui cet amour pour la femme idéale; il a couru le monde serrant et brisant de dépit dans ses bras toutes les imparfaites images qu'il croyait un moment aimer; et il est mort épuisé de fatigue, consumé de son insatiable amour." Prévost-Paradol, *Lettres*, 149.

[18] See Scott's (2d) edition of Swift, XIII, 310.

[19] Aimer c'est le grand point. Qu'importe la maîtresse?
> Qu'importe le flacon pourvu qu'on ait l'ivresse?

[20] It has been said that in the novels of George Sand when a lady wishes to change her lover God is always there to facilitate the transfer

[21] "Tous les hommes sont menteurs, inconstants, faux, bavards, hypocrites, orgueilleux ou lâches, méprisables et sensuels; toutes les femmes sont perfides, artificieuses, vaniteuses, curieuses et dépravées; le monde n'est qu'un égout sans fond où les phoques les plus informes rampent et se tordent sur des montagnes de fange; mais il y a au monde une chose sainte et sublime, c'est l'union de deux de ces êtres si imparfaits et si affreux. On est souvent trompé en amour; souvent blessé et souvent malheureux, mais on aime et quand on est sur le bord de sa tombe, on se retourne pour regarder en arrière, et on se dit: J'ai souffert souvent, je me suis trompé quelquefois, mais j'ai aimé. C'est moi qui ai vécu, et non pas un être factice créé par mon orgueil et mon ennui." (The last sentence is taken from a letter of George Sand to Musset.) *On ne badine pas avec l'Amour*, II, 5.

[22] *Table-Talk. On the Past and Future.*

[23] *The Plain Speaker. On Reading Old Books.*

[24] *The Round Table. On the Character of Rousseau.*

[25] "Aujourd'hui, jour de Pâques fleuries, il y a précisément cinquante ans de ma première connaissance avec Madame de Warens."

[26] Even on his death-bed the hero of Browning's *Confessions* gives himself up to impassionated recollection:

> How sad and bad and mad it was —
> But then, how it was sweet.

In his *Stances à Madame Lullin* Voltaire is at least as poetical and nearer to normal experience:

> Quel mortel s'est jamais flatté
> D'un rendez-vous à l'agonie?

ROMANTIC IRONY

[1] See especially *Lyceumfragment*, no. 108.

[2] A well-known example of the extreme to which the romanticists pushed their Fichtean solipsism is the following from the *William Lovell* of the youthful Tieck: "Having gladly escaped from anxious fetters, I now advance boldly through life, absolved from those irksome duties which were the inventions of cowardly fools. Virtue is, only because I am; it is but a reflection of my inner self. What care I for forms whose dim lustre I have myself brought forth? Let vice and virtue wed. They are only shadows in the mist," etc.

[3] *Beyond Good and Evil*, ch. IV.

[4] *On Contemporary Literature*, 206. The whole passage is excellent.

[5] M. Legouis makes a similar remark in the *Cambridge History of English Literature*, XI, 108.

[6] I scarcely need say that Wordsworth is at times genuinely ethical, but he is even more frequently only didactic. The *Excursion*, as M. Legouis says. is a "long sermon against pessimism."

[7] "Quia fecisti nos ad te et inquietum est cor nostrum, donec requiescat in te."

[8] *Eth. Nic.,* 1177 b.

[9] Cf. the chapter on *William Law and the Mystics* in *Cambridge History of English Literature,* IX, 341-67; also the bibliography of Boehme, *ibid.,* 560-74.

[10] See *Excursion,* I, vv. 943 ff.

[11] In his attitude towards sin Novalis continues Rousseau and anticipates the main positions of the Christian Scientist.

[12] Prune thou thy words,
    The thoughts control
That o'er thee swell and throng.
    They will condense within the soul
And change to purpose strong.
But he who lets his feelings run
    In soft, luxurious flow,
Shrinks when hard service must be done
    And faints at every foe.

[13] Wesley had no liking for Boehme and cut out from Brooke's book the theosophy that had this origin.

[14] Writing was often associated with magic formulæ. Hence γράμμα also gave Fr. "grimoire."

[15] *Thus Spake Zarathustra,* LXIX (The Shadow to Zarathustra).

[16] *Katha-Upanishad.* The passage is paraphrased as follows by P. E. More in his *Century of Indian Epigrams:*

> Seated within this body's car
> The silent Self is driven afar,
> And the five senses at the pole
> Like steeds are tugging restive of control.

> And if the driver lose his way,
> Or the reins sunder, who can say
> In what blind paths, what pits of fear
> Will plunge the chargers in their mad career?

> Drive well, O mind, use all thy art,
> Thou charioteer!—O feeling Heart,
> Be thou a bridle firm and strong!
> For the Lord rideth and the way is long.

[17] See Brandes: *The Romantic School in Germany,* ch. XI.

[18] Alfred de Musset saw his double in the stress of his affair with George Sand (see *Nuit de Décembre*), Jean Valjean (*Les Misérables*) sees his double in the stress of his conversion. Peter Bell also sees his double at the emotional crisis in Wordsworth's poem of that name.

[19] *Thus Spake Zarathustra,* LXIX.

[20] F. Schlegel: *Lyceumfragment,* no. 42.

[21] E.g., canto III, CVII-CXI.

[22] *Confessions,* Livre XII (1765).

ROMANTICISM AND NATURE

[1] Cf. Th. Gomperz, *Greek Thinkers,* I, 402.

[2] Wordsworth: *Miscellaneous Sonnets,* XII.

[3] In much the same spirit the Japanese hermit, Kamo Chōmei (thirteenth century), expresses the fear that he may forget Buddha because of his fondness for the mountains and the moon.—See article on nature in Japan by M. Revon in *Encyclopedia of Religion and Ethics.*

[4] *Confessions,* Bk. X, ch. IX.

[5] Cf. Cicero: "Urbem, urbem, mi Rufe, cole et in ista luce vive." (*Ad Fam.,* II, 22.)

[6] March 23, 1646.

[7] It was especially easy for the poets to go for their landscapes to the painters because according to the current theory poetry was itself a form of painting (*ut pictura poesis*). Thus Thomson writes in *The Castle of Indolence:*

> Sometimes the pencil, in cool airy halls,
> Bade the gay bloom of vernal landskips rise,
> Or autumn's varied shades embrown the walls:
> Now the black tempest strikes the astonish'd eyes;
> Now down the steep the flashing torrent flies;
> The trembling sun now plays o'er ocean blue,
> And now rude mountains frown amid the skies;
> Whate'er *Lorrain* light touch'd with softening hue,
> Or savage *Rosa* dash'd, or learned *Poussin* drew.
>
> (C. I, st. 38.)

[8] Disparaissez, monuments du génie,
> Parcs, jardins immortels, que Le Nôtre a plantés;
> De vos dehors pompeux l'exacte symmétrie,
> Etonne vainement mes regards attristés.
>
> J'aime bien mieux ce désordre bizarre,
> Et la variété de ces riches tableaux
> Que disperse l'Anglais d'une main moins avare.
>
> Bertin, 19ᵉ Elégie of *Les Amours.*

[9] Pt. IV, Lettre XI.

[10] *Nouvelle Héloïse,* Pt. IV, Lettre XI.

[11] *Ibid.*

[12] *Ibid.,* Pt. IV, Lettre XVII.

[13] *Confessions,* Livre V (1732).

[14] See especially *Childe Harold,* canto II, XXV ff.

[15] *Ibid.,* canto II, XXXVII.

[16] *Ibid.,* canto III, LXXII.

[17] *Ibid.,* canto IV, CLXXVII.

[18] See *La Perception du changement*, 30.

[19] Asia

> My soul is an enchanted boat,
> Which like a sleeping swan, doth float
> Upon the silver waves of thy sweet singing;
> And thine doth like an angel sit
> Beside a helm conducting it,
> Whilst all the winds with melody are ringing.
> It seems to float ever, for ever
> Upon that many-winding river,
> Between mountains, woods, abysses,
> A paradise of wilderness!
>
> . . . .
>
> Meanwhile thy spirit lifts its pinions
> In music's most serene dominions;
> Catching the winds that fan that happy heaven.
> And we sail on away, afar,
> Without a course, without a star,
> But by the instinct of sweet music driven;
> Till through Elysian garden islets
> By thee, most beautiful of pilots,
> Where never mortal pinnace glided
> The boat of my desire is guided;
> Realms where the air we breath is love—
>
> > *Prometheus Unbound*, Act II, Sc. v.

[20] "Si tu souffres plus qu'un autre des choses de la vie, il ne faut pas t'en étonner; une grande âme doit contenir plus de douleurs qu'une petite."

[21] Cf. Shelley, *Julian and Maddalo:*

> I love all waste
> And solitary places; where we taste
> The pleasure of believing what we see
> Is boundless, as we wish our souls to be.

[22] Cf. for example, the passage of Rousseau in the seventh *Promenade* ("Je sens des extases, des ravissements inexprimables à me fondre pour ainsi dire dans le système des êtres," etc.) with the revery described by Wordsworth in *The Excursion*, I, 200-218.

[23] O belles, craignez le fond des bois, et leur vaste silence.

[24] *Faust* (Miss Swanwick's translation).

[25] *Artist and Public*, 134 ff.

[26] Make me thy lyre, even as the forest is:
What if my leaves are falling like its own!
The tumult of thy mighty harmonies

Will take from both a deep, autumnal tone,
Sweet though in sadness. Be thou, Spirit fierce,
My spirit! Be thou me, impetuous one!

>   Drive my dead thoughts over the universe
>   Like withered leaves, etc.

Cf. Lamartine:

>   Quand la feuille des bois tombe dans la prairie,
>   Le vent du soir s'élève et l'arrache aux vallons;
>   Et moi, je suis semblable à la feuille flétrie;
>   Emportez-moi comme elle, orageux aquilons.
>
>   *L'Isolement.*

[27] Cf. Hettner, *Romantische Schule,* 156.

[28] See appendix on Chinese primitivism.

[29] G. Duval has written a *Dictionnaire des métaphores de Victor Hugo,* and G. Lucchetti a work on *Les Images dans les œuvres de Victor Hugo.* So far as the ethical values are concerned, the latter title is alone justified. Hugo is, next to Chateaubriand, the great imagist.

[30] The French like to think of the symbolists as having rendered certain services to their versification. Let us hope that they did, though few things are more perilous than this transfer of the idea of progress to the literary and artistic domain. Decadent Rome, as we learn from the younger Pliny and others, simply swarmed with poets who also no doubt indulged in many strange experiments. All this poetical activity, as we can see only too plainly at this distance, led nowhere.

[31] Grant Allen writes of the laws of nature in *Magdalen Tower:*

>   They care not any whit for pain or pleasure,
>   That seems to us the sum and end of all,
>   Dumb force and barren number are their measure,
>   What shall be shall be, tho' the great earth fall,
>   They take no heed of man or man's deserving,
>   Reck not what happy lives they make or mar,
>   Work out their fatal will unswerv'd, unswerving,
>   And know not that they are!

[32] Fragment de l'*Art de jouir,* quoted by P.-M. Masson in *La Religion de J.-J. Rousseau,* II, 228.

[33] If nature merely reflects back to a man his own image, it follows that Coleridge's celebrated distinction between fancy and imagination has little value, inasmuch as he rests his proof of the unifying power of the imagination, in itself a sound idea, on the union the imagination effects between man and outer nature—and this union is on his own showing fanciful.

[34] If I had had this consecration Wordsworth says, addressing Peele Castle,

>   I would have planted thee, thou hoary Pile,
>   Amid a world how different from this!
>   Beside a sea that could not cease to smile;
>   On tranquil land, beneath a sky of bliss.
>
>   .   .   .   .

A Picture had it been of lasting ease,
Elysian quiet, without toil or strife, etc.
Elegiac Stanzas suggested by a picture of Peele Castle in a storm.
⁸⁵ Cf. Doudan, *Lettres*, IV, 216: "J'ai parcouru le *Saint-Paul* de Renan.
Je n'ai jamais vu dans un théologien une si grande connaissance de
la flore orientale. C'est un paysagiste bien supérieur à Saint-Augus-
tin et à Bossuet. Il sème des résédas, des anémones, des pâquerettes
pour recueillir l'incrédulité."

ROMANTIC MELANCHOLY

¹ In his *Mal romantique* (1908) E. Seillière labels the generations that
have elapsed since the rise of Rousseauism as follows:
  1. Sensibility (*Nouvelle Héloïse*, 1761).
  2. Weltschmerz (Schiller's *Æsthetic Letters*, 1795).
  3. Mal du siècle (Hugo's *Hernani*, 1830).
  4. Pessimism (vogue of Schopenhauer and Stendhal, 1865).
  5. Neurasthenia (culmination of *fin de siècle* movement, 1900).
² *Eckermann*, September 24, 1827.
³ See *La Nuit de Mai.*
⁴ These lines are inscribed on the statue of Musset in front of the
Théâtre Français. Cf. Shelley:
  Our sweetest songs are those that tell of saddest thought.
⁵ Translation by J. E. Sandys of fragment cited in Stobæus, *Flor*,
CIX, I.
⁶ *Pythian Odes*, III, 20 ff.
⁷ *Pythian Odes*, III, 81-82.
⁸ *Song of the Banjo*, in the *Seven Seas.*
⁹ XVII, 446-47.
¹⁰ A brief survey of melancholy among the Greeks will be found in
Professor S. H. Butcher's *Some Aspects of the Greek Genius.*
¹¹ The exasperated quest of novelty is one of the main traits both of
the ancient and the modern victim of ennui. See Seneca, *De Tran-
quillitate animi:* "Fastidio illis esse cœpit vita, et ipse mundus; et
subit illud rabidorum deliciarum: quousque eadem?" (Cf. La Fontaine: Il me faut du nouveau, n'en fût-il plus au monde.)
¹² "A quoi bon m'avoir fait naître avec des facultés exquises pour les
laisser jusqu'à la fin sans emploi? Le sentiment de mon prix interne
en me donnant celui de cette injustice m'en dédommageait en
quelque sorte, et me faisait verser des larmes que j'aimais à laisser
couler." *Confessions.* Livre IX (1756).
¹³ *Nouvelle Héloïse*, Pt. VI, Lettre VIII.
¹⁴ "Encore enfant par la tête, vous êtes déjà vieux par le cœur." *Ibid.*
¹⁵ See the examples quoted in Arnold: *Essays in Criticism*, Second
Series, 305-06.
¹⁶ This is the thought of Keats's *Ode to Melancholy:*

> Ay, in the very temple of Delight
> Veil'd Melancholy has her sovran shrine,
> Though seen of none save him whose strenuous tongue
> Can burst Joy's grape against his palate fine.

Cf. Chateaubriand: *Essai sur les Révolutions*, Pt. II, ch. LVII: "Ces jouissances sont trop poignantes: telle est notre faiblesse, que les plaisirs exquis deviennent des douleurs," etc.

[17] See his sonnet *Les Montreurs*. This type of Rousseauist is anticipated by "Milord" Bomston in *La Nouvelle Héloïse*. Rousseau directed the engraver to depict him with "un maintien grave et stoïque sous lequel il cache avec peine une extrême sensibilité."

[18] "Qui es-tu? À coup sûr tu n'es pas un être pétri du même limon et animé de la même vie que nous! Tu es un ange ou un démon mais tu n'es pas une créature humaine . . . Pourquoi habiter parmi nous, qui ne pouvons te suffire ni te comprendre?" G. Sand, *Lélia*, I, 11.

[19] See p. 51.

[20] See *Lara*, XVIII, XIX, perhaps the best passage that can be quoted for the Byronic hero.

[21] Cf. Gautier, *Histoire du romantisme:* "Il était de mode alors dans l'école romantique d'être pâle, livide, verdâtre, un peu cadavéreux, s'il était possible. Cela donnait l'air fatal, byronien, giaour, dévoré par les passions et les remords."

[22] Hugo, *Hernani.*

[23] Lorsque, par un décret des puissances suprêmes,
Le Poète apparaît dans ce monde ennuyé,
Sa mère épouvantée et pleine de blasphèmes
Crispe ses poings vers Dieu, qui la prend en pitié.
>
> *Fleurs du mal: Bénédiction.*

Cf. *Nouvelle Héloïse*, Pt. III, Lettre XXVI:
"Ciel inexorable! . . . O ma mère, pourquoi vous donna-t-il un fils dans sa colère?"

[24] Coleridge has a side that relates him to the author of *Les Fleurs du mal*. In his *Pains of Sleep* he describes a dream in which he felt
> Desire with loathing strangely mix'd,
> *On wild or hateful objects fix'd.*

[25] Keats according to Shelley was an example of the *poète maudit*. "The poor fellow," he says, "was literally hooted from the stage of life." Keats was as a matter of fact too sturdy to be snuffed out by an article and had less of the quivering Rousseauistic sensibility than Shelley himself. Cf. letter of Shelley to Mrs. Shelley (Aug. 7, 1820): "Imagine my despair of good, imagine how it is possible that one of so weak and sensitive a nature as mine can run further the gauntlet through this hellish society of men."

[26] Euripides speaks of the Χάρις γόων in his Ἱκέτιδες (Latin, "dolendi voluptas"; German, "die Wonne der Wehmut").

[27] Chesterton is anticipated in this paradox by Wordsworth:

In youth we love the darksome lawn
Brushed by the owlet's wing.
Then Twilight is preferred to Dawn
And autumn to the spring.
Sad fancies do we then affect
In luxury of disrespect
To our own prodigal excess
Of too familiar happiness.

Ode to Lycoris.

[28] *Souvenirs d'enfance et de jeunesse,* 329-30.

[29] "[Villiers] était de cette famille des néo-catholiques littéraires dont Chateaubriand est le père commun, et qui a produit Barbey d'Aurévilly, Baudelaire et plus récemment M. Joséphin Peladan. Ceux-là ont goûté par-dessus tout dans la religion les charmes du péché, la grandeur du sacrilège, et leur sensualisme a caressé les dogmes qui ajoutaient aux voluptés la suprême volupté de se perdre." A. France, *Vie Littéraire,* III, 121.

[30] *Première Promenade.*

[31] *Ibid.*

[32] E.g., Hölderlin and Jean Polonius.

[33] A striking passage on solitude will be found in the *Laws of Manu,* IV, 240-42. ("Alone a being is born: alone he goes down to death." His kin forsake him at the grave; his only hope then is in the companionship of the Law of righteousness [Dharma]. "With the Law as his companion he crosses the darkness difficult to cross.")

[34] "Be good and you will be lonely."

[35] In the poem by the Swiss poet C. Didier from which Longfellow's poem seems to be derived, the youth who persists in scaling the heights in spite of all warnings is Byron!

Et Byron . . . disparaît aux yeux du pâtre épouvanté.

(See E. Estève, *Byron en France,* 147).

[36] In the *Mémoires d'Outre-Tombe* Chateaubriand quotes from the jottings of Napoleon on the island of Elba. "Mon cœur se refuse aux joies communes comme à la douleur ordinaire." He says of Napoleon elsewhere in the same work: "Au fond il ne tenait à rien: homme solitaire, il se suffisait; le malheur ne fit que le rendre au désert de sa vie."

[37] The solitude of the "genius" is already marked in Blake:

O! why was I born with a different face?
Why was I not born like the rest of my race?
When I look, each one starts; when I speak, I offend;
Then I'm silent and passive and lose every friend.

[38] Froude's *Carlyle,* II, 377.

[39] No finer lines on solitude are found in English than those in which Wordsworth relates how from his room at Cambridge he could look out on

> The antechapel where the statue stood
> Of Newton with his prism and silent face,
> The marble index of a mind for ever
> Voyaging through strange seas of thought alone.
>
> (Prelude III, 61-63.)

Cf. also the line in the Sonnet on Milton:

> His soul was like a star and dwelt apart.

40 *Eth. Nic.*, 1109 b.

41 James Thomson in *The City of Dreadful Night* says that he would have entered hell

> gratified to gain
> That positive eternity of pain
> Instead of this insufferable inane.

42 R. Canat has taken this phrase as the title of his treatment of the subject: *La Solitude morale dans le mouvement romantique.*

43 Decadent Rome had the equivalent of Des Esseintes. Seneca (*To Lucilius*, CXXII) speaks of those who seek to affirm their originality and attract attention to themselves by doing everything differently from other people and, "ut ita dicam, *retro vivunt.*"

44 Tennyson has traced this change of the æsthetic dream into a nightmare in his *Palace of Art.*

45 *Contemporains*, I, 332.

46 *Génie du Christianisme*, Pt. II, Livre III, ch. IX.

47 L'orage est dans ma voix, l'éclair est sur ma bouche;
Aussi, loin de m'aimer, voilà qu'ils tremblent tous,
Et quand j'ouvre les bras, on tombe à mes genoux.

48 Que vous ai-je donc fait pour être votre élu?

> .   .   .   .

Hélas! je suis, Seigneur, puissant et solitaire,
Laissez-moi m'endormir du sommeil de la terre!

49 Le juste opposera le dédain à l'absence
Et ne répondra plus que par un froid silence
Au silence éternel de la Divinité.

50 See Sainte-Beuve's poetical epistle *A M. Villemain* (*Pensées d'Août*, 1837).

51 See *Masters of Modern French Criticism*, 233, 238.

52 Wordsworth writes

> A piteous lot it were to flee from man
> Yet not rejoice in Nature.
>
> (Excursion, IV, 514.)

This lot was Vigny's:

> Ne me laisse jamais seul avec la Nature
> Car je la connais trop pour n'en avoir pas peur.

53 Madame Dorval.

54 *La Maison du Berger*. Note that in Wordsworth the "still sad music of humanity" is very closely associated with nature.

55 *La Bouteille à la Mer.*

⁵⁶ See Book IX of the *Nicomachean Ethics*.

⁵⁷ "All salutary conditions have their root in strenuousness" (appamāda), says Buddha.

⁵⁸ See *Masters of Modern French Criticism*, Essay on Taine, *passim*. Paul Bourget in his *Essais de Psychologie contemporaine* (2 vols.) has followed out during this period the survivals of the older romantic melancholy and their reinforcement by scientific determinism.

⁵⁹ "Le pauvre M. Arago, revenant un jour de l'Hôtel de Ville en 1848 après une épouvantable émeute, disait tristement à l'un de ses aides de camp au ministère de la marine: 'En vérité ces gens-là ne sont pas raisonnables.' " Doudan, *Lettres*, IV, 338.

⁶⁰ See Preface (pp. viii-ix) to his *Souvenirs d'enfance et de jeunesse* and my comment in *The New Laokoon*, 207-08.

⁶¹ Most of the political implications of the point of view I am developing I am reserving for a volume I have in preparation to be entitled *Democracy and Imperialism*. Some of my conclusions will be found in two articles in the (New York) *Nation: The Breakdown of Internationalism* (June 17 and 24, 1915), and *The Political Influence of Rousseau* (Jan. 18, 1917).

⁶² *Reden an die deutsche Nation*, XII.

⁶³ I should perhaps allow for the happiness that may be experienced in moments of supernormal consciousness—something quite distinct from emotional or other intoxication. Fairly consistent testimony as to moments of this kind is found in the records of the past from the early Buddhists down to Tennyson.

⁶⁴ I scarcely need say that I am speaking of the man of science only in so far as he is purely naturalistic in his point of view. There may enter into the total personality of Edison or any particular man of science other and very different elements.

⁶⁵ M. René Berthelot has written a book on pragmatism and similar tendencies in contemporary philosophy entitled *Un Romantisme utilitaire*. I have not read it but the title alone is worth more than most books on the subject I have read.

THE PRESENT OUTLOOK

¹ *Dedication of the Æneis* (1697).

² *Adventure of one Hans Pfaal*.

³ His attempt to rewrite *Hyperion* from a humanitarian point of view is a dismal failure.

⁴ There is also a strong idyllic element in *Paradise Lost* as Rousseau (*Emile*, V) and Schiller (*Essay on Naïve and Sentimental Poetry*) were among the first to point out. Critics may be found even today who, like Tennyson, prefer the passages which show a richly pastoral imagination to the passages where the ethical imagination

is required but where it does not seem to prevail sufficiently over theology.

⁵ XII, 74.

⁶ *Three Philosophical Poets*, 188.

⁷ After telling of the days when "il n'y avait pour moi ni passé ni avenir et je goûtais à la fois les délices de mille siècles," Saint-Preux concludes: "Hélas! vous avez disparu comme un éclair. Cette éternité de bonheur ne fut qu'un instant de ma vie. Le temps a repris sa lenteur dans les moments de mon désespoir, et l'ennui mesure par longues années le reste infortuné de mes jours" (*Nouvelle Héloïse*, Pt. III, Lettre VI).

⁸ The Church, so far as it has become humanitarian, has itself succumbed to naturalism.

⁹ *Sutta of the Great Decease.*

¹⁰ If a man recognizes the supreme rôle of fiction or illusion in life while proceeding in other respects on Kantian principles, he will reach results similar to the "As-if Philosophy" (*Philosophie des Als Ob*) of Vaihinger, a leading authority on Kant and co-editor of the *Kantstudien.* This work, though not published until 1911, was composed, the author tells us in his preface, as early as 1875-78. It will be found to anticipate very strikingly pragmatism and various other isms in which philosophy has been proclaiming so loudly of late its own bankruptcy.

¹¹ "C'est en vain qu'on voudrait assigner à la vie un but, au sens humain du mot." *L'Evolution créatrice*, 55.

¹² *Metaphysics*, 1078 b.

¹³ In the beginning was the Word! To seek to substitute, like Faust, the Deed for the Word is to throw discrimination to the winds. The failure to discriminate as to the *quality* of the deed is responsible for the central sophistry of *Faust* (see p. 331) and perhaps of our modern life in general.

¹⁴ "J'adore la liberté; j'abhorre la gêne, la peine, l'assujettissement." *Confessions*, Livre I.

¹⁵ *Analects*, XI, CXI. Cf. *ibid.*, VI, CXX: "To give one's self earnestly to the duties due to men, and while respecting spiritual beings, to keep aloof from them, may be called wisdom." Much that has passed current as religion in all ages has made its chief appeal, not to awe but to wonder; and like many humanists Confucius was somewhat indifferent to the marvellous. "The subjects on which the Master did not talk were: extraordinary things, feats of strength, disorder and spiritual beings" (*ibid.*, VII, CXX).

¹⁶ One of the last Chinese, I am told, to measure up to the Confucian standard was Tsêng Kuo-fan (1811-1872) who issued forth from poverty, trained a peasant soldiery and, more than any other one person, put down the Taiping Rebellion.

¹⁷ See J. Barthélemy Saint-Hilaire's Introduction to his translation of the *Nicomachean Ethics*, p. cxlix.

[18] *Eth. Nic.*, 1122-25.

[19] I have in mind such passages as *P.*, VIII, 76-78, 92-96; *N.*, VI, 1-4; *N.*, XI, 13-16.

[20] "Il n'y eut jamais pour moi d'intermédiaire entre tout et rien." *Confessions*, Livre VII.

[21] Some wag, it will be remembered, suggested as an alternative title for this work: *Wild Religions I have known.*

[22] *Letters*, II, 298; cf. *ibid.*, 291: "I have never known a life less wisely controlled or less helped by the wisdom of others than his. The whole retrospect of it is pathetic; waste, confusion, ruin of one of the most gifted and sweetest natures the world ever knew."

[23] *Nic. Eth.*, 1145b. The opposition between Socrates or Plato and Aristotle, when put thus baldly, is a bit misleading. Socrates emphasized the importance of practice (μελέτη) in the acquisition of virtue, and Plato has made much of habit in the *Laws*.

[24] *Analects*, II, CIV.

[25] This belief the Oriental has embodied in the doctrine of Karma.

[26] "La seule habitude qu'on doit laisser prendre à l'enfant est de n'en contracter aucune." *Emile*, Livre I.

[27] Emile was to be trained to be a cabinet-maker.

[28] *Eth. Nic.*, 1172b.

[29] *Doctrine of the Mean* (c. XXXIII, v. 2).

[30] See his poem *Ibo* in *Les Contemplations*.

CHINESE PRIMITIVISM

[1] La. 55, p. 51. (In my references La. stands for Lao-tzŭ, Li. for Lieh-tzŭ, Ch. for Chuang-tzŭ. The first number gives the chapter; the second number the page in Wieger's edition.)

[2] Ch. 22 C, p. 391.

[3] Ch. 12 n, p. 305.

[4] Ch. 11 D, p. 291. *Ibid.* 15, p. 331. See also Li. 31, p. 113.

[5] Ch. 19 B, p. 357.

[6] Ch. 19 L, p. 365.

[7] Ch. 10, pp. 279-80.

[8] Ch. 9, pp. 274-75.

[9] Ch. 29, pp. 467 ff.

[10] Ch. 2, p. 223.

[11] La. 27, p. 37.

[12] Ch. 8 A, p. 271.

[13] Li. 5, p. 143.

[14] Ch. 14 C, p. 321.

[15] For an extreme form of Epicureanism see the ideas of Yang-chu Li. 7, pp. 165 ff. For stoical apathy see Ch. 6 C., p. 253. For fate see Li. 6, p. 155, Ch. 6 K, p. 263.

[16] Ch. 33, pp. 499 ff.

[17] Ch. 33 C, p. 503.
[18] Bk. III, Part 2, ch. 9.
[19] Li. 3, p. 111. Ch. 24, pp. 225-27.
[20] Ch. 6 E, p. 255.
[21] See *The Religion of the Samurai: a Study of Zen Philosophy* (1913) by Kaiten Nukariya (himself a Zenist), p. 23.